Flows, Rhythms, and Intensities

of

EARLY CHILDHOOD EDUCATION CURRICULUM

Rethinking Childhood

Gaile S. Cannella
General Editor

Vol. 45

The Rethinking Childhood series is part of the Peter Lang Education list.
Every volume is peer reviewed and meets
the highest quality standards for content and production.

PETER LANG
New York • Washington, D.C./Baltimore • Bern
Frankfurt • Berlin • Brussels • Vienna • Oxford

Flows, Rhythms, and Intensities

of

EARLY CHILDHOOD EDUCATION CURRICULUM

EDITED BY VERONICA PACINI-KETCHABAW

PETER LANG

New York • Washington, D.C./Baltimore • Bern
Frankfurt • Berlin • Brussels • Vienna • Oxford

Library of Congress Cataloging-in-Publication Data

Flows, rhythms, and intensities of early childhood education curriculum /
edited by Veronica Pacini-Ketchabaw.
p. cm. — (Rethinking childhood; v. 45)
Includes bibliographical references.
1. Early childhood education—Curricula. 2. Postmodernism and education.
I. Pacini-Ketchabaw, Veronica.
LB1139.4.F56   372.19—dc22   2010014248
ISBN 978-1-4331-0900-3 (hardcover)
ISBN 978-1-4331-0899-0 (paperback)
ISSN 1086-7155

Bibliographic information published by **Die Deutsche Nationalbibliothek**.
Die Deutsche Nationalbibliothek lists this publication in the "Deutsche
Nationalbibliografie"; detailed bibliographic data is available
on the Internet at http://dnb.d-nb.de/.

Cover photo by Sylvia Kind, *Dialogues with nature* painting project,
Capilano University Children's Centre.

The paper in this book meets the guidelines for permanence and durability
of the Committee on Production Guidelines for Book Longevity
of the Council of Library Resources.

Printed in the United States of America

To my sister, Maria Angeles Pacini,

who has always showed courage

in her practice and life.

○ **Contents**

Acknowledgments   ix

Curriculum's Flows, Rhythms, and Intensities: A Beginning   xi
Veronica Pacini-Ketchabaw

■ FLOWS

1   Thinking beyond a Framework: Entering into Dialogues   3
Enid Elliot

2   These Ventriloquist Walls:
Troubling Language in Early Childhood Education   21
Cristina D. Vintimilla

3   Rethinking Children's Participation in Curriculum Making:
A Rhizomatic Movement   39
Kirsten Ho Chan

■ RHYTHMS

4   Extending the Notion of Pedagogical Narration
through Hannah Arendt's Political Thought   57
Iris Berger

5   A Story to Unsettle Assumptions about Critical
Reflection in Practice   77
Deborah Thompson

■ INTENSITIES

6   Is It Time to Put "Tidy Up Time" Away?: Contesting Routines
    and Transitions in Early Childhood Spaces   97
    Kathleen Kummen

7   Art Encounters: Movements in the Visual Arts
    and Early Childhood Education   113
    Sylvia Kind

8   A Curriculum for Social Change: Experimenting with Politics
    of Action or Imperceptibility   133
    Veronica Pacini-Ketchabaw with Fikile Nxumalo

9   Disrupting Colonial Power through Literacy:
    A Story about Creating Inuttitut-Language Children's Books   155
    Mary Caroline Rowan

10 Families and Pedagogical Narration: Disrupting Traditional
    Understandings of Family Involvement   177
    *Laurie Kocher with Paul Cabaj, David Chapman,
    Nancy Chapman, Carmen Ryujin, and Elizabeth Wooding*

Notes on the Contributors   203

○ Acknowledgments

This book has been the effort of many people. I would like to thank Rob Ketchabaw, who has provided much more than his time and support for this book to be possible, and Jacob Ketchabaw, who has provided me with the balance in my life without me asking. Their encouragement keeps me going. I am grateful to all the contributors to this book and to Leslie Prpich for her meticulous and insightful feedback and editing along the way. Finally, I would like to acknowledge the contributions of all the early childhood educators in British Columbia who have shared with me their practices and passions and have had the courage to try something new.

○ Curriculum's Flows, Rhythms, and Intensities: A Beginning

Veronica Pacini-Ketchabaw

> *It is possible to work with movement in subjectivity and learning, starting from the idea that it is already there and always continuously ongoing.*
> —Liselott Mariett Olsson, *Movement and Experimentation in Young Children's Learning: Deleuze and Guattari in Early Childhood Education*, 2009, p. 179

Engaging with movement and experimentation in young children's learning requires a curriculum that *invents* instead of predicts, that *moves* rather than controls. Then, it is not the curriculum's subject areas that come to matter but its *flows, rhythms,* and *intensities*. These, Gilles Deleuze and Felix Guattari (1987) suggest, are possibilities for other worlds.

This book is a collection of essays that highlights the flows, rhythms, and intensities—often imperceptible and difficult to capture—that run through early childhood education curriculum. It emerged from the authors' individual and collective work over the last 5 years of formal and informal collaboration. As is reflected in the various chapters, we come from different perspectives, viewpoints, and theoretical standpoints. This diversity has always enriched our conversations and I believe it enriches this book. The chapters can be read alone but also as a dialogue that gives voice to our beginning points. By beginnings, I do not mean *origins*, but rather what Edward Said (1985) refers to as *problems*: "Beginnings inaugurate a deliberately other production of meaning .... A beginning, therefore, is a problem to be studied..." (p. 13). This book was initiated with beginnings and, I hope, is a beginning in itself.

Seeking such an encounter, the book is addressed to students and practicing educators who are interested in opening up their practice and transgressing its limits. It will appeal to theoreticians and researchers in the early childhood education field. The book follows theory, uses theory, bends theory, does with theory, and transforms theory, but it is not a book *about* theory. Instead it troubles dualistic positions like theory/practice that constitute and perpetuate power relations within the field. While much of the literature in early childhood education views theory and practice as separate categories and refers to the application of theory to practice, this book, as Hillevi Lenz Taguchi (2009) might say, attempts to work within the intra-active nature of theory and practice.

○ Curriculum: How and Why?

Much of the literature on curriculum in early childhood education follows modernist understandings of childhood and early education, outlining ways that curriculum is to be developed (e.g., Marcus & Nyisztor, 2008). In fact, curriculum emerged as a "grand narrative" of the West, as part of the technical-rational or factory model to construct efficient and effective societies (Pinar, Reynolds, Slattery, & Taubman, 2000). By engaging in the intersections between postfoundational theories and everyday early childhood classroom practices, this book joins the dialogue that Shirley Kessler and Beth Blue Swadener (1992) bravely initiated in the early 1990s with their renowned volume *Reconceptualizing the Early Childhood Curriculum: Beginning the Dialogue*. This book, like theirs, responds to events within early childhood education studies and curriculum studies.

Modernist approaches to curriculum were based on a belief in a singular definition of "best"—the belief that a scientific approach to early childhood education would reveal a transcendent "truth." Early childhood reconceptualists question the modernist enterprise of curriculum development as too narrow an approach to the diverse ways of being and becoming (Dahlberg, Moss, & Pence, 2007; Kessler & Swadener, 1992). Curriculum studies theorists also dispute modernist perspectives of curriculum, and this book engages with their challenges. As Pinar and colleagues (2000) write:

> The field [of curriculum studies] no longer sees the problems of curriculum and teaching as "technical" problems, that is, problems of "how to." The contemporary field regards the problems of curriculum and teaching as "why" problems. Such a view requires that we understand what was before considered only something to be solved.

Now, the contemporary field is hardly against solving problems, but the view today is that solutions to problems do not just require knee-jerk, commonsensical responses, but careful, thoughtful, disciplined understandings. (p. 8)

The authors in this book engage in dialogues in "careful, thoughtful, and disciplined" ways to create new possibilities for early childhood education curriculum. We do not provide "how-tos" but embrace the idea of curriculum as a dynamic and fluid encounter. We challenge the concept of curriculum as an innocent solution to the complex landscape of early childhood education.

Following suggestions made by Pinar and colleagues (2000) almost a decade ago, this book speaks about engagements with curriculum, about acknowledging and struggling with its complexities, about deliberation, and about the necessity of viewing curriculum as a provocation to ask difficult questions. Curriculum cannot become a road map that educators follow, a one direction that will take them to one destination, or a description of what early childhood education services need to overcome or to manage or to conquer (Looney, 2001). Instead, curriculum can become an opportunity to resist, to make meaning, and to search out other (invisible, out-of-sight) meanings. As researchers and educators, this book's authors do not propose that readers follow the ideas presented here as solutions for early childhood classrooms. Rather we hope that readers will be sparked to meaningfully and critically engage with, contest, and resist everyday discourses by asking questions that will bring early childhood practice to "other" spaces.

The curriculum that is reimagined in this book is historically, socially, and politically situated within, not outside of, relations of power as social constructions (not truths). Dussel, Tiramonti, and Birgin (2000) suggest thinking of curriculum as part of "new maps of relations between the centre and the periphery of the educational system" (p. 537). Therefore, the authors engage with questions rather than answers: What new cartographies of power do postmodern curricula establish? How are young children and educators repositioned and reshaped within these new cartographies? What new languages are created and for what purposes?

We invite the reader to think of curriculum as "intensely historical, political, racial, gendered, phenomenological, autobiographical, aesthetic, theological, and international. Curriculum becomes the site on which the generations struggle to define themselves and the world" (Pinar et al., 2000, pp. 847–848). These chapters inspire us to rethink curriculum as "an extraordinarily complicated conversation" through which it "ceases to be a thing, and…is more than a process. It becomes a verb, an action, a social practice, a private meaning, and a public hope" (Pinar et al., 2000, p. 848). It becomes flows, rhythms, and intensities.

○ From Curriculum to Frameworks

Many of the chapters engage with an interesting trend in recently published Canadian curriculum frameworks: an attempt to move away from long-debated guidelines, such as developmentally appropriate practice (DAP), that have dominated thinking within early childhood education for many decades in North America (see Cannella, 1997; Dahlberg et al., 2007 for an analysis of DAP). Responding to the critiques of DAP guidelines, some Canadian governments have demonstrated an interest in embedding aspects of postmodern practices/theories in frameworks for practice (e.g., Early Childhood Research and Development Team, 2007; Government of British Columbia, 2008; Saskatchewan Ministry of Education, 2008).[1] These documents speak of children's identities as complex, multiple, and situated within historical, cultural, and social contexts. They challenge standardized testing, acknowledge diversity, and propose tools such as pedagogical documentation (see Dahlberg et al., 2007) as preferred methods for engaging in practices that value depth and context. Given this opening up to postmodern ideas, this book considers what it might mean to think and work within the context of these frameworks.

The authors do not do so uncritically, however. Frameworks are viewed as spaces for critical engagement for *beginnings*. In *Beyond Quality*, Dahlberg et al. (2007) suggest that we cannot "fool ourselves about what frameworks of normalization are or what they can do" (p. 116). They propose that we "recognize their limitations and dangers, their assumptions and values. Let them not be at the expense of ignoring other ways of thinking about and making sense of early childhood institutions and the work they do" (p. 116). This book's authors believe that we need to bring similar concerns when engaging with postmodern frameworks. This is not to suggest that frameworks are inherently bad and should be forgotten—they are here to stay. Rather, the chapters in this book attest that we need to reimagine the ways we engage with their meanings, their implications, and our uses of them.

○ Working with Educators and Students

Like in any other text, the ideas we explore were developed in conversations with many others beyond the authors included here. In particular, ongoing dialogues with educators and early childhood students enriched this book. Everyday engagement with the field brought these chapters together and created spaces for the authors to meaningfully engage in thinking *otherwise* about curriculum. As many of the chapters attest, educators and early childhood education students have worked with us, challenged us, and been challenged by us. Alejandra Sanchez, an instructor in an early childhood education program in British Columbia and a colleague who contributed greatly to the discussions that sparked this book, describes as follows the complex and uncertain processes of engaging with students to disrupt dominant ways of understanding early childhood education:

> It has been a thought-provoking endeavour to critically reflect on the students' work produced in my classroom. It seems that their pedagogical understandings have been contested and changed. The students' reflections occur when they encounter, get familiar with, and reflect collaboratively on the proposals, language, tools, and strategies of poststructural perspectives. Their thinking expresses the complexities of problematizing what they have considered their "will of truth" (MacNaughton, 2005).
>
> On one hand, the students realize they are immersed in disrupting a developmental psychology body of knowledge that is a logical and a familiar discourse for them. They realize they have been subjects of study under this lens and have also been subjects that reproduce the same dominant discourse when they interact and interpret children's identities and discourses. On the other hand, the students become aware that familiarity with this dominant discourse—its linearity and its universality—has restricted the possibilities of multiple readings when examining and interpreting the images of the child.
>
> The students also express the complexity that the poststructural literature presents to them. Becoming familiar and comfortable with poststructural statements such as the "truth does not exist" (MacNaughton, 2005, p. 5); "uncertainty is the state to live and act" (MacNaughton, 2005, p. 74); and the understanding of how "uneven power relations operate in different regimes of truth through specific discourses" (MacNaughton, 2005, p. 74) in relation to their experiences with children, teachers, families, and learning communities in the early childhood education field in which they are situated presents many challenges. Yet, the students have adopted an attitude of inquiry that allows them to engage in disrupting truths. For me it has been rewarding to see shifts in the students' interpretations and the connections they make with their own realities.
>
> Alejandra Sanchez

○ About the Book

The book is organized in three strands that reside in curriculum's creative and productive practices: flows, rhythms, and intensities. These strands are intended to be productive, to put curriculum in motion.

Flows repositions educators and children in curriculum, disrupting notions of them as mere knowledge transmitters and receivers. In Chapter 1, Enid Elliot challenges the very idea of frameworks in early childhood education. She argues that the dynamic processes of relationships cannot be represented in a framework—relationships require dialogue and meaningful interactions, while frameworks are monologues. In Chapter 2, Cristina D. Vintimilla examines a group of student productions that hang on "ventriloquist walls" to provoke the reader to consider language's performativity in the discursive formation of educators' identities. She challenges images of the early childhood educator as a child, as a "chaos avoider," or as always in control. In Chapter 3, Kirsten Ho Chan shifts attention to the image of the child, specifically the concept of children's participation in curriculum development. She challenges uncritical conceptualizations of children as competent, and argues that we have to push our theoretical approaches to crack open the concept of participation.

Rhythms is about the *doings* of curriculum. It critically engages with the ethical and political dilemmas of how curriculum is performed. In Chapter 4, Iris Berger extends the concept of pedagogical documentation or pedagogical narration to political spaces, arguing that curriculum needs to become a tool for political action. In Chapter 5, Deborah Thompson describes her experience of attempting to engage in critical reflection. She points the reader to the impossibility of reflecting critically without challenging the idea of a knowable subject.

Drawing on a range of postfoundational theories, *Intensities* reenvisions the spaces in which curriculum is performed. In Chapter 6, Kathleen Kummen provides a critical perspective on everyday routines and transitions in early childhood education. She links the emphasis on consistent classroom routines and transitions to the unquestioned truths of modernist understandings of child development. In Chapter 7, Sylvia Kind engages in the intersection between early childhood education and the visual arts. She argues that unpredictability and difficulty are not problems to be resolved but engagements to make possible new beginnings. Art in early childhood education, she contends, is immanent to its effects and the very possibilities it opens. In Chapter 8, in collaboration with Fikile Nxumalo, I propose a pedagogy of action or imperceptibility to rethink the ways early childhood education has approached social justice. I experiment with the concepts of force and materiality to rethink social action. In Chapter 9, Mary Caroline Rowan explores a bookmaking project with Inuit early childhood educators from the perspective of postcolonial discourses. She opens a space to think about the imprint of colonialism in contemporary Inuit life. In Chapter 10, Laurie Kocher writes with a group of families to trouble the idea of partnerships between educators and families. She argues that learning communities in which families and children are meaningfully involved require close attention to building relationships that are ethically and politically situated.

The book should not be read as a final capture of curriculum's movements, but as a "passing by" that generates flows, rhythms, and intensities.

ENDNOTES

1 Because the majority of the authors' work is locally situated in the province of British Columbia, Canada, several of the chapters engage with the *British Columbia Early Learning Framework* (Government of British Columbia, 2008).

REFERENCES

Cannella, G. S. (1997). *Deconstructing early childhood education: Social justice & revolution.* New York: Peter Lang.

Dahlberg, G., Moss, P., & Pence, A. R. (2007). *Beyond quality in early childhood education and care: Postmodern perspectives.* London: Falmer.

Deleuze, G., & Guattari, F. L. (1987). *A thousand plateaus: Capitalism and schizophrenia.* Minneapolis, MN: University of Minnesota Press.

Dussel, I., Tiramonti, G., & Birgin, A. (2000). Towards a new cartography of curriculum reform: Reflections on educational decentralization in Argentina. *Journal of Curriculum Studies, 32*(4), 537–559.

Early Childhood Research and Development Team. (2007). *Early learning and child care: English curriculum framework for New Brunswick.* Fredericton, NB: Family and Community Services.

Government of British Columbia. (2008). *British Columbia early learning framework.* Victoria, BC: Ministry of Education, Ministry of Health, Ministry of Children and Family Development, & British Columbia Early Learning Advisory Group.

Kessler, S., & Swadener, B. B. (Eds.). (1992). *Reconceptualizing the early childhood curriculum: Beginning the dialogue.* New York: Teachers College Press.

Lenz Taguchi, H. (2009). *Going beyond the theory/practice divide in early childhood education: Introducing an intra-active pedagogy.* New York: Routledge.

Looney, A. (2001). Curriculum as policy: Some implications of contemporary policy studies for the analysis of curriculum policy, with particular reference to post-primary curriculum policy in the Republic of Ireland. *Curriculum Journal, 12*(2), 149–162.

MacNaughton, G. (2005). *Doing Foucault in early childhood studies: Applying poststructural ideas.* London: Routledge.

Marcus, B., & Nyisztor, D. (2008). *Balanced curriculum for young children.* Toronto: Prentice Hall.

Olsson, L. M. (2009). *Movement and experimentation in young children's learning: Deleuze and Guattari in early childhood education.* New York: Routledge.

Pinar, W. F., Reynolds, W. M., Slattery, P., & Taubman, P. M. (2000). *Understanding curriculum: An introduction to the study of historical and contemporary curriculum discourses.* New York: Peter Lang.

Said, E. (1985). *Beginnings: Intention and method.* New York: Columbia University Press.

Saskatchewan Ministry of Education. (2008). *Play and exploration: Early learning program guide.* Saskatoon, SK: Early Learning and Child Care Branch, Ministry of Education.

Flows

Always follow the rhizome by rupture; lengthen, prolong, and relay the line of flight; make it vary, until you have ... broken directions. Conjugate deterritorialized flows.

—Deleuze and Guattari,
A thousand plateaus: Capitalism and schizophrenia, 1987, p. 11

CHAPTER ONE

Thinking beyond a Framework: Entering into Dialogues

Enid Elliot

By sharing stories we share ourselves, we encourage our listeners to remember their own narratives, and we begin a dialogue. Before I make claims about where this chapter will go and what it will possibly say, I want to share a story. This incident took place nearly 35 years ago, and I continue to wonder about it—

Sam arrived early that morning at the preschool full of bounce and enthusiasm. Having just turned 3 years old he had been coming to the toddler program for a year. After lunch it was clear he was ready for a nap. He was rubbing his eyes and slowing down. But once he was on his cot he squirmed and wiggled. While the others had quickly fallen asleep, he seemed to be fighting sleep; in fact, he was actually holding his eyelids open. I sat beside him and patted his back, but he seemed unable to relax, despite his yawns. This was not his usual pattern.

Finally, I picked him up, wrapped him in his blanket and held him like a baby. "Sam, it's okay to shut your eyes. I'm right here. If you see anything scary when your eyes are shut, just open them and I'll be here." I said this several times and he finally gave a shudder, an enormous sigh, and closed his eyes.

Later, having a cup of tea, I mentioned Sam's difficulty falling asleep to the social worker who visited the families in our program. Half seriously, I said to her, "If I didn't know better I would think his mother had taken him to see *The Exorcist*!" *The Exorcist* was a 1970s horror film about a young girl possessed by demons that were playing nearby.

"She did," replied the social worker. "It was what they did to celebrate his third birthday."

While there may have been no connection, I wondered what images Sam saw as he shut his eyes. I cannot wholly articulate why I responded to Sam as I did, but he relaxed and slept. At the time I felt certain he was tired, very tired. I felt I knew his "tired signals," as I knew those of the others in my small group of six 2 year olds. With hindsight I might attempt to explain myself, but I am uncertain to this day what was actually at work. Paley (1979) tells a similar story in her book *White Teacher*, about an incident at the beginning of her teaching career when the correct soothing words came to her as she spoke with a young girl in her class. Perhaps rocking Sam and murmuring as I did calmed him, and perhaps he worried about images from *The Exorcist*, but perhaps not. I don't remember speaking of it again with him or his mother and he did not have trouble at naptime after that. My memory of this incident has stayed with me, as I never knew how I came up with those words and actions. I responded to him within the context of our year long relationship, a long time with someone who has just turned 3. Sam's response gave meaning to my words and actions and furthered my understanding of him. He relaxed and fell asleep, and I understood that to mean that what I had said made him more comfortable.

This is not a situation that can be held up as a model or template for acting, nor can Paley's story. Yet both of these stories illustrate the power of intuitive action taken within a relationship of care. Being engaged with children and their families in an early childhood program requires being in relationship with them. While there may be social or political agendas to get children "ready for school," to rescue them from their situations of poverty or to improve their health, it is often the educators' relationships with children and their families that are the key to success in attaining these goals.

The current interest in the early years has led to policies, curricula, and frameworks designed to create and regulate optimal experiences for children. I suggest that encouraging dialogue within the field among researchers, policymakers, educators, parents, and children has far greater potential than these frameworks, texts, or curricula to create conditions for learning and understanding.

Educators, parents, and children bring rich and varied stories and abilities to the relationships they form. The stories we bring of childhood, of families, of the work of caring influences the dialogue in which we engage. The images we hold of an early childhood educator, a parent, or a child will give shape to our discussion. The nature of a dialogue is dynamic and engaged; relationships also are about engagement, responsiveness, and responsibility. Being alert to all aspects of another person requires a welcoming attitude and an open heart.

Frameworks and curricula cannot mandate attitudes, assumptions, and reflection; unable to engage dialogically they cannot know or respond to individual and local concerns. A framework or curriculum, even a chapter, fails to engage educators in a dialogue where thinking can shift and new ideas can be formulated.

Using Bakhtin's concept of dialogue and his construction of the responsibility to be *answerable*, I would like to look closely at the failure of frameworks and curricula to engage shifts in thinking. As a member of the early childhood community in British Columbia, I will focus on the BC Early Learning Framework (Government of British Columbia, 2008) to explore this failure. The framework was developed over 2–3 years in discussions with educators, researchers, and policymakers. A great deal of effort went into creating the framework, though the discussion was never taken widely to the community at local levels. The document is conscientious about acknowledging diversity and it encourages parents and caregivers to reflect on their children's learning. Aboriginal communities are creating a parallel document to reflect their visions and beliefs, and this is acknowledged in the document. While it is a thoughtful document, it cannot engage in a dialogue that is "answerable" or that might effect changes in thinking that will be reflected in practice.

Bakhtin offers us a vocabulary and a conceptual framework with which to discuss the dynamics of relationships created with children, families, and colleagues. His writing spoke to my own small conversation with myself of this incident and other aspects of practice. By sharing my narrative and inviting the reader to remember her own stories of practice and care, I am hoping to create a small internal dialogue within the reader to accompany the reading of this text, reminding the reader of personal stories in order to engage in a discussion of Bakhtin's ideas and the growing use of curricula and frameworks for guiding practice.

Our stories make visible our internal dialogues. Remembering our own stories of our practice can provide us with a deeper awareness of what needs to be shared and understood about this work. I hope my story will provide an opportunity, a space, for readers to remember their stories about children and about working and caring in an early childhood program, thus hopefully creating an internal small dialogue.

○ Creating Conditions of Learning and Caring

Children come to early childhood programs bringing their stories, their beliefs, and their curiosity. The early childhood setting is often their first experience of community outside their home, and the child looks to the educator for reassurance, support, and explanations. Like most people going into a new situation, children want to feel they can trust the new place, its people, and the materials.

Malaguzzi writes that "the aim of teaching is not to produce learning but to produce the conditions for learning" (Rinaldi, 2006, pp. 173–174). An educator who welcomes children into a dialogue, who is curious about their views and perspectives creates an environment of learning, an environment that values mutual learning and understanding. Within such an environment, children and families can feel that their stories will be valued and considered and that they in turn can listen and evaluate the stories offered to them.

The BC Early Learning Framework (Government of British Columbia, 2008) envisions a child who is capable, curious, and complex. I imagine an educator who is equally capable, curious, and complex engaged in dialogue using imagination, empathy, and caring to create a setting that encourages young children to learn and grow. By listening, caring, and encouraging dialogue we will create the conditions that nurture children, families, and ourselves. Since each of us is unique, dialogues will be particular to the participants, the place, and the time. Bakhtin (1993) urges us to look upon a human being as the centre of our attention and to gaze upon her or him with "aesthetic seeing": "In aesthetic seeing you love a human being not because he is good, but, rather, a human being is good because you love him" (p. 62).

o Images of Early Childhood Educators: Technicians, Experts, Custodians

Working as an infant/toddler teacher I had a small group of children for whom I cared and with whom I interacted. Sam was just one of the six children in the group and within that group each child was different, each mother or father or grandparent was different and with each I had a different relationship. Working within the context of a unique relationship I had to respond to each in a manner appropriate to that person, which meant I had to pay attention and often I needed to use imagination to begin to understand another's perspective.

The responsibility of caring for and about another is complex and presents unique challenges and rewards within each relationship. The complexity of this practice is often obscured by popular-culture images of educators as technicians, experts, or custodians. While each of these images can perhaps be meaningful or useful in particular situations, they often oversimplify the work of engaging with children and families, directing attention away from the difficult and often ambiguous aspects of connecting deeply within relationship.

Children's growth and development is often represented as sequential and predictable, with a primary focus on children's acquisition of skills (e.g., Bredekamp & Copple, 1997; Copple & Bredekamp, 2009; Meisels & Atkins-Burnett, 2005). Children's growth, as measured through articulated norms of skills and behaviours, appears simple, even straightforward. Within this vision of normatively ranked children, the image of the educator appears as a technician whose job is to ensure the achievement of children's demonstrable skills and abilities; her role is to facilitate children's movement from one stage to the next. Within a developmental viewpoint (Copple & Bredekamp, 2009) is an implicit belief that each progressive stage is "better" as children move to the end product of *adult*. The child's contribution to society as an adult is valued as part of the future. When judging children in terms of a prescribed set of norms, lost within this view are the children's individual patterns of growth, diverse histories and perspectives, and possible contributions in the present moment.

The current emphasis in early childhood education on readiness for school (Hertzman, 2000; Hertzman & Kohen, 2003) implies that to improve our society (country), children need to succeed in school and to succeed at school they must have a prescribed set of skills that will guarantee their success. As a result, pressure is placed on educators who are (strongly) encouraged by government agencies to ensure that all children have the necessary skills for school (Bowman & Moore, 2006). These specific skills have been defined as applicable to all children; they are largely skills believed to achieve academic accomplishment. This emphasis on academic skills narrows educators' focus in their interactions with children (Hertzman, 2000). When we focus on readiness skills, educators become *technicians* who, in turn, must develop a specific set of skills. Thus early childhood education programs become "training programs" to provide educators with the required set of skills that will promote children's skills for school success.

The developmental discourse can also position the educator as *expert* with specialized skills and knowledge of young children over and above parental knowledge. This expert knowledge implies that the educator already understands children in general, knows what they need, and can apply her knowledge for the general good of all children; specific knowledge and understanding of a particular child is seen to be less important. The title of expert also suggests knowledge or power to which others must defer and whose opinion holds greater weight than, for example, parents or a community.

As *custodian* the educator is expected to keep children safe and healthy. Requirements for hygiene, nutrition, and safety are carefully prescribed and educators are expected to adhere to them. Custodial images of educators abound in places as diverse as licensing regulations and the media. Expectations for preparing children for school or providing enriched experiences give way to discussions of safety, health, and hygiene.

The roles of technician, expert, and custodian give the perception that the work of interacting with young children and their families is simply a matter of mastering a finite set of skills and knowledge that define early childhood. Keeping children safe and healthy and preparing them for school are limited goals which can distract attention from the more complex dynamics that occur in early childhood programs. It is my contention that *working with children and families requires entering into and sustaining diverse relationships.* An approach and attitude other than that of expert, technician, or custodian is required to develop deep and meaningful connections with children and their families. The skills, knowledge, and imagination that are critical to building a community of children, families, and educators vary and are dependent on individuals and context. An educator needs to enter into relationships with care, imagination, and thought. Responding as an individual with an open mind and heart, an educator is interested in entering into an ongoing dialogue with children and families that can go far beyond the roles of expert, technician, or custodian. When we understand child development to be "messy" and unpredictable rather than straightforward and simple (Carr, 2001), narrow images of experts, technicians, or custodians constrain our thinking.

○ Images of the Child and the Early Learning Framework

The Early Learning Framework (ELF) of British Columbia presents an alternative to the child development perspective that has dominated our field. Committed to a vision of the child as capable and able to engage fully with the world, the ELF acknowledges that each child is uniquely situated within a particular family and within space and time, while the educator exists in relation to the child as provider, constructor, and reflector. The framework presents an image of the child as "capable and full of potential," complex, and curious. The ELF defines children as learners rather than seeing them more broadly as actors; while we are all learners, we are also doers and creators within our lives. As whole people with histories, communities, beliefs, and values, educators bring all of these influences into their interactions with children. The ELF aims to encourage thinking and reflection—for example, guidelines are provided for educators in the form of questions, such as "In what ways are toddlers' questions and concerns respected?"— but *without a space for dialogue and without others with whom to discuss,* it may be hard for educators to challenge their own thinking or acknowledge the range of abilities and skills they bring with them to the relationships they create with children and their families.

Relationships are acknowledged in the ELF as "essential to children's well-being" (Government of British Columbia, 2008, p. 15), but the emphasis is on relationships as an abstract element, beneficial to children only, rather than a dynamic and rich interaction between unique individuals who will create unique and particular moments. The document's focus, perhaps reflecting the current school readiness focus, is on cognitive learning rather than on community membership and connection to one's particular and unique place in history and space.

It is possible to have relationships with children in a role as an expert defining their stage of development or their level of academic skills, or as a custodian concerned with their safety, but in my discussions (Elliot, 2001, 2002, 2007) with educators, I found that they deeply valued the intimacy and the richness of the relationships they created with individual children. I spoke with women who had worked with children for over 5 years or more and were committed to creating good experiences for children; none of them spoke in terms of caring solely for children's health or their intellectual skills. Having experienced the power of connecting with children on a deep and personal level, these educators found meaning and satisfaction in their work from the relationships. None of them spoke of children in terms of the totalizing language of generalized child development, but rather in terms of each individual child. Each child was an individual and each relationship took on different meanings for the caregivers, and they had learned there was no one template for building that relationship.

If, as it seems abundantly clear, children cannot be neatly defined and their development cannot be categorized, we must construct a different vision of children (Burman, 2008; Rogoff, 2003; Singer, 1992). The caregivers I interviewed developed an individual image of a particular child; each was seen as a unique individual with whom caregivers created a singular relationship. As one educator who cared for infants said, "each child has a different cry and different cries for different reasons" (Elliot, 2007, p. 85). Each of these educators saw the children as capable of being in relationship and able to communicate. Within each relationship, there was a dialogue.

○ Acting within the Dialogue of Relationship

M. M. Bakhtin (1895–1975) speaks a great deal about language and dialogue and how our view of the world is shaped by our words and our interactions with others. A Russian sociolinguist who wrote through the 20th century, his writings have slowly filtered out to a more general audience and can give us some possible ways of imagining and articulating the work of being in relationship. While he did not write about pedagogy per se, his philosophical writings have the possibility of enriching and extending our thinking about our work with children and families (White & Nuttall, 2007).

Comprehending another's actions or understanding another's words has many levels and complexities. The one speaking and the one hearing, each have a unique set of meanings and beliefs. As Bakhtin says, "the word in language is half someone else's" (Bakhtin, 1994, p. 77). Bakhtin remarks that we cannot see ourselves, but others can. Because of that they can give us the gift of their sight of us and the context in which we are embedded, and, in turn, we can share what we see of them and their context.

The words we use, as well as the discourses within which they are embedded, structure our vision, understandings, and perspectives. As O'Loughlin (2009) reminds us, "subjectivity is actively constructed at the vortex of ancestral memory, sociohistorical circumstance, local discursive practices, and the mediating influences of language, schooling and other official regulatory processes" (p. 22). Meanings can shift and fracture depending on the context, speaker, and history; any utterance is "overlain with qualifications, open to dispute, charged with value, already enveloped in an obscuring mist" (Bakhtin, 1994, p. 75).

Bakhtin acknowledges that some discussions or perspectives are considered "truer" than others, pulling our attention in one direction, while more personal or historical perspectives can pull meaning and understanding in yet another direction. All of this pulling results in a tension, which is brought to any dialogue. In the field of early childhood education, developmental psychology has been a dominant voice for a long period of time, creating a pull in a particular direction by structuring the vision we have of children and weighting our dialogues in the direction of a universal vision of children and their families. Yet underneath this dominant voice there are diverse personal voices that run parallel or counter or at oblique angles to the generalizing, universalist discourse. All of these layers become part of the multiple voices engaged in the discussions we have within the field.

The current challenges to the developmental perspective (Burman, 1994, 2008; Cannella, 1997; Dahlberg, Moss, & Pence, 1999) have moved us away from the linear, sequential, "ages and stages" language of child development to a more complex and holistic view of children and families. As multiple perspectives become more apparent, we have an opportunity to examine and reflect on our practice of building relationships with children and families.

As early childhood educators, we have a vision of the children with whom we live and work. That vision influences how we enact our role with children and at the same time guides our thinking and engagement. As we enter into a relationship with a family or a child, the dialogue into which we enter impacts that vision while the vision also colours the nature of the dialogue. The dialogues are infinite, building the potential for new relationships and meaning.

Within a dialogic relationship people can create new meanings and ideas. From dialogues each of us can continue to learn and grow. Approaching children and their families in a spirit of dialogue, open to listening and considering multiple voices, can keep educators growing and learning, not settling for easy definitions or solutions. As Grumet (1988) says, "as we share the care of a child with her parents we engage in a mimetic and empathetic relation with them as well as with the child, gaining access to their hope as well as to their habits of nurture" (p. 179).

Out of our dialogues new understandings and ideas grow, change, and are never finalized. Together, through dialogue, educator, parents, and children construct new meanings because we have the opportunity to see and interpret the other's experience. Beyond the ways in which they understand themselves, while they can do the same for us. As we respond to another, we set the ground for understanding; in listening to each other and understanding what we can about the other's perspective we are then called, according to Bakhtin, to act in response to our understanding, or to act *responsibly*.

Responsibility to Listen

When we enter what Bakhtin calls a dialogic relationship with another person, we come to a constantly emerging understanding through the process of dialogue. The speaker constructs an image on the horizon of the listener and it is in the "borderzone" between participants that new ideas and understandings are formed. Both participants are needed in the dialogue; without the listener the speaker does not have another person with whom and to whom s/he must shape her/his ideas. Shaping the ideas in anticipation of the responses of the listener(s) changes the speaker's understanding. According to Bakhtin (1994), "understanding comes to fruition only in the response. Understanding and response are dialectically merged and mutually condition each other; one is impossible without the other" (1994, p. 76). Coming to understanding is a continuing, ongoing process, the relationship evolving as both people strive to comprehend but never arrive at a final understanding of the other.

Dialogue is not solely word-based; dialogue includes different modalities, different modes of expression. We can view children's play as one of their ways of creating a dialogue with each other, with adults, and with objects. While children may take on particular roles or ask particular questions, we can listen to hear what is being asked of us. We may wonder how we will respond in a manner that encourages dialogue or answers a question that opens up possibility rather than oppresses opportunity. Listening with care and empathy, we can respond in a manner that expands understanding. As I *listened* to Sam's struggle to stay awake and responded to him, his answering relaxation gave me further knowledge of him and his concerns; clearly, it seemed as if Sam's concern was *heard*. While there is a temptation to draw conclusions of his possible dreams and nightmares, I must hesitate and not settle on a conclusion; there might be other ways to understand the incident.

When we engage with children and families, a variety of voices need to be heard, and in listening to them we create a dialogic space within which to welcome the voices of parents and other family members. We must carefully consider our responses, as each response will set up another one. How we respond will be unique to each situation and will lead us to the next conversation. As we listen closely and carefully, we will confront our own images of families and challenge our assumptions.

Entering into relationship with others is an uncertain enterprise and listening helps to guide us in the uncertainty. Edmiston (2008) reminds us:

> Listening with compassion requires us to project into the lives of other people and to contemplate actions from their viewpoint. Listening with the heart is the beginning of ethical action because we can't treat people or other creatures as objects when we view the world as if we were them. Listening to people who aren't actually there requires an act of the ethical imagination, a human faculty that develops in play, especially child-adult play. (p. 171)

"Answerability" as Ethical Practice

Acting ethically within our relationships, listening to all the voices, even those of people who "aren't actually there" but may be part of our family, workplace, or community, takes imagination and care. Within a dialogue we are responsible or "answerable" for our response and our actions. Each encounter has its own context and meaning; that moment in time happens only once and is unique. Our response to each encounter and individual is different. We answer them within a particular time and setting; each one of us is answerable for our actions.

Bakhtin argues for an ethics of the particular moment rather than universal ethical principles. He says, "any universally valid value becomes actually valid only in an individual context" (1993, p. 36). While each of us needs the other to create understanding, we alone are responsible for our actions, whether thought or deed. There is an interconnection and a merging of "response-ability" here. Within an interaction we are constructing meaning with others, our responses being sensible of the other person(s) and, while we are working in concert with others, we are still alone and answerable for our actions.

In our interactions with children and with families, we are answerable to them in each moment that we are in dialogue. Bakhtin sees our ethical behaviour as contextualized and relational. Since we are constantly in dialogue with others, if not face to face then in our imaginations, our ethical positions are never static and our interactions with families will inform them as well as ourselves. As we grow, we develop voices within to which we listen and they help us to form our responses in the moment.

Edmiston (2008) further explains that, for Bakhtin, "when people are answerable their ethical understandings are affected and transformed because they allow themselves to be addressed by another person's ideas that dialogically affect and shape the framework they use to make meaning" (p. 17). Here is the significant point in Bakhtin's thinking—he suggests that we imagine the others' viewpoint and in that imagining, we are changed. As well, as we can offer insights to the other person that can change their perspective; it can be an infinite process of dialogue.

Bakhtin's view of the relational and contextual nature of action in the world fits comfortably with the discussions in the early childhood field of an *ethic of care*. An ethic of care "is not a system of principles, rules or universalizable maxims; instead, it is a mode of human responsiveness that is manifest in particular situations and types of relationships" (Cole & Coultrap-McQuin, 1992, p. 4). For example, caring for Sam and his perceived need for sleep meant being aware of his signals and finding the words to reassure him.

As we look more closely at early childhood work, the complexity of the practice becomes visible. As Bowden (1997) writes, "understanding is directed towards consideration of the particularity of concrete situations, and their complex interconnections in the fabric of their unique participants' lives" (pp. 3–4). Caring for children and for families often entails making a judgment from information gathered in the moment from observations, discussions, or imagination. Often Sam did not take a nap as he arrived later in the morning; on those days he and I went to watch subway trains while the others slept. My focus was on Sam, and not that it was nap time.

Focusing on relationships as central to early childhood practice means caring about the children, families, and co-workers and caring about what is important to the person, family, and community with which one is engaged. Dahlberg and Moss (2005) continue the discussion: "At its heart, therefore, the ethics of care is about how to interpret and fulfill the responsibility to others. Ethics does not involve conforming to a code but seeking answers to situated questions" (p. 76).

Imagination, Empathy, and Attitude

Living with the tension and uncertainty of being continually in dialogue and answerable requires imagination along with an attitude of openness and empathy. Bakhtin's concept that we see another person and offer that person an understanding of her/him that s/he did not have before requires us to be empathetic and to proceed with care. Bakhtin (1981) urges us to use our "dialogic imagination" to understand our actions from the viewpoints of others and respond accordingly. Taking us outside the rational response, empathy helps us to view the other with a curiosity and an openness that precludes immediate judgment. Empathy, says Papastergiadis in an interview with Zournazi (2002), "shouldn't be confused with a completely mindless or uniform absorption into the other because it isn't a non-critical adoption of the other…empathy is a much more dynamic process: of going closer to be able to see, but also never forgetting where you are coming from" (pp. 95–96).

Aware of the need for empathy, the renowned pediatrician and child psychiatrist D. W. Winnicott describes his conscious efforts to become empathetic with babies; he is quoted in Shepherd, Jones, and Robinson (1996) as saying,

> When I myself started, I was conscious of an inability in myself to carry my natural capacity for empathy with children back to include empathy with babies. I was fully aware of this as a deficiency, and it was a great relief to me when gradually I became able to feel myself into the infant-mother or infant-parent relationship. I think that many who are trained in the physical side must do the same sort of work in themselves in order to become able to stand in a baby's shoes. (p. 40)

It takes openness and imagination to continue to entertain other ideas and perspectives and to allow them to modify our own ideas. Imagination includes our emotional, rational, historical, experiential, and cultural selves as a unified whole, each of these elements influencing the other. While in a single moment we act in unification of the different aspects of our being, we are not a unified, fixed presence since we are continually in dialogue within ourselves and with others. Thus we change and act differently in different moments.

Through others we can imagine other possibilities. Bakhtin (1981) says, "the semantic structure of an internally persuasive discourse is not finite, it is open; in each of the new contexts that dialogize it, this discourse is able to reveal ever new ways to mean" (pp. 345–346). We step into their shoes to see the world from their perspective and then we step outside to understand the situation from another vantage point, giving us a richer and deeper understanding. Working with children and families there are an infinite variety of shoes into which to step in order to challenge our perspectives. Rather than a framework to stimulate our imaginations, we need dialogues and interactions (and maybe shoes).

It is our answerability and our imagination to think about another's perspective that helps us to act ethically and aesthetically. Bakhtin (1993) believes that acting consciously, answerable to another, is where life and art meet. As we accept our unique place-in-being we begin to act from a centre that is ours, but we have to develop "a certain ought-to-be attitude of consciousness, an attitude that is morally valid and answerably active" (p. 36). Rather than generating rules or regulations, Bakhtin tells us that we must create values and understandings that inform our actions, reflecting our own unique position in history. These values, understandings, and perceptions will emerge through our continuing dialogues and interactions.

Through our individual actions and responses to others, we unify or bring together "the moment of what is universal (universally valid) and the moment of what is individual (actual)" (Bakhtin, 1993, p. 29). Each moment is unique to us and to the children with whom we work, and in these moments we author or shape our identities. We also shape the identity of others with whom we are in dialogue and they in turn do the same for us. It is an endless spiral.

In my exchange with Sam at nap time, my imagination suggested possibilities. Having had a relationship with him and knowing he was tired, I imagined what might be hindering his ability to shut his eyes and sleep. In that moment of imagining, I found words that came from our interaction. There is no framework to guide this interaction and yet it provided me with an understanding that enriched our continuing relationship. Benner and Wrubel (1989), speaking of good nursing practice, say that "we cannot generalize by isolating effective actions and transferring the same interventions to another situation" (p. 4). There was no framework, no generalizations, to help me with Sam; rather, there was my relationship, attentiveness, and engagement that helped me find the thing to do.

Uncertainty and Multiple Ways of Knowing

The experience with Sam helped me to begin to develop a sense of trust that if I waited and listened, I would find the right response. I learned to trust that an answer would emerge from a place of uncertainty and hesitation. Claxton (2000), quoting from John Keats, explains the capability "of being in uncertainties, mysteries and doubts without any irritable reaching after fact and reason" (p. 49). When we are able to trust we will learn from our interactions from others and our empathy, caring, and imagination, we will respond ethically.

Claxton discusses the role of intuition in educators' work, suggesting that intuition is a way of knowing that enriches and complements a strictly rational way of knowing. Our rational selves act in the moment with our emotional, social, historical, and cultural selves. Separating the selves undermines the authenticity of the moment. Similar to Bakhtin's notion of the unity of the event—the "theoretical validity, historical factuality and emotional-volitional tone" are all part of the "performed act" (Bakhtin, 1993, p. 28). In other words, we operate from multiple levels in our interactions with others, not just a rational mode. By acknowledging our multiple perspectives, our own mutability, and our engagement in dialogues that continually shift and move our thinking, we can begin to create a dialogue that articulates the work within the early childhood field; we can move beyond the framework.

○ The Early Learning Framework: A Monologue

The image of an intuitive educator with access to multiple ways of knowing is not present in the Early Learning Framework. A framework is unable to reflect the richness and diversity of the early childhood community. Nor can this or any framework enter a dialogue with others. A framework cannot listen and respond to families or to the particular concerns or issues that educators may have with it. As a static document, the ELF does not engage in dialogue through which we can develop understanding or new thinking; it is not "answerable" to us.

It is through dialogue that ideas come into being. Bakhtin writes

> An idea does not *live* in one person's *isolated* individual consciousness—if it remains here it degenerates and dies. An idea begins to live, i.e., to take shape, to develop to find and renew its verbal expression, and to give birth to new ideas only when it enters into genuine dialogical relationships with other ideas. (1973, p. 71)

In the end, the framework is a monologue, setting out guidelines and static ideas. The vigorous and varied discussions that went into the creation of the framework have been quieted and the tensions and diversity of voices are not reflected within the final document. While it encourages readers to engage with its ideas and it acknowledges different perspectives, it does not present an example of multiple voices or perspectives. Instead it claims the authority of the government and academe. This unified voice allows no space for dialogues or modification of ideas.

The document's guiding questions are not questions of a deep or curious nature, but rather are designed to encourage practitioners along a designated path. This monologic set of guidelines does not recognize that reflection and thinking need space, time, and others with whom to think in order for people to change their ideas or their practice.

Challenges to our ideas and understandings happen within a relationship, with the voices of others who speak to us from their vantage point of history, values, culture, and experience. Staying in dialogue with children and with their families encourages us to continually engage with different perspectives and different viewpoints; staying in dialogue with policymakers, researchers, and academics will also increase our understandings and knowledge, as well as theirs. In this engagement we continually reevaluate our own position and we add another conversation to our repertoire of voices. These dialogues and relationships can move us beyond the framework.

○ Beyond a Framework

Acknowledging the important role of relationships within the work of early childhood education shifts the emphasis from a standardized set of skills and knowledge to a dynamic process that requires attention, imagination, and care to particular people in particular situations. I suggest that while curricula and frameworks such as the BC Early Learning Framework can support the idea of developing relationships with children, they are unable to engage with educators on developing a deep understanding of *relationship*. Educators, like children and families, are diverse in skills, stories, and concerns. Developing a deeper understanding of relationship will come from diverse dialogues that engage heart and mind.

If early childhood practice is relationship based, educators will enter into dialogues with children and with families. Using imagination along with thought and care, they can create conversations that increase their understandings and lead to new ideas. Within these dialogues they will be answerable to the other with whom they are in dialogue. MacNaughton (2005) speaks of providing educators with time and space to grow their own understandings of "the messiness, uncertainties and ethical dilemmas of relationships in teaching" (p. 193). LeGuin (1989) suggests that we go "back to feeling our way into ideas, using the whole intellect not half of it, talking with one another, which involves listening...to offer our experience to one another. Not claiming something: offering something" (p. 150).

We must encourage dialogue at all levels that impact early childhood—within government, within the university, within professional organizations, within the field—and avoid the monologism that results from unitary voices in official documents. We can generate new thinking and new ideas when we enter "into genuine dialogical relationships with other, foreign ideas" (Bakhtin, 1973, p. 71). Others have called for early childhood educators to step away from universal truths to values and beliefs that fit within particular communities and selves (Cannella, 1998; Dahlberg & Moss, 2005; Moss, 2006; Moss & Petrie, 2002). By entering this discussion we can each become more aware of our own values and of the perspectives from which we act. As each of us affirms our own unique place and relationship in life, we can begin to transform impersonal and universal values and ethics into our own and they can become part of our actions and interactions.

Bakhtin (1994) claims that "one's own discourse and one's own voice, although born of another or dynamically stimulated by another, will sooner or later begin to liberate themselves from the authority of the other's discourse" (p. 79). We can have our own unique relationship with the values and beliefs that we actively accept as having meaning for us, and this relationship will continue to evolve and change over time. Similarly, Rinaldi (2001) says, "our theories need to be listened to by others. Expressing our theories to others makes it possible to transform a world which is not intrinsically ours into something shared. Sharing theories is a response to uncertainty" (pp. 79–80).

As we move beyond the framework to develop these dialogues among educators, with children, and with families we will begin to develop a richer, more creative image of an early childhood educator. In dialogue with government and academia, the dialogue will deepen and understanding of the work of relationship-based practice will expand and be made more visible.

Creating relationships, environments, and meaning within an early childhood setting takes more than a framework; it requires imagination, attentiveness, and love. Staying alive to the possibilities within practice and relationships entails a continual striving towards and a searching for new understandings. Through dialogues within our communities with children, with other educators, and with families we can collaborate, think together, and come to new perspectives on our visions for children within our communities. We can listen and challenge each other; we can listen and resist old images and patterns; we can listen and transform our practices.

REFERENCES

Bakhtin, M. M. (1973). *Problems of Dostoevsky's poetics* (R. W. Rotsel, Trans.). New York: Ardis.

Bakhtin, M. M. (1981). *The dialogic imagination* (C. Emerson & M. Holquist, Trans.). Austin, TX: University of Texas Press.

Bakhtin, M. M. (1993). *Toward a philosophy of the act* (V. Liapunov, Trans.). Austin, TX: University of Texas Press.

Bakhtin, M. M. (1994). The dialogic imagination (M. Holquist & C. Emerson, Trans.). In P. Morris (Ed.), *The Bakhtin reader: Selected writings of Bakhtin, Medvedev, Voloshinov* (pp. 74–80). London: Arnold.

Benner, P., & Wrubel, J. (1989). *The primacy of caring, stress and coping in health and illness.* San Francisco: Addison-Wesley.

Bowden, P. (1997). *Caring: Gender-sensitive ethics.* London: Routledge.

Bowman, B., & Moore, E. K. (Eds.). (2006). *School readiness and social-emotional development: Perspectives on cultural diversity.* Washington, DC: National Association for the Education of Young Children.

Bredekamp, S., & Copple, C. (Eds.). (1997). *Developmentally appropriate practice in early childhood programs* (Revised ed.). Washington, DC: National Association for the Education of Young Children.

Burman, E. (1994). *Deconstructing developmental psychology.* London: Routledge.

Burman, E. (2008). *Developments: Child, image, nation.* London: Routledge.

Cannella, G.S. (1997). *Deconstructing early childhood education: Social justice & revolution* (Vol. 2). New York: Peter Lang.

Cannella, G.S. (1998). Early childhood education: A call for the construction of revolutionary images. In W. Pinar (Ed.), *Curriculum toward new identities* (pp. 157–184). New York: Garland.

Carr, M. (2001). *Assessment in early childhood settings: Learning stories.* London: Sage.

Claxton, G. (2000). The anatomy of intuition. In T. Atkinson & G. Claxton (Eds.), *The intuitive practitioner: On the value of not always knowing what one is doing* (pp. 32–52). Buckingham, UK: Open University Press.

Cole, E. B., & Coultrap-McQuin, S. (Eds.). (1992). *Explorations in feminist ethics: Theory and practice.* Bloomington, IN: Indiana University Press.

Copple, C., & Bredekamp, S. (Eds.). (2009). *Developmentally appropriate practice in early childhood programs.* Washington, DC: National Association for the Education of Young Children.

Dahlberg, G., & Moss, P. (2005). *Ethics and politics in early childhood education.* London: RoutledgeFalmer.

Dahlberg, G., Moss, P., & Pence, A. R. (1999). *Beyond quality in early childhood education and care: Postmodern perspectives.* London: Falmer.

Edmiston, B. (2008). *Forming ethical identities in early childhood play.* New York: Routledge.

Elliot, E. (2001). The sensual side of caregiving. The first years. *New Zealand Journal of Infant and Toddler Education, 3*(1), 32–34.

Elliot, E. (2002). *A web of relationships: Caregivers' perspectives on working with infants and toddlers.* Unpublished doctoral dissertation, University of Victoria, Victoria, British Columbia.

Elliot, E. (2007). *"We're not robots": The voices of infant/toddler caregivers.* Albany, NY: State University of New York Press.

Government of British Columbia. (2008). *British Columbia early learning framework.* Victoria, BC: Ministry of Education, Ministry of Health, Ministry of Children and Family Development, & British Columbia Early Learning Advisory Group.

Grumet, M. (1988). *Bitter milk: Women and teaching.* Amherst, MA: University of Massachusetts Press.

Hertzman, C. (2000). The case for an early childhood development strategy. *Isuma, 1*(2), 11–18.

Hertzman, C., & Kohen, D. (2003). Neighbourhoods matter for child development. *Transition, 33*(3), 3–5.

LeGuin, U. (1989). *Dancing at the edge of the world: Thoughts on words, women, places.* New York: Grove Press.

MacNaughton, G. (2005). *Doing Foucault in early childhood studies: Applying poststructural ideas*. New York: Routledge.

Meisels, S. J., & Atkins-Burnett, S. (2005). *Developmental screening in early childhood: A guide* (5th ed.). Washington, DC: National Association for the Education of Young Children.

Moss, P. (2006). *Bringing politics into the nursery: Early childhood education as a democratic practice*. Paper presented at the European Early Childhood Education Research Association, Reykjavik, Iceland.

Moss, P., & Petrie, P. (2002). *From children's services to children's spaces: Public policy, children and childhood*. London: RoutledgeFalmer.

O'Loughlin, M. (2009). *The subject of childhood*. New York: Peter Lang.

Paley, V. G. (1979). *White teacher*. Cambridge, MA: Harvard University Press.

Rinaldi, C. (2001). Documentation and assessment: what is the relationship? In C. Guidici, C. Rinaldi, & M. Krechevsky (Eds.), *Making learning visible: Children as individual and group learners* (pp. 78–93). Cambridge, MA: Project Zero and Reggio Emilia: Reggio Children.

Rinaldi, C. (2006). *In dialogue with Reggio Emilia: Listening, researching and learning*. London: Routledge.

Rogoff, B. (2003). *The cultural nature of human development*. Oxford: Oxford University Press.

Shepherd, R., Jones, J., & Robinson, H. T. (Eds.). (1996). *Thinking about children/D. W. Winnicott*. Reading, MA: Addison-Wesley.

Singer, E. (1992). *Child care and the psychology of development* (A. Porcelijn, Trans.). London: Routledge.

White, J., & Nuttall, J. (2007). The potential of Bakhtinian dialogism to inform narrative assessment in early childhood education. The first years: *New Zealand Journal of Infant and Toddler Education, 9*(1), 21–25.

Zournazi, M. (2002). *Hope: New philosophies for change*. New York: Routledge.

CHAPTER TWO

These Ventriloquist Walls: Troubling Language in Early Childhood Education

Cristina D. Vintimilla

We die. That may be the meaning of life. But we do language. That may be the measure of our lives.
—Toni Morrison. *Nobel Lecture* delivered at the award ceremony for the Nobel Prize in Literature 1993. Stockholm, Sweden.

As a graduate student and an early childhood pedagogue, I walk each day through narrow faculty corridors. These long hallways seem to shudder with an accumulation of voices, even when they are empty and serene. Their walls and my eyes find themselves always in subtle altercations. To me these walls are ventriloquists of a history, of the discourses that appear in each of the artifacts that get *pinned down*, posted to them, the notices and assignments on display, particularly inside the classrooms. I recognize these artifacts as public testimonies, as traces that evoke what was created, what was thought, and what was taught. They evoke a historicity, a structure of interpretation, and a way of understanding that intrigues and sometimes troubles me. Reading them I wonder: Who was involved in their conceptualization? To which truth do they respond and why were they chosen?

In the name of what responsibility were they selected? How did these artifacts come to be called forth to cover the walls of a university classroom from where they *talk to me* now?

In this chapter, I pause at a particular classroom wall to try to relate to the images (constructions) in a group of three student assignments, not only to understand the meaning of their language, but also to point out the consequences. Often my conversations with early childhood education students, in-service educators, and colleagues provoke me to question how we relate to language. Quite regularly such conversations point to a tendency to relate to language as a production of the autonomous I that is easily presumed to be the manifestation of an ego-centered self. By making this presumption it is easy to neglect our own historical construction, which not only precedes what is being uttered, but also conditions the ways language is used. Often there is a tendency to take for granted the use of language and discourses, and to remain unaware of language's constitutive character. I would suggest that in early childhood education it is rare to pause with the language being used to understand its genealogy, to trace its meaning and understand to which traditions of thought (epistemologies) and to which theories it responds. Which truths does it vow? What is this language actually doing? Which identities, knowledge, and "realities" are being produced by it? So, in this chapter, I approach this wall as if it could talk, and in so doing I relate the work of three authors: Michel Foucault (specifically his work in the area of discourse analysis), J. L. Austin, and Judith Butler. I relate to the work of these thinkers and I also juxtapose them. Their work forms the theoretical position I take when analyzing the discourses presented to me on this wall.

My intention is, on one hand, to underline as others have done (Dahlberg & Moss, 2005; MacNaughton, 2005; Pacini-Ketchabaw & Armstrong de Almeida, 2006) the importance and the *analytical potential* these theorists have for early childhood education. On the other hand, I want to open a space to challenge the ideas of sovereignty that haunt educational thought in order to challenge the conception of the autonomous, ahistorical subject as the origin of what is said. In this way I will question the consequential presentism that we keep reproducing in education, and particularly in teacher education programs.

○ J. L. Austin, Butler, and Language

J. L. Austin (1962) highlights the concept of *performativity* in language, pointing out that certain speech does not just describe an action but actually *performs* or produces that action. He sheds light on the fact that when we speak, we are *doing* something with language, and we can distinguish *illocutionary* acts from *perlocu-tionary* ones. As Butler (1997) explains,

> the former [illocutionary] are speech acts that, in saying, do what they say, and do it in the moment of that saying; the latter [perlocutionary] are speech acts that produce certain effects as their consequences; by saying something a certain effect follows. The illocutionary speech act is itself the deed that it effects; the perlocutionary merely leads to certain effects that are not the same as the speech act itself. (p. 3)

Austin is not concerned with understanding utterances as merely transporting meaning, but asks us to consider the ways in which the utterances produce effects. Moreover, he is less concerned with whether an utterance is true or false than he is with its performative force.

Butler takes up Austin's work and, at the same time, distances herself from it. Where Austin "consistently discusses utterances, Butler considers speech among other forms of discourse that all have performative force" (Ruitenberg, 2008. p. 264). Broadening the notion of performative force to other forms of discourse is particularly meaningful in discourse analysis, especially in an educational context, since this invites us to reconsider and acknowledge the force our discourses have.

Austin (1962) argues that the way to determine an utterance's performative force is to recognize the total situation of the speech act. But how can we determine that totality? It is especially difficult if we consider that utterances go beyond the moment in which they are used. The moment of an utterance

> is never a single moment…it exceeds itself in past and future directions, and in effect of prior and future invocations that constitute and escape the instance of utterance. (Butler, 2002, p. 3)

There will always be future invocations, iterations, and citations that challenge the concept of context as something circumscribed and replete with meaning.

According to Ruitenberg (2008), Butler does not focus on single utterances as Austin does; in fact Butler underlines performativity's cumulative power. For Butler, an utterance's force, and in particular its illocutionary force, happens through repetition in customary ways and in the day-by-day discourses that maintain convention. Ruitenberg (2008) writes

> Most illocutionary force does not stem from such single acts that are easily recognizable as performatives, but rather from "ordinary" discourse that conforms to convention that has been built up, over time, by repetition and the sedimentation of layer upon layer of discourse. (p. 260)

Discourse will have effect in this repetition, in the conventionality of the discourse and in its sedimentation. The repetitions or citations that come to life in different contexts do not necessarily result in exact reproductions of previous utterances, in fact the citations we make are "iterations, repetitions that alter" (Ruitenberg, 2008, p. 261). When analyzing discourse, especially within educational contexts, I think we attend less than we should to shades of meaning that are layered over time and through various iterations. Pausing to consider this sedimentation would widen the horizon of possibilities for early childhood students who might then be inclined to question the implications of the language they use and are taught to use.

My intention in this chapter is not just to approach the texts to understand the meaning of their discourse. I point to texts as places of reaffirmation, and the citation of a certain conventionality—an epistemology —that speaks to certain understandings about education and the educator's identity. Through analyzing the discourse of these texts, I want to ascribe agency to language by underlining its performativity and not just by approaching text as a deliberate act done by a subject. Following these ideas, then, it is important to consider that for Butler (1993), discursive performativity

> must be understood not as a single or deliberate act, but rather, as the reiterative and citational practice by which discourse produces the effect that it names…performativity not as the act by which a subject brings into being what he/she names, but, rather, as the reiterative power of discourse to produce the phenomena that it regulates and constrains. (p. 2)

Consequently, Butler's words invite us to consider the subject as performatively formed by discourses through constant discursive creations and interactions. Discursive performativity means not that

> I, as autonomous subject, *perform* my identity the way an actor performs a role, but rather that I, as subject, *am performatively produced* by the discourse in which I participate. (Ruitenberg, 2008, p. 261)

Before moving further, I want to recall the fact that when Austin refers to performative utterances he refers to them as the speech act of a subject that produces what is being said. When I read Austin's speech act theory it seems to me that he is putting the subject and its will as the center of the performative force. Butler (1993) pushes this conceptualization further by making clear that "this power is not the function of an originating will, but is always derivative" (p. 13), it is always a reiteration of a conventionality and certain norms.

○ Foucault and Discourse

Echoes of Foucault are strong in Butler's work. Foucault (1982) considered that subjects are not entities outside discourses. They are positioned by discourses, by the articulation of specific statements held in place by normative rules, and by the variety of discourses that are related to the subject's historicity. Fairclough (1992) argues that by attributing a major role to discourse in the constitution of subjectivity, the implications are that "questions of subjectivity, social identity, and selfhood ought to be of a major concern in theories of discourse and language and in discursive and linguistic analysis" (p. 44). This kind of work is important for early childhood education, and education in general, if we consider, for example, early childhood education as a discursive activity wherein every act, event, text, and assignment, has been positioned. Within this discursive activity, we have performatively produced, and continue to produce, conceptions and identities regarding the early childhood educator and teaching. In ascribing agency to language, and in understanding discourse the way Foucault and Butler invite us to do, one question surfaces for me: If we take up the invitation of Butler and Foucault, how should we interpret the display of "teacherly" texts I find on the walls, whether these walls are from an early childhood education program or a K-12 teacher education program? And furthermore, what kind of responsibility will be called upon when an assignment is presented, or an activity occurs, or a text is displayed on an early childhood education classroom wall?

For Foucault (1982), knowledge is formed by and produced in discourses. Through this formation and knowledge production, discourses shed light on different understandings of truth reproducing different epistemologies and social systems that constrain or enable our thinking and produce our identity. Hence knowledge, truth, and power are intimately related. Foucault's theories are part of an enormous amount of work in the social sciences, but I think we in education have not sufficiently taken up the possibilities inherent in a *history of the present*—a genealogy "that interrogates the present to examine its values, discourses and understandings with recourse to the past as a resource of destabilizing critical knowledge" (Foucault, 1982, p. 211).

This work could offer an antidote that might help to overcome the sense of presentism that pervades early childhood education, for example. This interrogation of the present ought to be considered as a way to open up deeper and wider spaces for dialogue and for an alternative philosophical consciousness, one that brings a different sense of agency and expands the way we relate to truth.

In the specific case of discourse analysis, Hook's (2001) words resonate with my argument when he suggests that when analyzing discourses (in this case in early childhood education) we need to go beyond "what was thought or said per se" (p. 522). We need to relate to "all the discursive rules and categories that were a priori assumed as a constituent part of discourse and therefore of knowledge" (p. 522). What is being asserted here is that in discourses we can uncover the roots from which truth-claims are fed by questioning how truth is being perpetuated and attained through them.

Hook (2001) points out that Foucault also argues with and pushes further the concept of discourse, considering it not as a creation but as an event in order to trouble assumptions about the origins of discourses. Although I am suspicious of Foucault's consideration of discourses as oppositional, I think that understanding discourse as an event reaches out to opportunities of analysis that overcome the illusion of autonomy with which the concept of creation tends to be associated. It also

> enables us to look beneath the alibis of creation, and to isolate very different (and multiple) origins of discourse, which Foucault (1981) suspects will reveal functions of exclusion. (Hook, 2001, p. 531)

In early childhood education and in its educators' formation, spaces that open up to relate to our discourses as events and to acknowledge the multiplicity of their origins are rare. We rarely acknowledge the multiple *origins* of our discourse as something that goes beyond the self-centered *I* as the *origin* of its creations. I posit that opening up this type of space could lighten the burden of our sense of personal ownership over our discourses, which sometimes may interpose with the possibility for pedagogical dialogue. By dislocating and decentering the origin of discourses from the sole responsibility of the autonomous *I*, Foucault introduced us to the possibility to recognize and re-relate discourse to broader affiliations and power-relations such as ideology, institutions, practices, and groups. Furthermore, Hook (2001) points out that by recognizing discourse as event,

> one should approach discourse less as a language, or as textuality, than as an active "occurring," as something that implements power and action, and that also is power and action. Rather than a mere vocabulary or language, a set of instruments that we animate, discourse is the thing that is done. (p. 543)

This quote is a reiterative testimony of the concept of performative force that was discussed in light of Austin's and Butler's work. They repeat the invitation to consider not merely the meaning of language but also its performative consequences, its active occurring or its doing.

Throughout this chapter, I have stressed the importance of the quality of the performative because the concept is pregnant with possibility for early childhood education and curriculum. There, what is defined as crucial tends to be the acquisition of pedagogical knowledge and skills that will guarantee that early childhood educators are prepared for being with children. At the risk of sounding reductionist, I will argue that rarely does such curriculum open up to wider horizons of possibility that result from deeply considering and engaging with poststructuralist theories of language and discourse. These theories invite us to question and engage in dialogues that go beyond the ideological arena and reach out to the ontological arena. In other words, they invite us to consider not only the ideologies in play, but what and who the educator—the early childhood educator—is allowed to be. I will consider these points when I analyze specific texts displayed on a teacher education classroom wall.

Foucault asked us to consider the conditions of possibility that discourses bring to life and also the intricate conditions of possibility (which for him are the bases of power) that allow certain discourses to be positioned as truthful and accountable as knowledge. Such conditions cannot be revealed by considering only our present condition. We need to trace back to "the multiple institutional supports and various social structures and practices underlying the production of truth" (Hook, 2001, p. 526). In the latter part of this chapter, I discuss the theoretical traditions in which some of our discourses are embedded and what these might mean for the education of early childhood educators. What are the conditions of possibility for the discourses that are present today in education and, in particular, in early childhood education? How can we use discourse analysis as a tool to critically unpack such conditions? If discourses are instruments for the reproduction of certain truths, a reproduction that through citationality and iteration produces the effect that it names, then this conceptualization calls a responsibility to acknowledge a history of systems of thought that is intimately connected with such reproduction and to which in education we tend to remain foreign. Furthermore, such understanding of discourses brings into being a certain suspicion and estrangement or critical distance that, rather than freeing us from discursive power, gives us a new understanding of agency, about which I write further.

○ Subject, Objectification, and Analysis of the Text

Foucault asserts that it is through analysis and examination that the objectification of the subject occurs. Consequently, on one hand, as Fairclough referring to Foucault's work pointed out, the individual is constituted "as a describable [and] analyzable object" (Fairclough, 1992, p. 53). If such is the case, then does discourse analysis also reinforce the objectification of the subject? Or is it possible to approach discourse analysis in ways that are not reductionist of the subject? On the other hand, does the objectification of the subject happen only through analysis and examination? Can the assignments I am presenting here be considered as actions that arrange and treat individuals as objects and/or is it about a subjectivation? A subjectivation that for Foucault (2000) happens through a form of power that

> applies itself to immediate everyday life [and] categorizes the individual, marks him by his own individuality, attaches him to his own identity, imposes a law of truth on him that he must recognize and others have to recognize in him. (p. 331)

For the analysis, the ontological consequence of these words is important. They underline being as something that is bestowed; as Butler (1993) writes

> Here "being" belongs in quotation marks, for ontological weight is not presumed, but always conferred. For Foucault this conferral can take place only within and by an operation of power. This operation produces the subjects that it subjects. (p. 34)

I argue that the assignments that cover the wall of the classroom where future educators, particularly in early childhood, study every day and with which I now open a dialogue are discourses through which, due to their cumulative and reiterative power or their performativity, an ontological consequence is effected and performed. We ought to give more attention to this argument when considering the curriculum for teacher education programs. The questions that beat strongly in my thoughts are: Who is the early childhood student permitted to be in early childhood education programs? Who are educators allowed to be? And how can the analysis of these assignments be a testimony of the way education responds to these questions?

Before I open a more specific dialogue with some of the texts I have encountered over the years in Canadian education programs, I must observe that I am governed at the heart of my proximity to these ventriloquist walls by a spontaneous resistance, one that I want to claim and sign, to the ubiquitous *infantilization* of the early childhood student. When I am in the presence of such classrooms walls, it seems to me that there is an unspoken assumption that in order to work with children, the early childhood student must be educated in a curriculum that infantilizes their course experience (to sit like children would do, to use art materials as children would do, to sing as children would do, and so on). This, to me, becomes pedagogically and ethically problematic. I think the following texts will be a good example of what I am pointing to here.

I open a dialogue with these texts as a way into the analysis. I ask: Who is being identified in these assignments? There is a tendency to recognize these assignments as the manifestation of our own ideas, in this case, the students' ideas.

Following Foucault's and Butler's invitation, I start this analysis by pointing out the complex origin of these discourses that recognize, but go beyond, the ego-centered self. The students are the writers of the discourse of these assignments, but they are not its originators, and as Butler (1997) points out, their intentions in writing these assignments

> are not what control the meaning of that discourse .... Although the subject surely speaks, and there is no speaking without a subject, the subject does not exercise sovereign power over what it says. (p. 34)

These assignments are discursive places in which iterations and citations are presented. They reproduce discourses about teachers and teaching and consequently performatively produce certain identities, perpetuate certain truths and conceptions that define education today and that, as Butler asserts, through repetition in time maintain a sphere of operation. Repetition in time is one of the characteristics of these assignments/texts. They are displayed on a wall that belongs to a public space—the faculty of education or the early childhood department. Although they are different assignments, they repeat a similar discourse about teaching and education. They present and represent themselves as a repetition every time we enter and leave the classroom.

Ventriloquist Walls: What Is This Wall Discursively Performing?

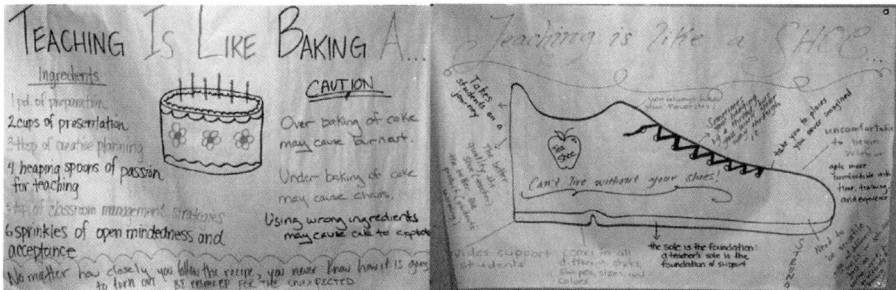

Identity and Conceptions of Education

The purpose of this chapter is not to critique the sort of assignments that are produced in an early childhood education program. These assignments can serve the purpose of helping pre-service educators express different meanings related to their decision to become a teacher and how they see themselves and understand teaching. What interests me is to hold more strongly Foucault's and Butler's understandings of discourse and the concept of performativity as openers of a different dialogue in and about early childhood education. I am interested in using discourse analysis not just to read a text, but to relate it to a broader context and to trace some conceptualizations about education. This is an invitation to welcome, in the preparation of early childhood educators, more theoretical work recognizing its potential revelatory power, especially if it will ask students not just to express their identity and their ideas but to recognize the performative power of their discourses.

The Journey of an Educator

This assignment is about the journey of an educator. Already the word journey is loaded with a modernist meta-narrative of progress that is understood as a progressive and linear evolution. Such an understanding of a journey in a progressive, linear, and developmental way is stated and visible in the path drawn at the center of the text. Citations such as "laughter is the best medicine," "live, love, laugh," "live it as if it were your last," and "think positive, be positive" are utterances in a prescriptive mode that cumulatively assert a predisposition of ontological lightness with which we should live life—and, more specifically, teaching—as an antidote against the roughness of the world. It is also a discourse that shadows and excludes a conceptualization of the world as contradictory, complex, and fractured.

This discourse of ontological lightness is present in early childhood teaching and also becomes visible in the wider cultural context, for example, through the way we relate to disagreement and conflict as if they were a threat to avoid in the name of positivism and politeness. Such discourses can be linked with an understanding of a liberal notion of selfhood as is also seen in the platitude "How can I make a difference?" and with which the previous citations contradict. This contradiction is also present in the slogan "Why is the world so cruel?" "How can I make a difference?" is not just rooted in a liberal notion of selfhood but also invokes a simplistic agency, an understanding of the world as something to affect without searching for awareness of our implication in it.

The "fun figure men" depicted throughout the text evoke the "fun god" that is present in contemporary discourses in education that understand teaching as entertainment and playfulness where the educator entertains and the children need amusement in order to learn. Such discourse is symptomatic of the larger cultural "truth" of Western liberal states that locates fun and amusement as life-style and as necessary qualities of life experiences. This point is iterated in the quote "I wish I was like you, easily amused." Such discourse performatively produces an image/identity of the educator as clown and the child as needy, consequently feeding both old power positions between educator/child and the anti-intellectualism that seems to characterize early childhood education nowadays.

The pronoun "I" is used repeatedly in the citations, echoing modern conceptions of sovereignty and reproducing an identity and conviction of the self based in liberal notions of autonomy and individuality, and in the power of the will. This "I" and its autonomy create inside the text an intertextuality with the system of certifications and accreditations that are displayed throughout the text, creating an interesting paradoxical tension of discourses. The strong presence of certification and accreditation is used to define the journey to become an educator, thus emphasizing, on the one hand, a consumerist approach to university and knowledge and, on the other hand, underlining an understanding of the university as a corporatized institution that grants "credits" as the tangible value in the economy of knowledge production. Such discourses on education create particular conditions of possibility and performatively produce a conceptualization of education and of early childhood education that feeds instrumentalist approaches to the meaning of education, profession, and thought.

The journey of an educator

Teaching Is Like a Shoe

The metaphor of the shoe to conceptualize teaching reveals some cracks and contradictions in the discourse. A shoe is a commodity, a simile used to conceptualize teaching, yet it obeys the command of the market economy and utilitarian consumerist qualities. The shoe as an accessory evokes a view of teaching as a consumer good, something to be purchased in the market of knowledge. This conceptualization of teaching is iterated and gains force in the utterances "you always have your favorites" and "comes in different styles, shapes, sizes, and colors," consequently reinvigorating understandings of teaching as both an acquisition of techniques and styles and as a judgment regarding which of those to apply. This instrumentalism is repeated in the sentence "need to be versatile, go with different outfits or activities just as teacher needs to go with variety of learning styles." The words "versatile" and "variety" refer to styles and activities evoking teaching as a managerial task within a behaviorist milieu. Consequently such discourses performatively produce an identity of an educator as a technician and behavioral expert. The educator is also one "who provides support to students." Such a statement creates a power position between an educator and a student or child that reinvokes conceptualizations of the educator as knowledgeable and strong and the child as needy of support.

Another aspect of the shoe metaphor is that a shoe protects vulnerabilities from dangers underfoot. This understanding of vulnerability as something to be protected from or to overcome is echoed in the sentence "Sometimes you're hanging by a thread, but you work your way through it." Vulnerability and danger interrelate in this sentence, calling upon the autonomy of the self to "work it out" from the discomfort and danger of "hanging" to the comfort of more stable and fixed situations. A preoccupation with the educator's comfort is clear in the utterance "uncomfortable to begin with…gets more comfortable with time, training, and experience." There is an anticipation of discomfort which this protection is expected to mediate in the hope that, with time, this essentially static shoe-self will become comfortable, not that the self within will change in ways unpredictable and limitless. Is this not a defensive fortress of self? What helps to diminish the discomfort are time, training, and experience.

To pursue a detailed genealogy of these terms in early childhood education is a meaningful purpose although it is beyond the scope of this chapter. Here, it suffices to point out that these terms are linked and embedded in an instrumentalist discourse that is presented and iterated throughout the text as well as in the other assignments that were displayed in the wall. Such texts are symptomatic of the broader discourse that is being reproduced in early childhood education with cumulative performative power each time it is iterated and cited. Time, training, and experience are taken as utilitarian means and instruments to an end, one that in this case is the educator's comfort. The word "training" connotes a conception of teacher education that is knowledge based, in skills acquisition and competences, to the exclusion of broader intellectual possibilities. Such utterances reinvigorate an understanding of the educator's preparation as a consumerist process based in the acquisition of such skills and competences. This understanding permits the comfort of the illusion of certainty.

Understanding teaching within a market economy framework is reiterated in the sentence "the better quality the shoe, the better the product," in which we may take for the shoe the teacher and, for the product, the student's learning. Such a sentence creates and performs a particular power relation between teacher and children. The quality of the educator is what guarantees the children's learning. At the same time, the concept of "quality" is used to refer to the educator as a product. This utterance sustains "truths" that identify the teacher as an expert who transmits knowledge and the child as the passive receiver of such truths, which, as previously mentioned, is also supported in the phrase "provides support for students." Learning is considered a final product, thus excluding more complex understandings of it as a nonlinear process or one in any way independent of teacher authority.

This understanding of the educator's role is reinforced in the phrase "takes students (children) on a journey." This statement contradicts the previous one in that the concept of a journey contradicts the concept of learning as a product, in implicit recognition that the journey's value is not in the path but in the arrival. As well, this evokes an understanding of a journey as progressive and developmentally driven. The power position that these utterances perform is reiterated at the center in the powerfully echoed quote "the sole is the foundation: a teacher's sole is the foundation of support." This sentence plays with "sole" and "soul." As such it is grounded in the Christian theological tradition underlying the value of the soul and calling upon the educator's essence. This quote repeats that tradition of Christian thought which produces an identity grounded in such discourses. One might well ask whose soul is being called upon here. Does this discourse exclude any who do not recognize such essence as a universal value? This is the soul as the foundation and support of learning, a recall to an interior world where a hidden source of meaning and presumed commonality might be found. Aside from the implicit exclusivity of this usage, this utterance appears to contradict the instrumentalism repeatedly brought to life throughout the text.

Teaching is like a shoe.

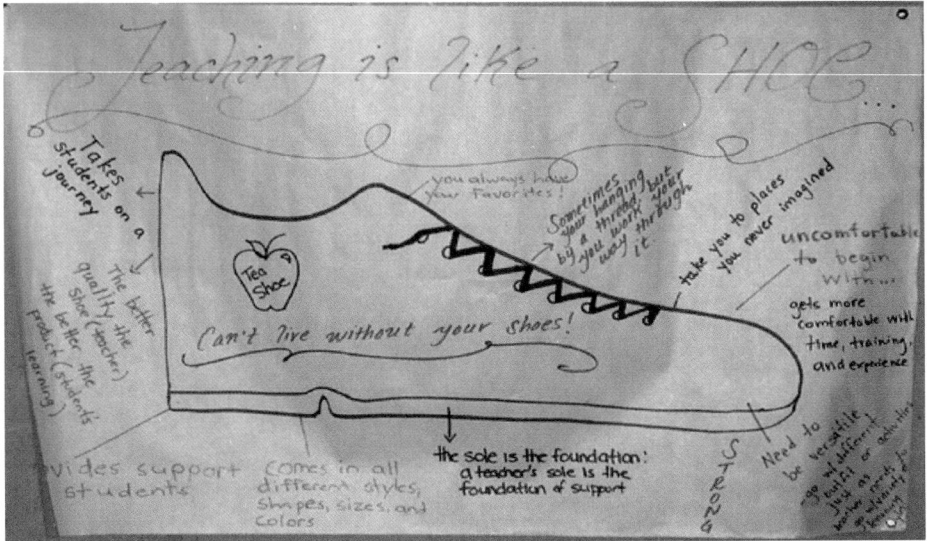

Teaching Is Like Baking a...

In this assignment the metaphor is teaching as baking a cake. Using a recipe to describe teaching implies the recognition of a process, although the process is predefined by the ingredients. The ingredients iterate a conceptualization of what an educator should know for teaching to happen. It is interesting how the measurements of the ingredients reveal the degree of importance they have in the teaching project. Preparation is the base of the recipe: "1 pd. of preparation" is followed by "2 cups of presentation," "3 tbsp of creative planning," "4 heaping spoons of passion for teaching," "5 tsp of classroom management strategies," "6 sprinkles of open mindedness and acceptance." These ingredients represent an understanding of the education of an educator as a technique and a managerial task; they reiterate the instrumentalism I have analyzed in the other assignments. Open-mindedness and acceptance are sprinkles in the whole endeavour of teaching. Passion, open-mindedness, and acceptance are presented as measured values in equal value relation with strategies and planning. Teaching as baking implies that something and someone is being cooked and, according to this recipe, the baker is the educator, repeating the power position between educator and student that was iterated in the assignment that understood teaching as a shoe.

The recipe comes with a caution: "over baking of cake may cause burnout." Burnout is evocative of mental instability; it is also a word related to too much thinking and this is something to be cautious about in the process of teaching, according to the recipe, consequently feeding the anti-intellectualism that corrodes teacher education. Another caution is that "under baking of cake may cause chaos." Chaos and its complexity and uncertainty need to be avoided. A good educator then will be a chaos avoider.

This text evokes a conceptualization of the educator as the controller of the teaching process in the "oven" of the classroom. It also perpetuates discourses that understand children as a "tabula rasa" ready to be shaped and "cooked" by the controlled hand of the educator. Pushing further this analysis, it might be underlined that such discourses are historically connected with totalitarian ideologies.

Another caution in the text says "using wrong ingredients may cause cake to explode." The ingredients are predefined and are in the educator's hands; the success of the process relies on a linear and uncritical pursuit of the steps. Such a conception is already performing and cumulatively repeating the value that is given in early childhood education to certainty and control, avoiding the uncertainty that lies in more critical thinking. This utterance also positions the educator as responsible for the learning process and gives force to the instrumentalism that is iterated in these assignments. The responsibility of the educator is reduced to following some steps and techniques, excluding a conceptualization of responsibility grounded in a less instrumentalized ethic.

Teaching is like baking a …

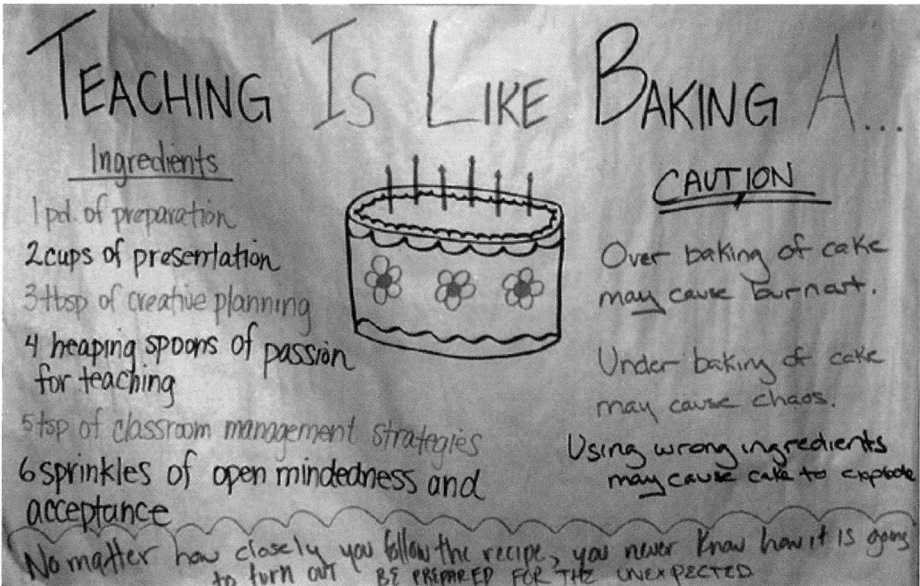

At the bottom of the text, the sentence "No matter how closely you follow the recipe, you never know how it is going to turn out; be prepared for the unexpected" is a final caution. The phrase "no matter how closely you follow the recipe" dismisses the recipe; its effectiveness loses power when confronted with the unexpected. The unexpected is something to be prepared for as if it were a threat, excluding unexpectedness as a rich possibility that opens up to what has not yet arrived and what may be a promising condition. This understanding of the unexpected is linked to the will for control that I mentioned before. Both represent, to some extent, modernist conceptions of the self as someone who needs to have control over the world through science and discipline; within such illusion lives the inherited fear of the unexpected.

○ Agency and Student Assignments

When reading these assignments, I asked the question "Who is the educator allowed to be?" This question is present in my thoughts; it arrives and is called upon by the discourses that come to life in those texts. I am concerned with its discursive performativity and the identities and conceptions that are performatively produced by those discourses. I am less concerned with the process of asking early childhood students to elaborate such assignments than with the narrow space and consideration given in education to language and its agency.

Agency is often attributed to the subject. In Butler's (1997) words, "agency has its origins in the subject" (p. 7), but rarely do we consider the agency that language has and that thinkers such as Austin, Butler, and Foucault invite us to consider. I started this chapter with the beauty of Toni Morrison's words: "We die. That may be the meaning of life. But we do language. That may be the measure of our lives" (cited in Butler, 1997, p. 7). These words are loaded with responsibility. At the same time, they are an invitation towards a responsibility in how language is used. They suggest a commitment towards a philosophical consciousness about the traditions of thought, the epistemologies, and the truths that motivate our speech acts and discursively form our identities. This way of thinking consequently dislocates the autonomous I, the subject, as the originator of what we consider to be our truths. Instead the subject "is formed in the Language that he/she uses" (Butler, 1997, p. 28). But why is it important to consider language's performativity and its inherent responsibility—responsibility towards the use of language—especially if, by giving agency to language, we tend to assume that we are taking away the agency of the subject? First we need to consider, following Butler (1997), that if the subject who speaks is also constituted by the language that she or he speaks, then language is the condition of possibility for the speaking subject, and not merely its instrument of expression. This means that the subject has its own "existence" implicated in a language that precedes and exceeds the subject, a language whose historicity includes a past and future that exceeds that of the subject who speaks. (p. 28)

Language constitutes us but is also the condition of possibility, as Butler asserts, evoking Foucault. The subject has no control over the historicity of language that exceeds and precedes the subject, but it is in language that the subject can find the condition of possibility for agency.

The second consideration we need to pause with is, as Butler (1997) points out, that

the one who utters…is responsible for the manner in which such speech is repeated, for reinvigorating such speech, for reestablishing contexts of hate and injury. The responsibility of the speaker does not consist of remarking language ex nihilo, but rather of negotiating the legacies of usage that constrain and enable that speaker's speech. (p. 27)

The subject does not lose agency by recognizing the agency of language. The subject is called upon to be responsible for the "manner in which such speech is repeated" and to recognize and negotiate the language use that constitutes us.

The implications for early childhood education of the theories I have discussed in this chapter are poignantly meaningful, especially if we recognize the discursive formation of our identities and that it is in the citational character of speech where the subject can "renew the linguistic tokens of a community, reissuing and reinvigorating such speech" (Butler, 1997, p. 39). My concern is that to recognize language's performativity we need to approach theories that shed light on such matters, and this is yet to come with stronger force in early childhood education programs. Early childhood education needs to reach out more to theories from educational philosophy, from philosophy and the humanities in general, to widen the horizons with which we can relate to teacher education. The analytical force of performativity is an example of the potential that theory has to widen our mentalities. Early childhood teacher education needs to consider this invitation more seriously in the name of a responsibility that goes beyond delivering competencies and preparing teachers to care for children.

REFERENCES

Austin, J.L. (1962). *How to do things with words*. Oxford, UK: Oxford University Press.

Butler, J. (1993). *Bodies that matter*. New York: Routledge.

Butler, J. (1997). *Excitable speech: A politics of the performative*. New York: Routledge.

Dahlberg, G., & Moss, P. (2005). *Ethics and politics in early childhood education*. New York: Routledge.

Foucault, M. (1981). The order of discourse. In R. Young (Ed.), *Untying the text: A poststructural anthology* (pp. 48-78). Boston, MA: Routledge & Kegan Paul.

Foucault, M. (1982). The subject and power. In H. L. Dreyfus & P. Rabinow (Eds.), *Michel Foucault: Beyond structuralism and hermeneutics* (pp. 208–226). New York: Harvester Wheatsheaf.

Foucault, M. (2000). *Power* (Vol. 3). New York: New Press.

Fairclough, N. (1992). *Discourse and social change*. Cambridge, UK: Polity Press.

Hook, D. (2001). Discourse, knowledge, materiality, history: Foucault and discourse analysis. *Theory and Psychology, 11*(4), 521–547.

MacNaughton, G. (2005). *Doing Foucault in early childhood studies: Applying poststructural ideas*. New York: Routledge.

Pacini-Ketchabaw, V., & Armstrong de Almeida, A.-E. (2006). Language discourses and ideologies at the heart of early childhood education. *International Journal of Bilingual Education and Bilingualism, 9*(3), 310–341.

Ruitenberg, C. W. (2008). Discourse, theatrical performance, agency: The analytic force of "performativity" in education. In B. Stengel (Ed.), *Philosophy of education 2007* (pp. 260–268). Urbana, IL: Philosophy of Education Society.

o Rethinking Children's Participation in Curriculum Making: A Rhizomatic Movement

Kirsten Ho Chan

Today, freedom of expression is viewed as both a right and a universal value. In the early childhood field, respecting children's views is seen as important for children to develop a sense of worth, make responsible decisions, and become active citizens. Children are no longer considered passive objects in the hands of their parents and society, but full-fledged persons to whom public authorities are accountable (Santos-Pais, 1999). Children's rights to be heard and to have their views taken into account are now embedded in education policy and practice.

For example, over the past two decades, considerable movement has been made on the global stage and in Canada to recognize children's right to participate in decision-making processes. Globally, the international policy landmark the 1989 United Nations Convention on the Rights of the Child is now used by many states to develop policies for children. These policies generally outline that young children can and should participate in matters that affect them, and suggest that children's early experiences influence their later abilities, identities, and well-being (Lansdown, 2005; Lindsay, 1998; MacNaughton, Hughes, & Smith, 2007).

In Canada, many of the recently developed curricula/frameworks involve ideas regarding children's participation, specifically in relation to curriculum development. The idea of child participation in curriculum making has its foundation in "an innovative model of the young child, in a new concern with young children's rights as citizens and in new knowledge about the significance of young children's early experiences" (MacNaughton et al., 2007, p. 458). This model is reflected in the BC Early Learning Framework (Government of British Columbia, 2008), which views young children as social actors who shape their identities, generate and communicate legitimate views about the world around them, and have a right to participate in that world. In this document, children are acknowledged as "capable and full of potential; as persons with complex identities, grounded in their individual strengths and capacities, and their unique social, linguistic, and cultural heritage" (Government of British Columbia, 2008, p. 4).

Despite this ideal of children as capable persons with the right to participate in decisions about their education, child participation in curriculum development has, for the most part, remained undertheorized and in practice it emerges in a tokenistic manner. Children are typically given few opportunities to engage in everyday discussions about issues that concern or directly affect them. Seldom are they asked to express their preferences in adult-dominated institutions. While children often appear to be given a "voice," they have little or no say about the subject matter or the method of communicating it. They have few opportunities to formulate their own opinions, never mind having these thoughts considered seriously or valued. Regretfully, more instances of tokenism exist than do genuine forms of children's participation in projects (Hart, 1992; Lankshear & McLaren, 1993).

At the same time, researchers in early childhood education have demonstrated that young children are competent at creating hypotheses, constructing theories, and envisioning possibilities for meaning making. Moreover, many scholars have argued that children possess knowledge about the world that differs from that of adults, and that engaging with that knowledge has the potential to improve adult understandings of children's experiences (MacNaughton et al., 2007). Young children can communicate their views about their daily lives and, specifically, about early childhood curriculum (e.g., Clark, 2000; MacNaughton, Barnes, & Dally, 2004). This perspective allows one to embrace a broader notion of education and curriculum development that includes aspects of learning and care based on children's rights and interests. For us to benefit from these understandings, however, we will need to further theorize the idea of children's participation in curriculum making. In particular we need to find new theories that would help us to move beyond tokenistic approaches to child participation.

By examining how child participation has been conceptualized and exploring alternative ways to think about it, this chapter seeks to contribute to an emerging literature about young children's participation and innovations in early childhood curriculum making. Specifically, the information presented in this chapter sets out to explore how young children's participation can be conceptualized using a rhizomatic perspective. My exploration will be guided by the concept of the rhizome presented by Deleuze and Guattari (1987) and developed in relation to early childhood education by Olsson in 2009.

In the first part of the chapter, I explore various perspectives on child participation. This section describes some practical and theoretical views of child participation and how they relate to curriculum making. The second part of the article addresses my emerging views on the concept of the rhizome in relation to children's participation.

○ Views of Child Participation in Early Childhood Curriculum Making

Images of the young child carry much ambiguity. On one hand, children may be seen as autonomous individuals. On the other, they are assumed to be vulnerable and in need of protection. Despite this ambiguity, proponents of child participation view children as active citizens whose capacity to learn and participate in their environment allows them to give meaning to the world around them. While most child-centred approaches to early childhood curriculum emphasize children's right to be listened do, the degree to which children should have a voice—and how that voice should be incorporated—is a subject of strongly divergent opinion.

The term "participation" generally refers to the process of sharing decisions that affect one's life and the life of the community in which one lives (Hart, 1992). A sociocultural perspective of early childhood conceptualizes young children primarily as members of social groups. Luff (2009), for example, sees early years practitioners as facilitators of children's participation in social life. Her research seeks to identify ways that educators enable young children's active, participatory learning (p. 129). While she argues that adults should respect and facilitate the rights of young children to be listened to, very little depth is taken in exploring how to incorporate children's thoughts, feelings, and ideas into everyday practice to validate and give value to their experiences. The primary focus is on adult–child relationships and on how adults can provide "a context for active growth while also instilling positive dispositions for future social participation and learning" (Luff, 2009, p. 130). In this model, children's right to be listened appears to be most important in terms of its contribution to positive, productive relationships.

It could be argued that this model is based in part on establishing a linear and chronological learning process, as it is primarily based on adult–child relationships.

Taking a different perspective, a rights-based approach views participation as the base on which a democracy is built and the standard against which democracies are measured. Hart (1992) suggests that

> a nation is democratic to the extent that its citizens are involved, particularly at the community level. The confidence and competence to be involved must be gradually acquired through practice. It is for this reason that there should be gradually increasing opportunities for children to participate in any aspiring democracy. (p. 4)

Similarly, Pais (2000) emphasizes gradually introducing children to opportunities for participation, with the child's age and maturity the determining factors in their involvement. And, while respecting children's views means not ignoring them, she states, neither should children's opinions be simply endorsed.

> Expressing an opinion is not taking a decision. But it implies the ability to influence decisions. Thus, a process of dialogue and exchange needs to be encouraged to prepare the child to assume increasing responsibilities and to become active, tolerant, and democratic—combining adults' direction and guidance to the child with the consideration of the child's views in a manner that is consistent with the age and maturity of the child, giving the child an opportunity and ability to understand why a particular option and not another is followed, why a particular decision is taken and not the one the child might have preferred. (Pais, 2000, p. 95)

Both of these rights-based educators see adults as requisite guides for children's participation in democratic decision making. While these perspectives do not assume that children are too immature to participate in decisions about their lives, they do imply that adults should decide for young children the knowledge, skills, behaviours, and experiences they need to become socially competent. In other words, to perpetuate the well-defined universal developmental stages, young children's participation is valued and examined using a predetermined content of culture, identities, and knowledge based on that which adults think is appropriate. In this format educators take on the role of an arbitrator, overseeing the children and evaluating them against predefined categories of normal development. Educators are then able to develop curriculum for the children based on these judgments, with the objective to help them develop "normally."

In a similar vein, an emergent curriculum model centres "children's interests, worries, desires, understandings, and misunderstandings and use[s] these as the beginning points for curriculum" (Wien & Stacey, 2000, p. 1). However, the model relies on "developmentally appropriate" standards and "well-developed observation skills of early childhood teachers" (Wien & Stacey, 2000, p. 1). For the purposes of this chapter, emergent curriculum can be thought of as beginning when something that fascinates children emerges from their ongoing activities, often in an unplanned way. The teacher then adapts the children's activities in ways that further stimulate, challenge, or expand their thinking (Riley & Roach, 2006). Rather than the child being an active participant throughout the whole learning process, the adult is expected to observe and interpret children's interests and to develop curriculum based on them, according to "developmentally appropriate" guidelines.

The emergent curriculum model often involves "normalizing the child"—that is, classifying and measuring children in linear and binary ways based on the concept of developmentally appropriate practice (DAP). The guidelines for DAP are the seminal framework of the National Association for the Education of Young Children (NAEYC; Copple & Bredekamp, 2009). DAP focuses on improving children's developmental outcomes, often articulated in terms of school readiness. According to Stonehouse (1994), DAP "lends itself to being interpreted simplistically, as a set of 'do's and don'ts' that are universal" (p. 76). A large amount of ongoing criticism questions DAP's contention that children's development unfolds in a universal manner (Kessler & Swadener, 1992; Ryan & Oschner, 1999; MacNaughton, 2003).

In contrast to developmental models, early childhood educators who work within a strengths-based framework tend to view children as "beings not becomings" (Qvortrup et al., 1994, p. 2, cited in Clark, 2005, p. 30). Young children are seen as providers of knowledge and co-constructors of meaning, while adults are envisioned as facilitators or opportunity providers rather than authoritative directors. Clark and Moss (2001), for example, place high importance on children's participation in early childhood education and insist that educators need to find practical ways to develop services that respond to the "voice of the child" and recognize young children's competencies (p. 2). Clark (2005) believes that child participation is essential to allow children's perspectives to become the "focus for an exchange of meaning between children, practitioners, parents and researchers" (p. 29). She emphasizes exploring children's experiences and perceptions of their own lives, as well as their interests, priorities, and concerns. She describes her "mosaic" approach, which is based on Reggio Emilia–inspired notions of the competent child, the pedagogy of listening, and the pedagogy of relationships, as

- □ multi-method, recognizing the different "voices" or languages of children;
- □ participatory, treating children as experts and agents in their own lives;
- □ reflexive, including children, practitioners, and parents in reflecting on meanings, and addressing the question of interpretation;

◻ adaptable, allowing practitioners freedom to adapt to their early years setting;

◻ focused on children's lived experiences, with the possibility to be used for a variety of purposes including examining the lives lived rather than the knowledge gained or received; and,

◻ embedded into practice, involving listening that seeks to establish a climate of listening. (Clark, 2005, p. 30)

A child-centred participatory rights-based approach prioritizes "making children's learning visible" and engaging young children as active citizens who are competent, capable, and socially responsible. MacNaughton and Smith (2008) outline the implications of such an approach for building a participatory, rights-based ethic for consulting children. It is not enough merely to observe and document what young children say, they argue: To engage them as active citizens we must take the *politics* of what has been heard and observed seriously and act on these thoughts accordingly. Doing so enables children to see their thoughts, feelings, and ideas as valid, and creates spaces to support young children to "learn about the complexities of acting on diverse ideas and perspectives in a democratic environment" (MacNaughton & Smith, 2008, p. 40).

For MacNaughton and her colleagues, the most successful consultations include young children's views about the consultation process itself (MacNaughton et al., 2007, p. 462). They bring attention to the notion that children's participation in a project can only be ethical, just, and rights honouring when the consultation processes are designed with care. Listening to children, MacNaughton and her colleagues contend, assists them to become active citizens who participate in public decision making, so the consultation process itself is as valuable as its outcomes (2007, p. 462). By using a methodology that attempts to be as sensitive as possible to the particular ages, contexts, cultures, and backgrounds of the children involved, MacNaughton and her colleagues create a space for all of the children involved to understand what is being proposed and to make reasonable decisions that reflect what they believe are their particular interests.

It is tempting to look for a single best approach to involving young children in curriculum making. However, the CREATE Foundation, an Australian organization committed to child empowerment and participation, cautions that

the consultation process can change over time, with different people wanting to participate in different ways at different times, and the success of any consultation process depends on the extent to which children and/or adults can translate their own perspective on the issue at hand into effective action. (CREATE Foundation, 2000b, cited in MacNaughton et al., 2007, p. 462)

Thus one must consider the many different ways to promote and encourage each child's participation in light of their individual abilities, confidence, and experience. Children will assess their situation, consider possible options, express their views, and therefore influence decision-making processes in myriad ways. Further, the child's evolving capacity represents just one side of the equation, while the other has to do with adults' evolving capacity and willingness to listen to, interpret, and give adequate weight to the views expressed by the child (Clark, 2000; Lansdown, 2005; Pais, 2000). For child participation to be ethical, those who live and work with children—educators, teachers, parents, family members, and society at large—must be prepared to give children as many opportunities as possible to freely participate in the societies of which they are part.

While the approaches to early childhood curriculum-development research discussed thus far in the chapter converge around similar ideals of child participation, often they follow a linear, hierarchical, and unidirectional pattern that centres adults as experts in the pedagogical planning process. They share similarities around the idea that concurrent with valuing children's self-expression is the responsibility to listen to and learn from them. However, many of the approaches are also based on the idea of subjectivity and of "learning as tameable: predictable and possible to plan, supervise and evaluate against predetermined standards" (Olsson, 2009, p. 118). As Olsson (2009) suggests, much learning appears to take place in the unconscious and does not involve a process of achievement. Therefore, a profound challenge lies in considering, interpreting, and understanding children's views enough to reexamine our own opinions and attitudes, and to be willing to transform our practice to both encompass children's ideas and remain open to that which is not yet known.

But how do we incorporate children's participation in curriculum making in ways that are just and ethical and that allow for transformation of early childhood practice? A fruitful starting point might be to engage in a different kind of thinking. For example, Olsson (2009) proposes that rather than finding answers we engage in a struggle—in this case a struggle in the participation process—in which teachers and researchers begin to

> imagine the child in more open and complex ways, trying to avoid falling into the trap of thinking, talking and acting in a simplified way through the notion of the "competent child." The ambition has been to open up this image of the child to many other expressions; to find more and unknown ways of being a child than being defined through one's competencies.... The ongoing struggle involves an ambition to avoid defining the child beforehand, either through theories of developmental psychology, or through the more or less outspoken definitions of competency. (p. 14)

From this viewpoint participation, for adults as well as children, is a dynamic process that involves continual transformation through learning.

○ A Rhizomatic Movement in Child Participation

To engage in the kind of struggle that Olsson proposes, Deleuze and Guattari (1987) seem to offer important concepts "capable of loosening a few long-established knots within research and social sciences" (Olsson, 2009, p. 93). According to Olsson, their rhizomatic way of thinking can be highly productive to reconceptualize curriculum making. Through it, curriculum making can be reenvisioned as a way to continually negotiate with shifting knowledge to broaden the learning experience (Olsson, 2009). In this section, I will experiment with these ideas to explore young children's participation in curriculum making. According to Olsson, this type of exploration attempts to do research by using and experimenting with "whatever seems to function so as to create an encounter between experiences" from the chosen world—in this case, the world of early childhood curriculum making—and the Deleuzian/Guattarian philosophy. She writes:

> It is a style of work that is not about imitating thought or telling practices what they are lacking. It is a style that includes looking at the world and human beings without letting the perception and affection constantly turn towards the negative by focusing on lack and need. It is a question of looking at ourselves and the world from another perspective than that of lack. (2009, p. 125)

As described in Olsson (2009), Deleuze and Guattari (1987) used a metaphor of rhizomes to conceptualize networks in knowledge creation. They described rhizomes as dynamic entities. Unlike tree roots, which have fixed origins, rhizomes are tuberous—multiplicitous, adventitious—and they connect in nonlinear and nonhierarchical assemblages to other things. With a rhizome, anything may be connected and interconnected to anything else. In relation to the social field, the work of Deleuze and Guattari consistently focuses on

> that which is not yet known. It attempts to go beyond the taken for granted and already defined, the predetermined positions and habitual ways of thinking, talking and doing. It is a philosophy that focuses upon ongoing creation of leakages and considers these as non-discursive, non-interpretative potentialities, inherent in any structure or system, that do not need to be deconstructed but rather to be activated. (Olsson, 2009, p. 24)

When applied to early childhood education, this movement in teaching and learning with young children suggests an alternative to models with predetermined outcomes and homogeneous assessments. The focus of child participation in curriculum making should be on whatever is going on in the process of learning at the time, not on attaining knowledge or achieving goals. Furthermore, learning should be treated as "impossible to predict, plan, supervise or evaluate according to predefined standards" (Olsson, 2009, p. 117).

Olsson (2009) argues that "one needs to find a way whereby the dualism individual/society is no longer treated as a cause-effect relationship, but rather find another logic for how to treat what takes place *in between* constructed and imagined entities such as individuals and society" (p. 31). The rhizome metaphor challenges traditional cause and effect relationships and creates a space for validating and framing knowledge creation in early childhood education. It is here that the idea of content of knowledge can be seen as part of a relational field. In this approach, "one avoids nailing down specific knowledge goals to serve as departure points for the learning process and to be used to evaluate each child" (Olsson, 2009, p. 21).

The intention of the rhizomatic movement is to create a space where everything is valued and can come together to form new and multiple thoughts. In this perspective the child is no longer a passive object to be shaped, developed, prepared, educated, and/or cared for. Instead, when children's desires are listened to and considered, educators can bring their ideas into activity planning in a way that makes children part of producing new realities (Olsson, 2009).

The rhizomatic way of thinking recognizes that "the child" is not homogeneously constructed. Deleuze and Guattari would not see the child as a subject distinct from the socialization frameworks and biological determinism of developmental science that reconstitute a subject which never becomes adult nor remains young (Tarulli & Skott-Myer, 2006). In their view, the child is constituted instead as "subjectivity extracted from chronological time or age in its intensities and productions; that is to say, as a subjectivity that never arrives but is constantly renewed as an idiosyncratic expressive extraction of both location and temporality" (Tarulli & Skott-Myer, 2006, p. 191). Everyone, regardless of chronological age, is in a constant state of "becoming." Becoming refutes binary divisions and enables further transformations, melding subjects and objects in close proximity (Tarulli & Skott-Myer, 2006). In other words, a child is not an image of the world. Instead the child forms a rhizome with the world, a parallel evolution of the child and the world; the child assures the deterritorialization of the world, but the world effects a reterritorialization of the child, which in turn deterritorializes itself in the world, and so forth.

Lines of Flight

Rhizomatic thinking connects multiple viewpoints in innovative and unanticipated ways, creating spaces for creative dialogue that troubles traditional views of child participation in early childhood curriculum development. Olsson explains that for Deleuze and Guattari, "lines of flight" run "like a zig-zag crack in between the other lines—and it is only these lines that, from the perspective of Deleuze and Guattari, are capable of creating something new" (Olsson, 2009, p. 58):

> When something new and different is coming about, when the lines of flight are created and activated in practices, it is never taking place as a relationally planned and implemented change by specific individuals. Rather, there are from time to time magic moments where something entirely new and different seems to be coming about. (p. 63)

A line of flight connects singularities, or planes. As "a fibre strung across borderlines" it is a means of deterritorialization, thinking innovatively. Lines of flight could be seen as networks that have the ability to cut across borders and build links between preexisting gaps and between nodes that are separated by categories and orders of segmented thinking, acting, and being.

In the context of early childhood curriculum making, Deleuze and Guattari might argue that it is these lines of flight that give opportunity for creative and inspired escapes from the standardization and stratification of early childhood education. In other words, young children and educators may seek to move beyond the "standard" or "traditional" planned curriculum to expand curriculum making in new and creative ways that are not relationally planned or specifically change oriented. The goal of rhizomaticism, then, is not the obliteration of existing strata (or organized, territorialized space) but the discovery of the available lines of flight within that space. These lines of flight challenge some of the boundaries and constraints that limit how ECE curriculum is created, thereby promoting spaces where action is possible and unobstructed. Because lines of flight can take place at any time and lead us in any direction, as educators we must not only allow for them to take place, but give them the appreciation they deserve by challenging ourselves to think and act in often unconventional ways. It is in this unconventional space where young children could become a fundamental part of curriculum development and where the "magic moments" described above might take place.

If we choose to understand people, specifically young children, as social actors who are experts in their own experiences, curriculum making must make these lines of flight visible through listening to individuals and having them directly participate in the planning process, allowing for creativity and experimentation. Tarulli and Skott-Myer (2006) contend that each time an adult "becomes a child"—by rejecting the binaries of developmental difference and embracing the common becoming of human life—young children's participation can be set into creative and productive flight. Creativity, in turn, "can be picked up and made use of through struggling with creating the most favorable conditions possible for lines of flight and leakages to appear" (Olsson, 2009, p. 75).

Desire as the Source of All Production

For Deleuze and Guattari (1987, as interpreted by Tarulli & Skott-Myer, 2006), desire is the principal and primal force in everything, the immanent source of all production. Tarulli and Skott-Myer (2006) write:

> Lines of flight are imbricated in the economy of desire; forming the "field of imma-
> nence," they are instantiations of desire, and as such constitute the productive force
> of change, of eventness, of becoming—of all that which would question, unsettle,
> undermine, evade, or break up the static molar codes that rigidly define, identify, or
> represent (and hence bind) the subject (subjectus). Desire does not simply flow beneath
> molar lines: one might say that it over flows, that it always exceeds the banks or chan-
> nels that strive to contain it, forever emerging as surplus and as the myriad site of
> ineradicable loopholes (cf. Bakhtin, 1984) out of the social categories and codes that
> otherwise pretend to fix bodies in time and space. (p. 190)

Deleuze and Guattari's concept of desire challenges the unified, rational, and expressive subject and attempts to make possible the emergence of new types of decentred subjects that are free to become dispersed, multiple, and reconstituted as new types of subjectivities and bodies. It could be suggested that terms such as "drive" and "impulses" imply a singularity, while desire implies a multiplicity. Deleuze and Guattari seek to modify the term desire from the usual usage: It does not refer to conscious desires, but rather to the state of the unconscious forces. The strangeness of desire without an object or subject, as desiring production, is what they seek to present (Tarulli & Skott-Myer, 2006).

When relating Deleuze and Guattari's concept of desire to early childhood education curriculum development, one might argue that young children may have an interest in becoming involved in the curriculum-making process. However, this interest exists as a possibility only within the context of a particular social formation. If children are capable of pursuing that interest, it is first of all because they desire to do so. They are invested in the social formation that makes that interest possible. Their interests have been constructed, assembled, and arranged in such a manner that their desire is positively invested in the system that allows them to have this particular interest. Therefore, Deleuze and Guattari reconfig-ure the concept of desire to describe that which we desire and invest our desire in as a social formation.

Consequently, in engaging the issue of early childhood participation in cur-riculum making in the context of becoming, those who identify themselves as "adult" must wrestle with the concept of desire. To ethically engage young children in curriculum development—that is, to go beyond simply giving the appearance of consultation and truly involve them in decision making—adults must move beyond "exploring early childhood education" in relation to conventional developmental, social, and economic indicators. Instead, we must consider the ways in which children's desires can be related to curriculum making. Doing this would require us to think, question, and critically analyze our ways of knowing and to open ourselves to otherness, complexity, and multiplicity.

Potentialities for Practice

With a rhizomatic approach, innovative ways to involve young children in curriculum making can become a reality. Following lines of flight, for example, experimenting and latching onto young children's desires requires the ability to connect any point to any other point through construction, deconstruction, and co-construction processes. Child participation research often seeks to explore what Deleuze and Guattari referred to as "states of meaning" where multiplicities change direction and undergo metamorphosis. The "non-closed" nature of the system—in this case, the consultation process—means it is not reducible to "the one or the multiple." The importance lies not in the components but in directions of motion and configuration that give rise to an emergent series of interpretations (Deleuze & Guattari, 1987). The experiential process that results provides a map that is "always detachable, connectable, reversible, modifiable, and has multiple entrance-ways and exits and its own lines of flight" (Deleuze & Guattari, 1987, p. 21).

This Deleuzian/Guattarian shift in thinking offers a flexible approach in which initial assumptions about curriculum and education can be challenged, can take on new forms, and can be modified to move in different directions as activities unfold. The rhizomatic perspective encourages us to attend to the multiplicity of events taking place at a particular moment, and new and unpredictable events are valued and expanded. This type of thinking challenges us to move past notions of truth and to think critically about the world in new ways. For many educators, this shift in thinking causes a "crisis in thought" as we struggle over how to give meaning to the world around us (Dahlberg, Moss, & Pence, 1999). Dahlberg et al. (1999) maintain that this crisis in thought and "struggle over meaning can produce opportunities and open up the possibility of viewing children, early childhood institutions, and early childhood pedagogy in new ways" (p. 123). These new ways of thinking have the potential to enliven the concept of child participation in curriculum development and transform early childhood policy making, training, research, and practice.

The rhizomatic model illuminates the complexities that exist within curriculum-development processes and asks stakeholders to consider moving beyond the linear logic that frames current education policy. But can a rhizomatic model be put into practice? Educators who try to move away from tokenistic child participation are often overwhelmed with the functionality of involving young children in curriculum development. Practical questions arise, for example: How can spaces be provided that allow children to feel confident and encouraged to express their opinions? What approaches are suitable? How can the experiences of non-verbal children be included? Which approaches will lead to findings that can transform practice?

By framing children's growth as occurring concurrently across a series of domains in an irregular, diverse, and constantly changing process (Deleuze & Guattari, 1987), consulting young children could embody the rhizomatic way of thinking to early learning. It is this "lateral" logic that recognizes the "complex and shifting ways in our 'becoming'" (MacNaughton, 2004, p. 94) and "replaces certain 'hard facts' with shifting and multiple truths" (p. 92), thereby opposing notions of standards-based programming that base young children's education on the achievement of a particular set of academic knowledge and skills. Children act in unanticipated ways that give rise to the unpredictable and unknown. Therefore, in the process of consulting with young children, lines of flight will be created concerning the role of the educator/researcher, the image of the child, and the making of curriculum. Consequently, there is no longer a defined teacher–student relationship, but rather an educational community that is in a constant state of change. This work must not focus on what has happened, but instead embrace the importance of educators and children working together in an ongoing process of constructing and reconstructing the problem.

○ The Possibility to Move beyond Tokenism

Involving young children in decisions regarding curriculum development is underpinned by the United Nations Convention on the Rights of the Child and is gaining support around the world. In Canada, the province of British Columbia, for example, has embedded children's right to participate in its early learning framework (Government of British Columbia, 2008). However, as outlined above, child participation in curriculum making is complex, and it requires both a clear commitment and ongoing, effective actions to make it a living reality.

A rhizomatic framing of curriculum making acknowledges this complexity and looks for ways to map it. In this movement, curriculum making is seen as a continuous, dynamic learning-teaching-experiencing process. All stakeholders in early childhood education—children, educators, parents, and community members—are given the opportunity to express their views on curriculum. Through the consultation process,

> the child is no longer understood as lacking or incomplete but, as they say in Reggio Emilia, intelligent: intelligent, that is, as a person capable of making meaning of the world from his or her own experiences, not as a person who scores more than so many points on an IQ test. (Dahlberg & Moss, 2005, p. 102)

A rhizomatic way of thinking about children's participation in curriculum making can shift attention from ways to create programs *for* children to ways to create programs *with* children. In this process, we can move beyond tokenistic forms of child participation to truly include, respect, and value children's voices.

REFERENCES

Clark A. (2000). Listening to young children: Perspectives, possibilities and problems. Paper presented to the 10th European Conference on Quality in Early Childhood Education, EECERA Conference, London, 29 August–1 September.

Clark, A. (2005). Ways of seeing: Using the mosaic approach to listen to young children's perspectives. In A. Clark, A. Kjorholt, & P. Moss (Eds.), *Beyond listening*, pp. 29–49. Bristol, UK: The Policy Press.

Clark, A., & Moss, P. (2001). *Listening to children: The mosaic approach*. London: National Children's Bureau.

Copple, C., & Bredekamp, S. (Eds.). (2009). *Developmentally appropriate practice in early childhood programs*. Washington, DC: National Association for the Education of Young Children.

Dahlberg, G., & Moss, P. (2005). *Ethics and politics in early childhood education*. New York: Routledge.

Dahlberg, G., Moss, P., & Pence, A. R. (1999). *Beyond quality in early childhood education and care: Postmodern perspectives*. London: Falmer.

Deleuze, G., & Guattari, F. (1987). *A thousand plateaus: Capitalism and schizophrenia* (Brian Massumi, Trans.). Minneapolis, MN: University of Minnesota Press.

Government of British Columbia. (2008). *British Columbia early learning framework*. Victoria, BC: Ministry of Education, Ministry of Health, Ministry of Children and Family Development, & British Columbia Early Learning Advisory Group.

Hart, R. (1992). Children's participation: From tokenism to citizenship. UNICEF Innocenti Essays. Florence, Italy: UNICEF.

Kessler, S., & Swadener, B. B. (1992). *Reconceptualizing the early childhood curriculum: Beginning the dialogue*. New York: Teachers College Press.

Lankshear, C., & McLaren, P. (1993). *Critical literacy: Politics, praxis and the postmodern*. Albany, NY: State University of New York Press.

Lansdown G. (2005). *Can you hear me? The rights of young children to participate in decisions affecting them*. Working Paper No. 36 in Early Childhood Development. The Hague, the Netherlands: Bernard van Leer Foundation.

Lindsay G. (1998). Brain research and implications for early childhood education. *Childhood Education, 75,* 97–104.

Luff, P. (2009). Looking and listening for participatory practice in an English day nursery. In D. Berthelsen, J. Brownlee, & E. Johansson (Eds.), *Participatory learning in the early years,* pp. 129–144. New York: Routledge.

MacNaughton, G. (2003). *Shaping early childhood: Learners, curriculum and contexts.* Maidenhead, UK: Open University Press.

MacNaughton, G. (2004). The politics of logic in early childhood research: A case of the brain, hard facts, trees, and rhizomes. *Australian Educational Researcher, 31*(3), 87–104.

MacNaughton G., Barnes S., & Dally S. (2004). Including young children's voices: Early years gender policy. Department of Education and Children's Services: State Government of South Australia, South Australia.

MacNaughton, G., Hughes, P., & Smith, K. (2007). Young children's rights and public policy: Practices and possibilities for citizenship in the early years. *Children and Society, 21*(6), 458-469.

MacNaughton, G., & Smith, K. (2008). Engaging ethically with young children: Principles and practices for consulting justly with care. In G. MacNaughton, P. Hughes, & K. Smith (Eds.), *Young children as active citizens: Principles, policies and pedagogies,* pp. 31–43. Newcastle, Australia: Cambridge Scholars Publishing.

Olsson, L. M. (2009). *Movement and experimentation in young children's learning: Deleuze and Guattari in early childhood education.* New York: Routledge.

Pais, M. (2000). *Child participation.* New York: UNICEF.

Riley, D. A., & Roach, M. A. (2006). Helping teachers grow: Toward theory and practice of an "emergent curriculum" model of staff development. *Early Childhood Education Journal, 33*(5), 363–370.

Ryan, S., & Oschner, M. (1999). Traditional practices, new possibilities: Transforming dominant images of early childhood teachers. *Australian Journal of Early Childhood, 24*(4), 14–20.

Santos-Pais, M. (1999). *A human rights conceptual framework for UNICEF.* Florence, Italy: UNICEF International Child Development Centre.

Stonehouse, A. (Ed.). (1994). *Not just nice ladies.* Castle Hill, Australia: Pademelon Press.

Tarulli, D., & Skott-Myer, H. (2006). The immanent rights of the multitude: An ontological framework for conceptualizing the issue of child and youth rights. *The International Journal of Children's Rights, 14,* 187–201.

Wien, C. A., & Stacey, S. (2000). Spring conference on emergent curriculum [brochure]. Certification Council of Early Childhood Educators of Nova Scotia.

PART II

Rhythms

There is a rhythmic character when we find that we no longer have the simple situation of a rhythm associated with a character, subject, or impulse. The rhythm itself is now the character in its entirety.
—Deleuze & Guattari, *A thousand plateaus: Capitalism and schizophrenia*, 1987, p. 318

⊙ Extending the Notion of Pedagogical Narration through Hannah Arendt's Political Thought

Iris Berger

Stories, through a process political theorist Hannah Arendt (1906–1975) conceptualized as *historying* (Kristeva, 2001), become part of a community's history once they are told and made public. Arendt conceptualized human life as political action revealed through the language of narration. By this token, the educator/storyteller who practices pedagogical narration is invited (while inviting others) to assume the position of political actor/leader.

This chapter explores the concept of pedagogical narration through Arendt's political thought in order to build on the view expressed by Dahlberg, Moss, and Pence (Dahlberg & Moss, 2005; Dahlberg, Moss, & Pence, 1999; Moss, 2007) that early childhood can be loci of political and ethical practice. The chapter's main goal is to extend the notion of pedagogical narration as a form of action and critical understanding by recalling Arendt's concepts of *public sphere, action, natality, plurality*, and *storytelling*. Four key ideas are explored: (1) pedagogical narration as reclaiming and sustaining a public sphere of engagement and contestation; (2) pedagogical narration as critical understanding; (3) pedagogical narration as a form of resistance; and (4) pedagogical narration as a provocation for "preserving" newness and plurality.

The term *pedagogical narration* has been inspired by concepts such as pedagogical documentation[1] (Dahlberg et al., 1999) and learning stories[2] (Carr et al.,
2000). In a nutshell, pedagogical narration is a process by which educational experiences in early childhood settings are narrated and made visible in the public
realm, thus becoming subject to public critical thought and dialogue. These narrations provoke us to think anew and to resist normalized and habitual conceptions of childhood, education, learning, and assessment. In so doing, they open
the *political space* for discussions of possible meanings of these constructs. When
viewed as a tool for political action, pedagogical narration presents an unprecedented opportunity for early childhood educators (as well as citizens) to deepen
and broaden meanings associated with early learning and to explore alternative
discourses of early childhood education.

○ Hannah Arendt: An Introduction

Hannah Arendt was born in Hanover, Germany in 1906. As a young Jewish
woman and an accomplished student of philosophy, she had to leave her home in
Germany with the rise of the Nazi government in 1933 and to live in exile. She
escaped to Paris and then to New York, where she was granted American citizenship in 1951, 10 years after her arrival.

In a television interview in 1964 (as described in Disch, 1994) Arendt revealed
how her personal experiences in Nazi Germany left her wondering about and dis-
turbed by the "inactivity" of the German intellectual milieu to which she belonged
(she referred to this inactivity as the rift between philosophy and polity). She was
particularly troubled by the fact that being a "good thinker" did not imply "good
judgment" (Coulter & Wiens, 2002), and she postulated that her colleagues were
able to separate their actions from their thinking. In the interview she described
how her sudden isolation from her community triggered her thinking about the
political meaning of the public realm and the speed with which it can disappear
from one's experience, as well as the swiftness with which one can be made superfluous (or disappear) within it.

For Arendt the Second World War and its atrocities signaled an epistemic
breakdown; being confronted with an event that had destroyed existing categories of thought and judgment presented, in Arendt's words, a "problem of understanding" (Disch, 1993, p. 670). The conceptual categories of the Western
tradition collapsed and did not enable comprehension of what occurred. At the
same time, this "epistemic breakdown" afforded an opportunity to look at the
world with eyes not distracted by traditional forms of thought (Canovan, 1994).

Arendt linked what happened during the war to a tradition of Western philosophy that formed an ideal of detachment toward politics[3] (Disch, 1994).

For Arendt this realization was critical. It signaled her loss of faith in the idea of the "professional thinker" who removes herself from community life in pursuit of abstraction. Despite her educational background, Arendt decided to become a political theorist and put her thoughts into action, rather than becoming the professional thinker she was trained to be (Kristeva, 2001). *Life* and *action* became central to Arendt's intellectual journey as well as to her textual/metaphorical vocabulary (Kristeva, 2001), hence her provocative offer to us to connect lived experiences[4] to critical understanding—a connection that comes to life, as will be argued later, through the practice of pedagogical narration.

Arendt's concern with the disengagement of philosophy from politics led her to propose a conceptual expansion of the notion of the political (Disch, 1994; Heller, 1991). She reconstructed the nature of political existence as a way of thinking and acting—as opposed to a removed abstractive contemplation. Responding to Arendt's provocation, Calhoun and McGowan (1997) ask, "Must politics be merely a matter of power relations, or can it embody the realization of some of the higher and most distinctive potentials of human life?" (p. 1). Arendt challenges us to think about politics in which "*questions of meaning, identity, and value take centre stage*" (Calhoun & McGowan, 1997, p. 1, my emphasis). By giving us a political theory with a richer meaning of politics, Arendt opened up the political/public sphere to questions that otherwise may not have entered into it. She suggests an engagement in "worldly" experiences which both give and are given meanings through perspectival storytelling and ceaseless questioning of what we encounter.

o **Arendt's Notion of the Public Sphere**

Arendt's concern for the decline of the public realm in the modern age is an ongoing theme in her writing. She was particularly troubled by the rise of mass or "normalized" society (Arendt, 1998, p. 40), in which "ways of being in the world" continuously diminish and where people's behaviours are homogenized by innumerable (implicit) rules (Schutz, 1999). Arendt saw in the public sphere a possibility to revive active public life, where differences of position and perspective are revealed and exchanged and where "worldly realities" are constructed. She described the public realm as a "place of appearances"; a place for "being seen and heard" (Arendt, 1998, p. 50); and, most importantly, a place where stories are told and relations between narratives occur:

> Being seen and being heard by others derive their significance from the fact that
> everybody sees and hears from a different position. This is the meaning of public life
> …. Each time we talk about things that can be experienced only in privacy or inti-
> macy, we bring them out into a sphere where they will assume a kind of reality ….
> The presence of others who see what we see and hear what we hear assures us of the
> reality of the world and ourselves. (Arendt, 1998, pp. 50/57)

Arendt recognized appearances in the public place as a political condition (Kristeva,
2001). The place of appearances where we reveal who we are through action and
speech calls upon us to show courage to disclose ourselves to others. Yet, for Arendt
(1998), the public sphere was by no means a naïve meeting place, but a place of
contestation where the political is enacted through the appearance of a plurality
of ideas and perspectives:[5]

> The reality of the public realm relies on the simultaneous presence of innumerable
> perspectives and aspects in which the common world presents itself and for which no
> common measurement or denominator can ever be devised. [For]…though the com-
> mon world is the common meeting ground for all, those who are present have differ-
> ent locations in it. (Arendt, 1998, p. 57)

As Calhoun and McGowan (1997) note, the public space is not seen as a community through which similarities are organized and recognized; political action is
focused on differences. Further, "what is crucial to public life is that public discussion continues indefinitely. Public discussion is a goal in itself, not merely a
means by which to arrive at decisions" (p. 10). This does not mean that decisions
are not made; it means they are made after critical consideration of multiple points
of view. The public sphere exists to offer occasions to reveal discourses; through
these revelations we come to understand not merely one another, but how to "look
upon the same world" from different points of view (Calhoun & McGowan, 1997,
p. 9).

o Action, Plurality, and Natality: Disclosing Who We Are in a Public Sphere

Understanding Arendt's conception of action[6] is crucial to understand her political thought. The Arendtian action is related to two conditions: natality and plurality. To act, for Arendt, meant to start something new, to begin, to lead, to set
something into motion (Arendt, 1998). She built this conception of action on a
metaphor of natality borrowed from Saint Augustine. Natality, a term for the
human capacity for renewal, holds that people are constantly born into the world
with the potentiality to initiate and are continually in need of introduction to that

world and to one another (Arendt's metaphor was of a "newcomer" or a "stranger"). This desire to contribute to the re-creation of the world, explains Levinson (2001), is what motivates political action.

"With words and deeds we insert ourselves into the human world," Arendt (1998) wrote, "and this insertion is like a second birth" (p. 176). Through this insertion into the human world, with speech and action, we reveal who, not what, we are as we disclose our distinctiveness. Action, in this sense, is an actualization of the human condition of plurality, which, for Arendt, was the condition of all political life:

> Action would be an unnecessary luxury, a capricious interference with general laws of behavior, if men were endlessly reproducible repetitions of the same model, whose nature or essence was the same for all and as predictable as the nature and essence of any other thing. Plurality is the condition of human action because we are all the same, that is, human, in such a way that nobody is ever the same as anyone else who ever lived, lives, or will live. (Arendt, 1998, p. 8)

The human condition of plurality is realized through ongoing, never-completed processes of communication. Action takes place in the space of appearance (or public space) and always encounters the questions "who are you?" and "what is the meaning of this action?" Kristeva (2001) suggests that narrative fulfills the role of responding to these questions.

Action and speech have another significant function: They give rise to "worldly interests" (Arendt referred to them as "inter-ests") that lie between people. Most action and speech is concerned with this in-between that "relates and binds" people together in a "web of human relationship" (Arendt, 1998, pp. 182–183). While the in-between may vary among groups of people, Arendt maintained, it should not be conflated with a notion of common identity because action still entails the capacity to disclose one's distinctiveness, thus "protecting" plurality and natality.

For Arendt, natality was the essence of education (Arendt, 1977, cited in Levinson, 2001), and she recognized its complexity and its paradoxical nature, that is, that the capacity to initiate, to bring the "new" to the world is tempered by the fact that the world not only precedes us but constitutes us (Levinson, 2001). In other words, we are heirs to particular histories; hence we experience ourselves as *belated* even though we are capable of being a *beginner*. Further, the condition of plurality implies that initiation always takes place in the midst of other acting human beings (in what Arendt calls the "web of relations") whose very presence mitigates against one's action coming to fruition. Belatedness positions us in relation to both the past and to others (Levinson, 2001). This idea does not necessarily negate agency. Instead it signals the place where education, and particularly pedagogical narration, can step in as a political action.

It is important to note that the "new" that is proposed here is not the same as the new in the modernist sense of innovation, that is, as progress toward an ideal (for Arendt this would have been impossible given the human conditions of natality and plurality). Levinson (2001) clarifies that according to Arendt, the "new" wants to begin, makes a suggestion, has no particular end in mind, poses many possibilities. It is our task as educators to "preserve newness," to invite the new to appear, and to lift, so to speak, the "weight of history" (Levinson, 2001, p. 30). Thus educators create possibilities where children are invited to experience themselves as unprecedented and extraordinary.

o Action as Narration and Narration as Action

Storytelling was integral to Arendt's political philosophy. Benhabib (1994) goes so far as to suggest that she conceived of political theory *as* storytelling. Kristeva (2001) contends that "Arendt rehabilitates *the praxis of narrative*...only action as narration, and narration as action, can fulfill life in terms of what is specifically human about it" (p. 8, my emphasis). Arendt endowed narrative with the capacity for action. Stories are both the *effects* of action (by disclosing the meanings of events, albeit not definitively) and action itself (Arendt, 1998). In seeking to explain Arendt's notion of narrative, Kristeva (2001) explicates the link between narrative and action:

> Through this narrated action that story represents, man corresponds to life or belongs to life to the extent that human life is unavoidably a political life. Narrative is the initial dimension in which man lives, the dimension of a bios and not of a zoe—a political life and/or an action recounted to others. The initial man-life correspondence is narrative; narrative is the most immediately shared action, and, in that sense, the most initially political action. Finally, and because of narrative, the "initial" itself is dismantled, is dispersed into "strangeness" within the infinity of narrations. (p. 27)

While action holds the capacity for renewal (to begin, to lead) it is at the same time described by Arendt as "boundless and unpredictable" (Arendt, 1998); it has no preconceived end (in fact, Arendt claims that action hardly ever achieves its purpose) and it is in danger of disappearing if not noted by spectators. Since actions themselves cannot contest meanings, as they are fleeting and limitless, it is the storyteller's role to make action public through narratives (Disch, 1994). Thus, narrative's initial role is to transform experience into a (tangible) "appearance," or to make action visible. Action can only appear, according to Arendt, if it is narrated by an attentive spectator who completes the story through thought that follows upon the act. This contemplation takes place through evoked memory, without which there is nothing to tell (Kristeva, 2001). But storytellers do more than "tell stories that accord permanence to fleeting actions"; importantly, they craft them into stories whose meaning can be opened to public disputation (Disch, 1994, p. 73). By doing so, storytellers initiate the process of public debate, and this, as Disch (1994) argues, is the "quintessential realization of natality, the condition that makes way to new beginnings" (p. 73).

The political value of storytelling and the power of documentation in its narrative form did not escape the educators in the Reggio Emilia schools (Edwards, Gandini, & Forman, 1998) or the initiators of New Zealand's learning stories project (Carr et al., 2000). When the practice of pedagogical documentation was adopted in Reggio Emilia in the 1970s, it was an attempt to share *publicly* through "stories" (at the beginning they appeared in the form of a diary) the lives of young children in one of the city's infant and toddler centres. The educators wanted to advocate to parents and community members about the educational value of relationships with others as well as the unique experiences infants encountered in their daily lives in the centres in order to impact the government's decision to publicly fund them (Edwards, 2006). Similarly, Podmore and Carr (1999) developed the learning stories assessment project to bring forth the idea that children learn through relationships and to emphasize the role of family and community in children's learning as resistance to a growing climate of concern with accountability and quality across New Zealand's educational sector.

To better understand the role of pedagogical narration as action and critical understanding, it is necessary first to return to the Arendtian notions of publicity, action, natality, and plurality, to complicate and enlarge their meanings and relate them to the practice of pedagogical documentation.

○ Theorizing Pedagogical Narration as Action

Through the act of pedagogical narration, educators take on the role of the attentive spectator and storyteller who initiate public disputation of meaning. The process begins with educators noticing children's actions (children's words and deeds) that evoke curiosity and thinking. Educators collect materials, such as photos, images, written notes, video or tape recordings, quotes, and other samples of children's experiences that act as "fragments of a memory" (Rinaldi, 2001, p. 84) from which arise possibilities for rethinking as narratives. These materials form the basis of a collaborative process of critical dialogue among actors who are related to the story to be told. The documentations are often reconstructed as written narratives and shared in the form of displays (e.g., posters, booklets, or pamphlets) typically consisting of text and images as a provocation to continue the discussion, reflection, and interpretation of the pedagogical work among teachers, children, parents, and community members.

Pedagogical Narration as Reclaiming and Sustaining a Public Sphere of Engagement and Contestation

By sharing the documented exemplars publicly, participants in the process have the potential to create and sustain a public sphere of engagement with questions concerning young children's education. Since, as Arendt makes clear, the possibility of a public sphere is not simply given, it must be created by action and narration. Following Arendt, Disch (1994) explains that "publics emerge not around an action itself but around the various stories that make it a public event" (p. 85). Action and narration become *interventions* in the *web of relations* that constitutes the public realm. The stories affect citizens so that they are moved to participate in the activity of "interpretive contestation that sustains the integrity of the public realm and its plurality" (Disch, 1994, p. 104). Inspired by Hannah Arendt's and her student Maxine Greene's writings about the public, Aaron Schutz (1999) posits that by listening to others and contributing interpretations to a common referent in a public space, participants enlarge and expand their *inter-est* as relations among narratives begin to appear and inspire further action. Thus the practice of pedagogical narration has the potential to broaden public perceptions about early childhood education.

Interestingly, Malaguzzi (as cited by Hoyuelos, 2004, in Moss, 2007) explains the political nature of documentation as a responsibility of the school, asserting that "what schools do must have public visibility," which, for Malaguzzi, meant the possibility of discussing and dialoguing "everything with everyone" (p. 14). It is important to note that while the narratives aid in constituting a common *inter-est* and a local public realm, presenting them to the public is not grounded in an attempt to achieve a "transparent consensus" (Schutz, 1999, p. 81), but is rather an invitation for contestation. Pedagogical narrations transform school experiences into "objects for thought" presented to a multitude of spectators so that the common interest can be discussed from a variety of perspectives to illuminate its "utter diversity" (Arendt, 1998, p. 57).

Arendt suggests that stories can be offered as exemplars (Disch, 1997). By offering exemplars to the public, the meanings of the story are dispersed into the web of relations and the story itself becomes a birth and "a foreignness that endlessly begins anew in the public space" (Kristeva, 2001, p. 25). Indeed, Arendt dared us to create stories that are fragmented, incomplete, and that launch "an infinite action of interpretation" (Kristeva, 2001, p. 18).

At the same time, storytelling for Arendt was about remembrance, about pre-serving citizens' words and deeds from oblivion and creating public memory. This public memory in the form of stories flows in the in-between of the web of human relations and acts as the ground from which the possibility for common action emerges (Arendt, 1998). Therefore, pedagogical narrations not only give shape to experience but also create history for the life of the school's community. Here lies the invitation and the challenge to actively collect and display traces of history made visible through pedagogical narrations in the shape of posters, photographs, children's work, and publications, which act together to preserve the educational project's history and identity, and, at the same time, give it direction and focus. In this manner, the collection of pedagogical documentation or narrations plays a crucial role in creating a community of remembrance.

Pedagogical Narration as Critical Understanding

Lisa Disch (1994) distinguishes the Arendtian concept of storytelling from more traditional conceptions of storytelling as a means for handing down tradi-tion or a vehicle for self-expression. For Arendt storytelling was a "practice of sit-uated critical thinking" and the storyteller's task was not to report objectively, but to tell a story that engaged the audience's critical faculties (p. 27). Thus, story is not about telling the truth. Stories are told "to stir people to think about what they are doing" (Disch, 1993, p. 671). A story "lays open to view the complexity" (Nussbaum, 1986, in Disch, 1994, p. 112) in a way that inspires spontaneous crit-ical thinking (Disch, 1994).

Arendt envisioned the process of critical understanding through a metaphor of visiting—a kind of thinking (or imagining) by which one rewrites the story of an event from a plurality of perspectives in a particular context (Disch, 1994). While Arendt imagined *visiting* as an intrapersonal process, pedagogical docu-mentation is enacted as both intra- and interpersonal (Rinaldi, 2001). Constructing documentation entails a kind of interpersonal visiting where diverse viewpoints (of children, teachers, consultants, parents, and community members) are in dia-logue about the event. This dialogic process is conducted not to defend a unify-ing principle, but to attempt to put together different views in relation to each other. This kind of thinking from a *public* rather than an "objective" vantage point is what gives the story or exemplar what Arendt would call "exemplary validity" (Disch, 1997). From this perspective, critical understanding becomes a process (not a destination) that entails judgment that is "situated but not standpoint bound" (Disch, 1994, p. 2). Moreover, claims for immediate understanding and certainty are suspect because they shut down communication and relieve citizens of their responsibility to participate and take action (Disch, 1994).

Indeed, narration is an act of critical understanding and judgment at a number of levels. First, in order to "story" an action it becomes necessary to "carve it out" from its boundlessness and from its diffusion within the web of human relations. Arendt recognizes this challenge. Rather than focusing on the technical aspects of narrative, she posits that what is important for "eyewitness" narrative is to recognize the moment of closure and to identify the story's agent (Kristeva, 2001). Building on Arendt's ideas, Kristeva notes: "The art of narrative, then, resides in the ability to condense the action into an exemplary moment, to extract it from the continuous flow of time, and reveal a who" (Kristeva, 2001, p. 17). This is not an easy task. A story is not an imitation of an action and narrated action is not about merely describing the experience. In a discussion about the practice of documentation as it is enacted in the Reggio Emilia pre-primary schools, Rinaldi (2001) clarifies this challenge that pedagogical narration as critical understanding presents for educators:

> At the moment of documentation...the element of assessment enters the picture immediately, that is, in the context and during the time in which the experience (activity) takes place. It is not sufficient to make an abstract prediction that establishes what is significant—the elements of value necessary for learning to be achieved—before the documentation is actually carried out. It is necessary to interact with the action itself, with that which is revealed and defined and perceived as truly significant. (p. 85)

In the process of pedagogical narration, educators make decisions about choosing an experience to be narrated and reflected upon. Even at this first stage there is an element of selection and an act of judgment with regard to the value and significance of the event that is chosen. Further, the educator has to make decisions about the choice of words that will frame the narrative and give it a particular meaning (considering the ethics and politics of the text). When the narrative is shared, the educator takes further responsibility in opening up the space for alternative interpretations and narrating the collective version of the story by being attentive to how others' perspectives might have changed/enlarged the story. Dahlberg et al. (1999) underline that pedagogical narration is not a means of capturing a single, neutral, picture of what children can do. Rather, pedagogical narration operates in relation to values, intersubjectivity, and multiple perspectives (Dahlberg et al., 1999). Through the process of pedagogical narration, educators become participants, co-constructors of the documented experiences.

In this light, pedagogical narration marks a shift from traditional understandings of observing and recording young children's behaviour. It also broadens the notions of teachers as reflective practitioners, as it sustains and makes visible the necessity for vigorous relationships between thinking and acting. Furthermore, the challenges of articulating and sharing the pedagogical work require that teachers debate, organize, and refine their own understandings in relation to, and in the context of, discussions with others who are familiar with the event and its protagonists (New, 1998). Through this process teachers clarify their stance. Moreover, they take a public stand by articulating their position toward the documented event. Maxine Greene (1973, cited in Schutz, 1999) stipulates that most of the time the individual teacher, who is immersed in the technical/mechanical aspects of daily routines, is not conscious of her standpoint. Recalling the notion of action as disclosing one's distinctiveness in the public sphere, it seems fitting to propose that through pedagogical narration, teachers begin to find out who they are (not what they are) as they develop the capacity to act and to be engaged in what too often seems to be a "determinate world" (Greene, 1995, cited in Schutz, 1999).

Malaguzzi (1998) understood that documentation can be an important tool to bridge acting and thinking. Thus he contended that "teachers must possess a habit of questioning their certainties…responding to all these demands requires from teachers a constant questioning of their teaching…they must discover ways to communicate and document the children's evolving experiences at school"; this as opposed to "an isolated, silent mode of working that leaves no traces" (p. 69). "This flow of documentation," Malaguzzi continues, "introduces parents to a quality of knowing that tangibly changes their expectations. They reexamine their assumptions about their parenting roles and their views about the experiences their children are living and take a new and more inquisitive approach toward the whole school experience" (p. 70). For children too, the flow of documentation creates a "second scenario" through which they become more interested and curious as they "contemplate the meaning" of their narrated actions (p. 70).

Pedagogical Narration as Resistance

For Arendt storytelling was not only a form of situated critical understanding, but also a form of resistance against the dictate that the thinker must withdraw to a vantage point beyond the world in order to understand it (Disch, 1993). Arendt saw objectivity and abstraction as a form of withdrawal from life and a detachment from the world (Disch, 1994); thus, she looked for a way of judging without losing the connection to lived experiences and without losing the possibility of offering a judgment that is open to questioning (Disch, 1994). Arendt maintained that story can perform this role because "to tell a story is to break the usual 'rules of caution' and refrain from rhetorical moves that would give one's position the appearance of unquestionability" (Disch, 1994, p. 4). Disch (1993) elaborates on Arendt when she claims that

under certain conditions, a story can be a more powerful critical force than a theoretical analysis. In a society where the abstraction of social theory and social science
sometimes masks real conflicts, a skillful narrative can bring to light the assumptions
buried in apparently neutral arguments and challenge them. Storytelling invites a
critical engagement between a reader and a text and, more important, among the various readers of a work, in a way that the social science "voice from nowhere" cannot.
(p. 665)

Arendt's proposition to see storytelling as resistance makes a significant contribution to viewing pedagogical narration as a site for challenging and resisting
the emphasis in early childhood education on the general over the particular and
on theory over practice. This issue becomes highly relevant in light of the fact
that, as Grieshaber and Cannella (2001) argue, historically the identity of the early
childhood field has been hierarchically tied to the field of developmental psychology, which has been used to guide early childhood practice. Early childhood educators were traditionally conceptualized as implementers of theories and
consumers of research conceived by experts (i.e., developmental psychologists)
outside of the realm of the daily classroom experiences and practice of the early
childhood educator (Grieshaber & Cannella, 2001). Malaguzzi (1998) recognized
the danger of relying exclusively on external educational theories; therefore, he
nudged educators to engage instead in critical dialogue that questions theories
from outside and relates them to the particular lived experiences in children's centres. He adamantly insisted that teaching involves continuous bridging between
children's experiences that unfold in the classrooms and the development of a local
pedagogical thought (Malaguzzi, 1998).

Here lies the potential of documented examples of children's learning to
become a rich platform from which educators negotiate theory and practice relations. Rather than relying solely on experts for their knowledge of children and
their learning, educators "need to build their own pictures of children as learners
that capture specific children in specific circumstances at specific times"
(MacNaughton, 2003, p. 77). Through pedagogical narrations the daily school
realities mediate relationships with external theories of education, as the stories
situate theories in relation to particular experiences, opening the space for questions and inquiry. Through the practice of collective narration, the educator
becomes a collaborator with the child and others to generate knowledge in the
world. Disch (1993) proclaims that "a well-crafted story shares with the most ele-
gant theories the ability to bring a version of the world to light that so transforms
the way people see that it seems never to have been otherwise" (p. 665). In a similar vein, Lenz Taguchi (2007) contends that in the process of textualizing practice, it is inevitably written into existence both as practice and as theory, "and in
that sense made accessible and even palpable, for being rewritten, re-talked, and

thereby re-performed and transformed" (p. 279). This assertion, perhaps more powerfully than others, affirms pedagogical narration as a form of action.

If words create actions and action creates words, then judgment and resistance can be enacted in the choice of words and in how we language the story. The relationship between words and action is critical. As Arendt (in Disch, 1997) puts it, language has a "disclosing quality"; it is not just a means of self-expression but also "the repository of a particular way of apprehending the world that grows out of collective symbols and memories" (p. 152). This plurality of meanings embedded in words requires "finding the right words at the right moment" (Arendt, 1998, p. 26). Disch (1994) notes that Arendt developed her own vocabulary both by introducing new words and by giving familiar terms an unfamiliar context. Disch (1994) posits that the development of a new vocabulary is not coincidental; rather it acts as a resistance to the norm, the universal, and the taken for granted. It is a tool for political leadership. Similarly, Dahlberg and Moss (2005) see the invention of a new vocabulary as the production of a counter discourse. Educators and researchers from Reggio Emilia and New Zealand created a new vocabulary with which to discuss early childhood education, childhood, and assessment in their contexts (e.g., documentation, pedagogy of listening, learning stories). Taking on an attitude of resistance to the taken for granted can be viewed as the challenge and the invitation for educators from various contexts to begin to develop distinctive early childhood pedagogical languages.

Pedagogical Narration as a Provocation for Preserving Newness and Plurality: Overcoming the Paradox of Natality

Arendt first gave us the hope of natality (to begin) and then problematized its possibility of arising because of the condition of plurality and the idea of belatedness. To understand how pedagogical narration can help us overcome the paradox of natality, it is necessary to return to Arendt's notion of history. For Arendt, history is the "the great story without beginning and end" (Arendt, 1998, p. 184). History is a "becoming," a "storybook" with many actors and speakers and without a tangible author. Stories continuously interrupt history because they carry the capacity to begin, even though they will be added to this great storybook of history. There is no better example to represent this idea of (hi)story than the practice of pedagogical narration. The power of pedagogical narration to "preserve newness" by narrating actions and beginning a dialogue, a conversation, and perhaps a new project for learning, is, at the same time, its ability to add to the "collective remembrance" of the life of the schools.

Borrowing from Levinson (2001), who advocates for teaching as "preserving of the new," we might say that pedagogical narration finds the "gap between past and future" (Levinson, 2001, p. 30). This gap represents not an escape from history but a "fissure" within time where children and educators do not feel determined and fated by history (Levinson, 2001), a time when they feel an opportunity to reconfigure themselves in response to history and are able to see, within the relational space of the school, new relations and new realities. We work in the "gap between past and future" says Arendt (1977, p. 94, in Levinson, 2001, p. 29); the past conditions us but it does not determine the future. Rinaldi (2001) discusses the possibilities that the practice of documentation affords in terms of natality and freedom[7]:

> Doubt and uncertainty permeate the context; they are part of the "documenters' context." Here lies true didactic freedom, for the child as well as the teacher. It lies in this space between the predictable and the unexpected, where the communicative relationships between the children's and teacher's learning processes is constructed. It is in this space that the questions, the dialogue, the comparison of ideas with colleagues are situated. (p. 85)

Inviting and encountering the new always threatens our present categories of understanding, making the existing standards and rules potentially inadequate. Can we rise to the challenge and begin to see, to use Levinson's (2001) words, natality as a site of potential provocation? This encounter with the new necessitates what Arendt called "thinking without a banister" (Arendt, 1979, cited in Disch, 1994, pp. 143–144). Banisters are a metaphor for abstractions (categories and formulas ingrained in our mind) that we tend to impose on events by force of habit (Disch, 1994). The capacity to think without a banister, explains Disch (1994), is a way of thinking critically where categories are not imposed but are rather inspired by one's engagement with a phenomenon. Pedagogical narration can give us the ground on which thinking without a banister can occur, because educators' thought is inspired and provoked by the documented event, and educators are challenged to reconceptualize and reconsider their previous assumptions about children.

Here lies also the provocation to view education as introducing the old (transmission) while actively preserving children's capacity to act (to begin) in ways that might renew the world without dictating to them how to renew it (Rinaldi, 2001). How can we become more attentive to the conditions that foster natality? How can we remain open to being surprised and amazed by children's actions, or, to use Arendt's words, how can we actively "expect the unexpected" (Arendt, 1998, p. 178)?

Through pedagogical narrations we can respond to the question posed by the conditions of natality and plurality, namely, "Who are you?" This is by no means a question that can be answered with certainty. Arendt (1998) emphasized the challenge or the impossibility of solidifying in words a person's living essence as it shows itself in the flux of action and speech:

> The moment we want to say who somebody is, our very vocabulary leads us astray into saying what he is; we get entangled in a description of qualities he necessarily shares with others like him; we begin to describe a "type" of a "character" in the old meaning of the word, with the result that his specific uniqueness escapes us. (p. 181)

Instead of trying to describe a universal child, by employing pedagogical narration as critical understanding and inquiry we can focus our attention as educators on provocative questions such as "What is your image of the child?" (Malaguzzi, 1994) and "Who is a human being?" (Rinaldi, 2001). These questions, which are ontological statements more than they are questions, open up the space for dialogue that has a direction but no limits; it signals a beginning with no predefined end. By posing these questions (ceaselessly) and responding to them continually through narratives, educators commit to a practice that embraces an ethics of plurality and natality. Each narration or documentation of children's actions offers a possibility to meet a new child. This is not the child who is defined by what she is or by what he will become. It is a child who appears to us as unique and unprecedented, a protagonist who gained the possibility of joining the "great storybook." Through pedagogical narrations, children's multiple identities can continually emerge in an unexpected and creative manner. This narration affords a kind of listening that allows children to *appear*. In this public arena children discover that they exist and can "emerge from anonymity and invisibility" (Rinaldi, 2001, p. 87). As Aaron Schutz (1999) puts it, "unless one's history is actualized or brought to language it can not matter" (p. 80). Disch (1994) offers that perhaps one of Arendt's most significant insights is that individuality is not a property of the self but a public achievement, "a possibility afforded by the regard of others" (p. 86).

Implications for Early Childhood Education

Rethinking the Political: Early Childhood Spaces Reconceptualized as Sites for Political Action

Arendt's way of thinking proposes to us a new view of the political: a political that permeates all social activities including those constituted by the very young, their teachers, parents, and communities. Pedagogical narration can play a critical role in politicizing early childhood by giving it a public arena. It is through the practice of pedagogical narration that we can insert into the public realm of appearances stories about the lives of children and educators. By opening the early childhood domain for deliberation, we can enlarge the common *inter-est* from which collective action can emerge.

Hannah Arendt can inspire us to see our role as early childhood advocates from the point of view of politics as raising and responding to questions about meanings, identities, and values. Questions such as: Who is the child? What does education mean in our particular context? What is the role of early childhood education in our society? These questions, which necessitate continual democratic attention, can and should be raised by early childhood educators, children, parents, and political leaders. Moss (2007) emphasizes the importance of these questions when he argues that "we could extend the areas opened up to politics that are re-politicized as legitimate subjects for inclusive political dialogue and contestation: the image of the child, the good life and what we want for our children" (p. 12).

Becoming a Storyteller: Pedagogical Narrations as Creating Possible Realities

Dahlberg and Moss (2005), in a similar vein, give us the concept of *minor politics*. These, they explain, are concerned with the here and now, with the everyday, as they seek to "engender a small reworking of their own spaces of action" (p. 138). Yet they further clarify that minor politics and the expansion of the political terrain involves a collective process of critical thinking and contestation. Here we return to the provocative offer from Arendt, Reggio Emilia, and New Zealand that critical understanding can be enacted through the process of narrating lived experiences when this process invites multiple perspectives and publicity.

These stories, told from the position of spectators and actors who are attentive to the life of the school, reveal children in creative, unexpected, and unprecedented ways. Additionally, making stories about children's actions and learning processes visible to the public entails constructions of children that are not abstract. Through these stories, children are released from their anonymity, they gain a multiplicity of identities, and they become foci for dialogue and interest.

The narratives can be offered as exemplars, as a collection of stories that tell about early childhood from the vantage point of plurality and from the contexts of various localities. These stories act as an inspiration and a possibility to enlarge our shared thought and our shared understanding of what early childhood education is and what it can be about. These stories are not offered as the "truth" or as an example of "best practice"; instead they suggest possible realities, ways of seeing children and education that invite conversation and that inevitably change the public dialogue about early childhood education.

Moreover, pedagogical narration opens new possibilities for transgressing the theory–practice binary, because educators are invited to see themselves beyond the metaphor of the "labourer" (Coulter & Wiens, 2002) as thinkers, actors, and storytellers. They become creators of new meanings, questioning theories from "out there" and offering their position with regard to school occurrences. This reflective and daring attitude can be seen as an appeal to upend the taken-for-granted hierarchical power construction in the educational realm of schooling in general and early childhood in particular, where teachers/educators are too often depicted within a technical and instrumentalist paradigm. It follows then, that we can begin to advocate for a broader image, not only of children, but also of early childhood educators.

Early Childhood Educators as Leaders

Arendt's notion of natality suggests that despite the seemingly insurmountable weight of habits, rules, and predictability, the possibility that the world can be renewed is always present as conditioned in action. In her seminal work *The Human Condition* (1998), Arendt also offers a unique conceptualization of a leader as a *beginner*. This (humble) notion of a leader implies that change is already embedded in the courage to begin. Courage, Arendt (1958/1998) suggests, which we often think of as a quality of the "hero," is already present in the willingness to act and speak, to insert oneself into the world and begin a story.

Schutz (2001) asserts that the importance of Arendt's work resides not only in what she asked us to think about, but in what she encouraged us to be. It seems fitting, then, to end this discussion by offering Arendt's provocation as a challenge to us as early childhood educators: By storytelling in the public sphere through enacting pedagogical narration, we may enact the courage to *begin*—and to become political leaders.

ENDNOTES

1 The inspiration for the practice of documentation comes from the pedagogical work that emerged in the Reggio Emilia pre-primary schools in northern Italy. See, for example, Edwards, Gandini, and Forman (1998), Malaguzzi (1998) *The Hundred Languages of Children: The Reggio Emilia Approach—Advanced Reflections*). Carla Rinaldi, one of the educational leaders of the Reggio Emilia approach, clarifies that Reggio educators consciously use the term *documentation* not as a collection of documents to demonstrate the truth of a fact, but rather as a "tool for recalling" and a "possibility for reflection" on educational events (Rinaldi, 2001). Dahlberg et al. (1999), who also distinguish documentation from its behaviourist connotation of child observation as means of assessing a child's development, termed the practice of documentation as it was practiced in Reggio Emilia *pedagogical documentation*. In British Columbia, we use the term *pedagogical narration*.

2 Learning stories are narratives of learning and teaching constructed in response to New Zealand's national early childhood curriculum Te Whariki. See, for example, Carr (2002) *Assessment in Early Childhood Settings: Learning Stories*; and Lee and Carr (2002) *Documentation of Learning Stories: A Powerful Assessment Tool for Early Childhood*.

3 Arendt claimed that this tradition of detachment from philosophy originated in Plato's abandonment of politics out of anger at the execution of Socrates (see Coulter & Wiens, 2002; Disch, 1994; Kristeva, 2001).

4 In this context "lived experiences" does not mean simply what happens to us, but the process by which we attribute meaning to what happens.

5 Lisa Disch (1994) maintains that for Arendt the political connotation of "publicity" is openness, which exists whenever a question, problem, or event is submitted to argumentation.

6 In *The Human Condition* (1998) Arendt distinguishes action from labour and work. The latter entail sustaining basic human needs and producing objects with a means–end purpose: The rationale for labour and work is technical and consumerist. Action is also distinguished from behaviour which implies that people are predictable, adaptable units.

7 Arendt also equated natality with freedom [see, for example, Arendt (1993)].

REFERENCES

Arendt, H. (1998). *The human condition*. Chicago: University of Chicago Press.

Arendt H. (1993). What is freedom? In H. Arendt, *Between past and future: Eight exercises in political thought* (pp. 143–171). New York: Penguin Books.

Benhabib, S. (1994) Hannah Arendt and the redemptive power of narrative. In L. P. Hinchman & S. K. Hinchman (Eds.), *Hannah Arendt: Critical essays* (pp. 111–138). Albany, NY: State University of New York Press.

Calhoun, C., & McGowan, J. (1997). *Hannah Arendt and the meaning of politics*. Minneapolis, MN: University of Minnesota Press.

Canovan, M. (1994). *Hannah Arendt: A reinterpretation of her political thought*. Cambridge, UK: Cambridge University Press.

Carr, M. (2002) *Assessment in early childhood settings: Learning stories*. London: Paul Chapman Publishing.

Carr, M., May, H., & Podmore, V. N., with Cubey, P., Hatherly, A., & Macartney, B. (2000). *Learning and teaching stories: Action research on evaluation in early childhood*. Wellington, NZ: New Zealand Council for Educational Research & Ministry of Education.

Coulter, D., & Wiens, J. R. (2002). Educational judgment: Linking the actor and the spectator. *Educational Researcher, 31*(4), 15–25.

Dahlberg, G., Moss, P., & Pence, A. (1999). *Beyond quality in early childhood education and care*. London: RoutledgeFalmer.

Dahlberg, G., & Moss, P. (2005). *Ethics and politics in early childhood education*. London: RoutledgeFalmer.

Disch, L. J. (1993). More truth than fact: Storytelling as critical understanding in the writing of Hannah Arendt. *Political Theory, 21*(4), 665–694.

Disch, L. J. (1994). *Hannah Arendt and the limits of philosophy.* Ithaca, NY: Cornell University Press.

Disch, L. J. (1997). Please sit down but do not make yourself at home: Arendtian visiting and the prefigurative politics of consciousness raising. In C. Calhoun & J. McGowan (Eds.), *Hannah Arendt and the meaning of politics* (pp. 132–165). Minneapolis, MN: University of Minnesota Press.

Edwards, C. Gandini, L. & Forman, G. (Eds.) *The hundred languages of children: The Reggio Emilia approach—Advanced reflections.* Westport, CT: Ablex.

Edwards, C. (2006). A Keynote presentation: Laura's diary. The Second NAREA Summer Conference. *Advocacy, Diversity and Alliance for the Rights of Children: Documentation, Reflection and Transformation.* University of Calgary, Alberta, Canada.

Grieshaber, S. J., & Cannella G. S. (2001). *Embracing identities in early childhood education: Diversity and possibilities.* New York: Teachers College Press.

Heller, A. (1991). The concept of the political revised. In D. Helm (Ed.), *Political theory today* (pp. 330–343). Palo Alta, CA: Stanford University Press.

Kristeva, J. (2001). *Life is a narrative.* Toronto, ON: University of Toronto Press.

Lenz-Taguchi, H. (2007). Deconstructing and transgressing the theory-practice dichotomy in early childhood education. *Educational Philosophy and Theory, 39*(3), 275–290.

Lee, W. , &Carr M. (2002). *Documentation of learning stories: A powerful assessment tool for early childhood.* Paper presented at the Dialogue and Documentation: Sharing Our Understanding of Children's Learning and Developing a Rich Early Years Provision, Pen Green Corby, United Kingdom.

Levinson, N. (2001). The paradox of natality: Teaching in the midst of belatedness. In M. Gordon (Ed.), *Hannah Arendt and education* (pp. 11–36). Boulder, CO: Westview Press.

MacNaughton, G. (2003). *Shaping early childhood: Learners, curriculum, and contexts.* Maidenhead, UK: Open University Press.

Malaguzzi, L. (1994). Your image of the child: Where teaching begins. *Child Care Information Exchange, 96,* 5–9.

Malaguzzi, L. (1998). History, ideas, and basic philosophy: An interview with Lella Gandini. In C. Edwards, L. Gandini, & G. Forman (Eds.), *The hundred languages of children: The Reggio Emilia approach—Advanced reflections* (pp. 49–98). Westport, CT: Ablex.

Moss, P. (2007). Bringing politics into the nursery: Early childhood education as a democratic practice. *European Early Childhood Education Research Journal, 15*(1), 5–20.

New, R. S. (1998). Reggio Emilia's commitment to children and community: A reconceptualization of quality and DAP. *Early Years, 18*(2), 11–18.

Podmore, V., & Carr, M. (1999). *Learning and teaching stories: New approaches to assessment and evaluation.* Paper presented at the AARE—NZARE Conference on Research in Education, Melbourne, Australia, 1 December, 1999. Retrieved October 18, 2009, from http://www.aare.edu.au/99pap/pod99298.htm

Rinaldi, C. (2001). *Making learning visible: Children as individual and group learners.* Reggio Emilia, Italy: Reggio Children and Project Zero.

Schutz, A. (1999). Creating local "public spaces" in schools: Insights from Hannah Arendt and Maxine Greene. *Curriculum Inquiry, 29*(1), 77–98.

Schutz, A. (2001). Theory as performative pedagogy: Three masks of Hannah Arendt. *Educational Theory, 51*(2), 127–150.

CHAPTER FIVE

A Story to Unsettle Assumptions about Critical Reflection in Practice

Deborah Thompson

Stories can illuminate particular personal truths, allowing a reader, a listener, or the storyteller to gain insight. "Little stories" (Cotton & Griffiths, 2007) show what it is like to be in a particular place at a particular time. Ledwith (2005) suggests that these little stories add depth to everyday lives, creating bigger pictures in the process. The "little story" I will tell in this chapter reveals what emerged while I was in the process of critically reflecting on my early childhood practice. Through this story I explore, from my position as an early childhood educator, the tensions embedded in processes of reflexive practice within the context of a curriculum framework. Engaging in critical reflection in the midst of practice challenged my assumptions about critical reflexive practice and illuminated how using a curriculum framework as a tool can both challenge practices and reconfirm prejudices.

Susan Smith (2006), in a discussion of reflexivity's place in writing up qualitative research, identifies two approaches to positioning the writer in the research. A realist tale, Smith suggests, positions the writer as an impersonal source, without bias or judgment. In contrast, a *confessional tale* highlights the writer's voice and reveals tensions and dilemmas that emerged in the research process. Confessional tales, according to Smith, explicate the ways in which the researcher transforms during the research process. Each of the two approaches serves a different purpose; used together, they strengthen the knowledge the research generates.

In this chapter, I employ two narratives—a realist and a confessional tale—to describe my involvement with a particular curriculum framework. The *realist tale* outlines the British Columbia Early Learning Framework Implementation Project 2007–2009, which involved a group of early childhood practitioners, including myself, in learning about curriculum models, postfoundational theories, and critical reflection. The *confessional tale* describes my personal journey through the project. In particular, it explores my engagement with pedagogical narration—a method of documenting "little stories" in early childhood practice. Creating pedagogical narrations and revisiting them allowed exploration of the "truths" that I bring to my practice and my reflections. Through my negotiations with the British Columbia Early Learning Framework (BC ELF) in my practice with young children, I was forced to reconsider the process of critical reflexive practice. In particular, I discovered that engaging in critical reflection in the midst of practice challenged my taken-for-granted understandings. For example, I assumed that critical reflection would always reveal "best practice," making decision-making easier. In practice, however, I discovered that it always leads to more questions, thus decisions that flow from critical reflection are tentative and subject to constant revision. Further, while in some instances critically reflecting on my practice allowed me to destabilize dominant discourses, in other instances it permitted normalization of practices and truths I take for granted. Following my two tales of engaging with a curriculum framework, I explore these tensions, as well as others contained in Early Childhood Care and Education (ECCE) work—work that requires decisions, action, *and* reflexivity.

o Two Tales of a Working with a Curriculum Framework

Context (The Realist Tale)

The British Columbia Ministry of Education, in partnership with the Ministries of Health and of Children and Families, developed the BC Early Learning Framework (ELF) to guide and support those working with young children. The framework's primary purpose is to support

Positioning Myself (The Confessional Tale)

My involvement in the BC ELF Implementation Project was that of an early childhood field leader. When the project began I was the supervisor in a program that provided care for children *early childhood practitioners in creating rich early learning experiences and environments that reflect the latest knowledge on how best to support young children's learning and development. Its vision is based on an image of the child as capable and full of potential, and it envisions early learning as a dynamic process actively supported by families and other caregivers (Government of British Columbia, 2008).*

Early childhood field leaders and college instructors were recruited to participate in a 2-year, three-phase implementation project. The first phase engaged the field leaders in online learning and face-to-face workshops to explore the framework and the reconceptualist understandings of ECCE practice in which it is grounded. In the second phase, the field leaders presented the framework to the college instructors. In the final phase, the field leaders and instructors worked in teams to present workshops on the framework to early childhood practitioners in their home regions around the province.

The ELF project highlighted critical reflection on early childhood practice and presented a tool (pedagogical narration) to broaden and deepen understanding of children's learning. Throughout the project, participants created pedagogical narrations by documenting ordinary moments in their practice settings. An exemplar (Water and Sand, by Deborah Thompson) is included in the implementation guide that was developed through the project (Government of British Columbia, 2009).

between the ages of 18 months and 3 years. In this position I supervised childcare staff and worked along with them as a caregiver. I also taught several evening courses in an Early Childhood Care and Education certificate program at a local community college. I had been involved in the ECCE field for many years as a caregiver, college instructor, unionized worker, and childcare advocate. During that time I coordinated programs, developed new childcare centres, taught courses, and completed a masters degree in ECCE while continuing to work as an early childhood educator directly caring for children.

Throughout my long involvement in the field, I had developed firm opinions and "truths" about early childhood and ECCE curriculum. My certainties included the belief that children learn best when they have the freedom to choose what to do. I evaluated programs that heavily rely on preplanned curriculum as less innovative, interesting, and valuable than programs that encourage spontaneity, flexibility, and originality. When I considered becoming involved in the BC ELF project, I had reservations about curriculum guides and frameworks. I feared that a framework could quickly become a dictated top-down plan that would hinder relationships and prevent both adults and children in early childhood settings from choosing anything at all. But the framework's format highlighted questions rather than answers, and that appealed to me. The implementation project appealed to me even more because it would provide an opportunity to work with pedagogical narration, a practice I was interested in. So I plunged in and applied to be part of the project.

Critical Reflection

Critical reflection, as described in Understanding the British Columbia Early Learning Framework: From Theory to Practice, *is "the art of thinking deeply about our own fundamental beliefs, with the goal of understanding the various cultural and social forces and factors that shape our own sense of self" (p. 11). Throughout the ELF and its implementation guide, questions are posed to educators and caregivers to facilitate their critical reflection on practice and to help them plan experiences and environments for children. As examples, in the learning area* Social Responsibility and Diversity, *educators are asked to consider How are children made aware of the relationship between themselves and the environment? In what ways do children have the opportunity to participate in day-to-day practices such as recycling, reducing waste, water conservation, etc. (p. 36)?*

During the implementation project, participants engaged with these questions as they created pedagogical narrations in their programs and critically reflected on the documentation.

Curriculum Models

The project participants worked through seven online modules intended to deepen their understanding of concepts

Critically Positioning Myself

The various roles that I take up—caregiver, instructor, supervisor—often position me as "the expert" who "knows": my knowledge is placed above that of children, families, students, and other caregivers. Responsibility and commitment demand knowledge, but "knowing" can limit my ability to learn new ways and new ideas. On the other hand, resisting the impulse to know sometimes challenges my ability to respond in the midst of practice and to commit. And, while I strive to be open to new ideas and to others' beliefs and values, I also have passionate ideals (my own beliefs and values) that sometimes work to close off particular practices.

My positions of instructor and supervisor often allow me time to consider possibilities and reflect on my actions. As a caregiver, though, I engage in practices that require choice and action. While reflecting on past actions helps me to make decisions about future practice, in the present I must choose one response or action over another.

Confronting Curricular Positions

I related MacNaughton's conforming position to the nature/nurture debate. I've had endless discussions with other *introduced at an introductory workshop. To begin, three models (of the learner, of curriculum, and of curriculum contexts) were considered through MacNaughton's (2003) three curricular positions (conforming, reforming, and transforming). MacNaughton's categories are based on Habermas's three domains of human interest, in which technical interests focus on how things happen, practical interests focus on what things mean, and critical interests question whether our knowledge is biased. Similarly, MacNaughton describes the conforming position as following general rules of biology or culture, whereas a reforming position seeks improvement and a transforming position involves changing something into something new.*

Conforming positions in ECCE are exemplified by theories of maturationism, behaviourism, and social learning. According to MacNaughton, the image of the child contained in maturationist theories relies on appeals to nature; the child is viewed as naturally unfolding into an adult. In contrast, the images contained in behaviourism and social learning theory rely on appeals to culture, in which others shape the child into an adult.

Reforming positions present an image of a child who "improves" through interactions between nature and culture. In this image, the child is viewed as incomplete, innocent, and vulnerable. Constructionist and psychodynamic theories are examples of reforming positions.

The transforming position in ECCE contains the idea that we can transform culture and nature through interactions with each other; it is that transformative capac-

ECEs about children's gendered behaviour. These discussions frequently appeal to either nature (e.g., boys will be boys) or nurture (e.g., girls adopt the behaviours of their mothers and other female role models). In both types of explanation, the status quo of gendered lives appears as "normal." Coming to understand these as "conforming" positions helped me to comprehend my disregard for nature/nurture explanations of gender, because for most of my adult life I have passionately resisted conforming to stereotypical gender roles. But I wondered what explanations I dispassionately accept, without reflection. What did I not contest or even see?

I understood the reforming position's theories as the basis of most current early childhood curriculum. I rely on some theories more than others. For example, challenges to developmental psychology's hegemony in ECCE curriculum resonate with me because developmental theories fail to describe many of the children I have met over the years. I have often joked that particular children had "apparently not read the book"; over time I seemed to make that quip about every child. Those same theories, however, support the play-based curriculum that I hold near and dear.

The transforming position challenged my taken-for-granted ideas and offered new possibilities to confront old concerns—how to challenge gendered behaviours and the injustices of childhood poverty, how to reconcile my ideal of children's freedom to choose with

ity, MacNaughton (2003) believes, that "holds the key to maximizing young children's learning" (p. 71). In this position the child is imagined as a citizen, an agent, and a meaning maker. Childhood is viewed as an important stage of life in its own right. Social constructionism, postmodernism, poststructural feminism, and critical race and postcolonial theories are examples of transformative theories. Reggio Emilia preschools exemplify a transformative practice.

A Theoretical Basis for ECCE Practice

Stage theories of development dominate ECCE practice. Vygotsky, Bowlby, Piaget, Erickson, and other stage theorists provide support for the concept of developmentally appropriate practice (DAP), on which ECCE practice in many settings is based. For example, Erickson's psychosocial theory positions young children as resolving crises related to trust, autonomy, and initiative, suggesting a curriculum that offers opportunities to make choices and take risks within supportive adult–child relationships. Piaget's constructivist theory emphasizes an active learner who, in the "preoperational" (preschool years) stage, discovers knowledge through play, thus providing support for a play-based curriculum.

Stage theories have been criticized because they describe a universal path of human development. Various authors have argued that a focus on these theories—and on DAP—silences other ways of thinking about young children and their education (Cannella, 1997; Dahlberg, Moss,

learning about social responsibility. The transforming position engaged my interest, but I felt the risk of placing it on a pedestal, of wandering into lazy, uncritical acceptance while dismissing the other positions. For several years I have been drawn to practices inspired by the Reggio Emilia preschools, but sometimes I wonder if the "Reggio pull" is yet another ECCE bandwagon.

Struggling to Understand

Engaging with postmodern theories created some anxiety. My anxiety came from moving toward the idea of multiple truths while immersed in everyday practice that required actions. These actions involved choices that I could now see as choices between truths. But if I chose one action and not another, wasn't I privileging one truth over others? The desire to be confident about my choice (based on one truth) competed with the desire to remain open to the possibility of multiple truths.

My involvement in the world of ECCE had led me (in poststructural terms) to hold the discourse of development as my taken-for-granted truth. I had been introduced to other ideas in recent years, but the developmental knowledge base of ECCE—which assumes a "universal" child and ignores the effects of differences based on gender and class, for example—still dominated most of my unreflective moments of practice and many reflective moments

& Pence, 1999, 2007; MacDonald, 2007).
Early childhood reconceptualists draw on
postfoundational theories, including those
of Michel Foucault, who conceptualized
discourse as a body of thinking and writing
about a topic that shares language, con-
cepts, and methods of examination
(MacNaughton, 2005). Critics of DAP argue
that it functions as a dominant discourse
or "regime of truth" (Foucault, 1972), limit-
ing the types of experiences that children
are offered in early childhood settings.
Educators who adhere to DAP, for example,
offer children particular types of learning
experiences based on their perceived devel-
opmental needs.

Foucault understood truth and knowl-
edge as a human inventions that "are
always changing and constructed by
human beings in multiple forms" (Cannella,
1997, p. 13). Thus he challenged the idea of
an essential, foundational, "true" knowl-
edge and argued instead that truth is pro-
duced. He held that power is a relational
struggle to authorize truth (MacNaughton,
2005) and that power constitutes knowl-
edge from multiple possible truths
(Dahlberg, Moss, & Pence, 2007). Early child-
hood reconceptualists apply Foucault's
questions to ECCE practice, asking: "What
knowledges have been excluded [by this
discourse]? Whose knowledge has been dis-
qualified as beneath our hierarchical sys-
tems? Whose truths have been hidden
through our rhetorical methods? How have
particular groups gained control over oth-
ers through the construction of discourse
knowledges and truths?" (Foucault, 1980,
cited in Cannella, 1997, pp. 13–14).

as well. Like many ECCE practitioners, I have privileged play as a desired activity in early childhood settings. I believe children learn through play and are harmed by activities that encroach too much on play. I also understand that no child learns only through play and that not all children learn through play. The latter was brought home to me several years ago when a parent of a child who faced extreme developmental challenges expressed frustration about her daughter's experience with play-based curriculum in another childcare centre. She remarked that her daughter didn't play and wouldn't learn if play was the only experience provided. Her comments made me uncomfortable because, although I could understand her frustration, I could imagine myself providing the same type of program.

My involvement in the ELF project pushed me to look at this and other dilemmas in terms of universal and multiple truths. The anxiety and confusion I experienced came from recognizing that my beliefs and assumptions—about play, for example—guide my practice, but that my belief in the possibility of a universal truth, even about play, has evaporated. How would I ever hold a conviction again? And how would I act without convictions?

Images of the Child, the Family, and the Educator

Through the readings assigned in the implementation project, the early childhood practitioners explored the BC ELF's underlying themes regarding the image of the child. Three approaches are apparent in the framework: a rights-based approach (i.e., an image of a child with rights); a listening approach (i.e., an image of a child who can be listened to instead of being already "known"); and a non-preparedness approach (i.e., an image of a child who does not have to live in a constant state of preparation for the next stage of life; Ryan & Grieshaber, 2004).

Practitioners were also asked to consider, through MacNaughton's three curricular positions, images of the family and of the educator. A conforming position invites ECCE practitioners to shape parents into "good, knowledgeable" parents through parent education. Practitioners typically do this through informing parents about current knowledge of children. Examples might include newsletters that contain information about nutrition, workshops about effective disciple strategies, or informal conversations in which caregivers share their knowledge base. The image of the parent in this case can include a learner, a seeker of advice, one who does not know the "best" way to care for children. The image of the educator is of one who has specialized (correct) knowledge. A more critical version of this position portrays caregivers' image as that of experts who save children from their parents' inexpert care.

Contesting Images and Uncovering Power Relations

I struggled with the idea of children's rights, as it appeared to be an argument for understanding individuals as separate from their family or community. Possibilities emerge if we consider the rights of a family, or even a community, as containing within them children's rights. Thinking about a child's right to an education reminded me of the heated and frustrating debates I have been involved in regarding the concepts of "care" and "education" and the titles "caregiver" and "teacher." A child's right to an education could be interpreted as privileging education and teaching over care and caring. But a right to education does not preclude or diminish a right to care. Nor does it preclude a family's need for childcare. What we believe is a "right" reflects the "truths" we have chosen to defend.

In the past I have prided myself on my ability to form warm, supportive relationships with parents. In the course of creating pedagogical narrations, which I describe later in the chapter, I was surprised to discover how the warmth of those relationships covered over their knower/seeker nature, where I am positioned as the knower and parents as the seekers. Parents frequently ask me for advice and I give it. Now I wonder what that suggests about power relations.

In my narration, I recount two different interactions with parents. The first was with a parent who took the docu-

Within a reforming position, ECCE practitioners may attempt to learn about the child from the family, for example, by asking questions about cultural practices. Within this perspective, caregivers acknowledge that the parent is the "expert" with regard to their own child. Caregivers attempt to understand the parents' perspective so as to provide the best possible care for an individual child. The ideal is an image of shared knowledge and responsibility.

The transforming position challenges practitioners to consider power relations between families and caregivers. This perspective focuses on the interrelationships of children, their families, and early years practitioners, examining how our images impact those relationships. The images of the family and the educator contained within this idea positions everyone—children, parents and other adult family members, and caregivers—as learners who don't "know" but learn together, opening up creative curriculum possibilities.

Pedagogical Narration

Understanding the British Columbia Early Learning Framework: From Theory to Practice (2008) defines pedagogical narration as a process in which children and adults co-construct interpretations of a series of "ordinary moments"—common, habitual occurrences. From Theory to Practice *explains that "observing and interpreting what children do and why they do it probes the connection between thinking and questioning, and shows or makes visible the way children are making meaning*

mentation I was creating home, reflected on it, and brought back reflective questions and interpretations. She included in the interpretive section information about her child's life experience (with wild flowers but not with gardens) that we at the centre didn't know. The information she provided enriched my understanding of how this child was making meaning of her experience.

In the second instance, a parent gently and humorously (evidence of the warm relationship) challenged my use of the word "discovered" in relation to a particular action (splashing), pointing out that her child had long used that skill! What was especially unnerving to me was that in spite of my espoused position that I thought of parents as "experts" regarding their children, I was still surprised to recognize that they had more knowledge about their children than I did.

Telling a Story: Water and Sand

The environment in which I worked contained a water feature that consisted of a long hose, a pipe, a fence, and an enormous sand box set in a large yard containing two climbing structures, plants, grass, logs, boulders, pathways, and a hill. The kindergarten teacher had attached the hose to a tap and strung it along the top of the fence. Water flowed through the hose into a plastic pipe and emerged at a child's shoulder level, providing a constant source of running *of their learning or of their interaction with the world" (p. 12). The process is similar to ones known variously around the world as pedagogical documentation (Sweden and Italy), learning stories (New Zealand), and action research (Australia).*

The process of pedagogical narration begins when an educator first observes an ordinary moment with a child or children. She or he then documents the moment with words and pictures; these can include written field notes, audio recordings of conversations with the family and/or the child, photographs, video clips, and drawings or other creations that the child or children make.

During the implementation project, participants documented ordinary moments that occurred in their own programs and then shared the narrations with each other, with their colleagues, and with the children and their families. An exemplar (Water and Sand, *by Deborah Thompson) is included in* From Theory to Practice.

Critical Reflection to Deepen Interpretation

Critical reflection is key to the pedagogical narration process. According to From Theory to Practice, *pedagogical narration involves eight steps, and six of the eight involve critical reflection: (1) be curious about how the BC ELF relates to one's practice; (2) observe ordinary moments; (3) record and describe an ordinary moment; (4) reflect and interpret an ordinary moment to make learning visible; (5) share the description with colleagues, children,*

water and creating a "river" around the edge of the sand box.

To create a pedagogical narration for the project, I chose to observe children playing in this setting, as I thought it offered possibilities for interesting moments to emerge. A lovely warm day and the running water together produced a calm but engaging environment. The children became deeply engrossed in playing with the water. A practicum student and I took pictures and recorded the conversation of a child who was collecting the water and pouring it onto the grass. While the other children waded in the "river," this child intently filled pails with water, carried them to the grass and dumped them, returning to the tap again and again. Completely absorbed in her task, she did not engage with anyone else. When questioned, she replied that she was watering the flowers (dandelions in the grass) to make them grow. She explained that it required a lot of water.

Giving Up the Dream of Perfect Play

I loved the "moment" we recorded. It contained all the elements I like best about working with children—an outdoor environment, children completely engrossed in play with simple natural elements or engaged in focused interactions with adults. While choosing photographs for the narration and writing my personal reflections, I focused on showing how well the moment demonstrated compo-

and families; (6) consider the comments of others to add to and deepen interpretation; (7) link the pedagogical narration to the ELF; (8) evaluate, plan, and start the process again.

In the implementation project, participants critically reflected on the narrations they created by relating them to learning goals in each of the ELF's four learning areas, and by answering reflective questions posed in the framework. Participants were encouraged to engage their colleagues and the children's families in reflecting on the narrations. They did this by posting the narrations on the wall or sending materials home with parents. They also posted their documentations (photographs and text) online so that others in their study groups could contribute ideas. After receiving feedback from others, the authors revised their narrations with thought to how they could use what they had learned to improve their practice.

nents of the ELF. I selected photographs that illustrated a positive answer to various questions within each of the framework's four learning areas. The areas represented ideas that I strongly supported as indicative of good practices, and it was pleasurable to show how our practices "measured up." As I worked through the first three learning areas, I cheerfully reified my beliefs while "passing the test."

When I reached the area focused on social responsibility, I chose to examine the goal of helping children to "understand how their own actions may affect nature and the planet" (Government of British Columbia, 2008, p. 38). Associated with this goal was the question "What steps are taken to make children aware of the relationship between human activities and environmental challenges?" I realized then that at the same time I was providing a rich environment focused on meaningful play-based learning, I was also teaching the children to waste resources. This realization interrupted my dream of perfect play.

Critical Reflection or Self-Affirmation?

As I reflected on the steps I had taken in relating the pedagogical narration to the ELF, I realized that I hadn't engaged critically in any way with the first three areas of learning identified by the framework. In fact, my critical gaze had disappeared as soon as I understood that the framework contained my version of "good" ECCE practice, and I let go of my initial critical response to the idea of a framework to guide practice. Unexpectedly, during the project a pull away from provisionality and toward certainty had surfaced. Because the assumptions embedded within the framework reinscribed my own beliefs, I neglected to critically analyze them, choosing instead to accept to them as indicators of truth.

Fendler (2003) describes the problem that emerged for me while creating the exemplar for the implementation guide: "Some reflective practices may simply be exercises in reconfirming, justifying, or rationalizing preconceived ideas" (p. 16). I gradually became aware that I was engaged in a process of self (or perhaps centre) congratulations. In the past I had been reluctant to use accepted "quality measurement" tools such as the ITERS (Harms, Cryer, & Clifford, 2003) to evaluate the practice in our centre as it seemed obvious that we would score high, which I believed would lead to complacency. Yet I had quickly become complacent (and perhaps even smug) using a tool explicitly designed for critical reflection! The awareness that I had easily slid into reconfirming what I already thought—in spite of understanding myself as practicing critical reflection for the purpose of improving practice—shocked me and led to this writing.

My experience reveals several tensions embedded in processes of reflexive practice within the context of a curriculum framework. Some of those tensions might be attributed to the attempt to reconcile multiple truths. Others relate to contradictory conceptions of reflection employed in various contexts; the action demands of practice; the desire to validate practice; and the effects of self-expression. Each of these tensions contributed to unsettling my taken-for-granted assumptions about engaging in critical reflection on early childhood practice.

o   The Attempt to Reconcile Multiple Truths

According to Foucault, "truth is not some objective reality, but what comes to be accepted as true at a particular time and in a particular place" (Dahlberg & Moss, 2005, p. 141). Particular times and places create the conditions by which a given idea becomes accepted as truth. Local truths frequently become viewed as universal, challenged only when they conflict with other accepted truths.

For example, in the environment in which I live, the southwest coastal region of British Columbia, concerns about careless water consumption can seem irrelevant as variations of precipitation (light showers, heavy rain, torrential downpour) dominate winter weather reports. Other experiences in different environments, however, had exposed me to various discourses that discouraged waste. Living in dry environments without easy access to running water had taught me to think about water consumption and conservation. An open tap for the purpose of play fit within the discourse of a child-centred, play-based ECCE curriculum but it didn't fit a conservation discourse. Each of these discourses contained a "truth" and the truths contradicted each other: unfettered exploration of running water was "good" because it facilitated children's learning; unfettered exploration of running water was "bad" because it depleted resources in a frivolous way. These truths appear to be mutually exclusive, which makes reconciling them a challenge—one that requires a reconsideration of the valuations of "good" and "bad" and a problematization of practices.

○ Contradictory Conceptions of Reflective Practice

The term *reflective practice* "covers activities from deep life, work and organization-changing critique to rote box-ticking practices seeking to make professionals accountable to and controllable by increasingly bureaucratic and market-led organizations" (Bolton, 2006, p. 204). Fendler (2003) applies the same notion to reflective teaching:

> Today's discourse of reflection incorporates an array of meanings: a demonstration of self consciousness, a scientific approach to planning for the future, a tacit and intuitive understanding of practice, a discipline to become more professional, a way to tap into one's authentic inner voice, a means to become a more effective teacher, and a strategy to redress injustices in society. Reflective teaching has become a catchall term for competing programs of teacher education reform. It is no wonder then that current research and practices relating to reflection tend to embody mixed messages and confusing agendas. (p. 20)

Definitions of reflexivity contain ideas both of unthinking reflexes and of turning back on self more deliberately. These conflicting ideas perhaps hint as to how reflection can be taken up in many ways. Relying on past experience to decide how to act in the future conceivably could involve reflexes, or habitual, uncritical repetition of what "worked" before. Habitual practice refers back to initial interpretations of experience, which then become reified as the truth. As a college instructor, I have frequently listened to frustrated students who have been discouraged from a particular practice with the reason "We tried that before and it didn't work." *Critical* reflection, however, would require examining the experience—what happened, who took part, what might be different this time, and other questions specific to the situation. For many of us who are practitioners, though, critical reflection on every action might not be possible.

○ Action Demands of Practice

Typically, reflection happens after an activity or event has occurred. For example, following my crisis of conflicting discourses around the children's water play, the childcare program still needed to function. Each week, my colleagues and I planned activities and events. Our meetings focused on what we intended to accomplish, allowing space for concerns, *but ending in decisions*. We had to choose whether to provide environments that included play with water or not provide them. If we chose to include water play, my critical reflection on practice now demanded that we incorporate concern with resources into the play environment. Ideally, such decisions will result from group reflection. Each member of the childcare team may subscribe to a different discourse; inviting feedback from parents and children allows access to non-ECCE discourses. But when and how will this group reflection occur? It is easy to picture a practitioner reflecting informally after the work day has finished. Likely, most working people do this every day. But group reflection would require organization, commitment, and time. In many ECCE sites, commitment may be abundant but time is not. The demands of practice, of action, of caregiving are strong. Thus actions may be based on habitual practice rather than critical reflection. If all actions are habitual, practice will not change even when it should. The tension lies in resisting the ease of tried and tested practice to engage in time- and energy-consuming critical reflection.

○ The Desire to Validate Practice

Another tension arises from practitioners' desire (including my own) to be "right." This appears to me to be a frequent occurrence—and a dangerous habit—in the ECCE field. Binaries of right/wrong or good/bad seem to be part of our habitual thinking. Perhaps this is so because our work is practical more than theoretical. We choose to offer children particular materials, activities, and environments because we understand them to be good for children. "Right" choices might include unit blocks, dolls, books, and puzzles arranged in relation to each other so that children can choose what to use without interfering with others' activities. "Wrong" choices might include toy weapons, television, or dolls that reinforce stereotypes that we believe may "shape" children in an undesirable way. Our choices depend on our values, beliefs, and goals. Sometimes we make these decisions in partnership with parents, further validating our choices as right and good. Our roles require us to take responsibility for our actions, and we often have to justify our decisions to ourselves and to others, including colleagues, parents, or administrators. However, the need to be accountable and responsible for our actions may create a desire to "get it right" at the cost of being open.

○ **The Effects of Self-Expression**

In both this chapter and in the pedagogical narration that I write about in the chapter, I used story as a tool to reflect. Following Smith's (2006) idea that combining narrative approaches strengthens the knowledge that the research generates, I claim that both the pedagogical narration and this chapter make explicit a personal transformation in understanding. When I created the pedagogical narration, I relied on my reactions and feelings to make intuitive understandings explicit. Paraphrasing Fendler (2003), I attempted to use intuitive understandings of practice to become an effective caregiver addressing an issue of social responsibility. To explore my experience of engaging in critical reflection in the midst of practice, I attempted both a neutral story (the realist tale) and a highly personal, situated story (the confessional tale).

Both stories, however, are partial. The realist tale hides the subject, as if telling an objective, "true" account. The confessional tale, in contrast, foregrounds the subject, as if personal intuition and emotion represent "the real truth." Each tale contains interpretations of experience that can be reinterpreted, deconstructed, and reconstructed to tell other truths. As Scott (1991) reminds us, "experience is at once always already an interpretation and something that needs to be interpreted" (p. 797).

I am conscious, too, that confessions function to shape me—and my thinking—in particular ways. Swan (2008) suggests that an authority to whom (or to which) the confession is made is always present. Confession may appear to be an innocent statement of actual experience to a neutral, benign audience. Burman (2003) demonstrates, however, that in the act of giving voice to emotional expression, the emotionality of confession can function to regulate, normalize, and circumscribe that expression. The focus of emotional confession becomes to shape the confessor and the tale so that both please the audience/authority. In this way confession cannot be understood as either innocent or a recounting of an actual experience. Neither can the audience be understood as benign. The audience becomes an authority whose hidden presence shapes what can be told.

Burman (2003) cautions against a confessional reflexivity as it tends to locate problems in the self and thus to ignore other issues. Fendler (2003), too, suggests that "the simultaneous skepticism and support for autobiography constitutes reflection as a complex form of normalization in discourses of education" (p. 22). In this way reflection can validate or disregard experience as needed in the process of normalizing particular discourses.

Davies and Gannon (2006) understand experience not as unquestionably reliable and valid, but rather as providing texts. In a process they call *collective biography,* they work on a particular topic within a group of researchers,

> drawing on [our] own memories relevant to that topic, and through the shared work
> of telling, listening and writing ... move beyond the clichés and usual explanations to
> the point where the written memories come as close as [we] can make them to "an
> embodied sense of what happened." In working in this way we do not take memory
> to be "reliable" in the sense of providing an unquestionable facticity, nor do we take
> what initially surfaces as being truer, or more valid, than the texts that are worked
> and reworked in this approach. We take the talk around our memories, the listening
> to the detail of each other's memories, as a technology for enabling us to produce,
> through attention to the embodied sense of being in the remembered moment, a truth
> in relation to what cannot actually be recovered—the moment as it was lived. This is
> not a naive, naturalistic truth, but a truth that is worked on through a technology of
> telling, listening and writing. In a sense it is the very unreliability of memory that
> enables this close discursive work. (p. 17)

Just as Davies and Gannon understand "experience" "not in the sense of individuals having experiences, but about subjects who constitute themselves and are constituted as experiencing subjects" (p. 17), I recount two tales of engaging in a curriculum framework as versions of an experience in which I constitute myself as the subject of particular experiences and work with those versions of experience to interpret critical reflection in practice.

○ Critical Reflection in ECCE Practice: A Never-Ending Story

Bolton (2006) argues that narratives, in an attempt to create a sense of order and security, "can only too easily be essentially self-affirming and uncritical" (p. 204). In relating my pedagogical narration to the ELF, it was not until I considered an alternative discourse (an environmental responsibility discourse) that I noticed how my reflection worked to validate my own practices and those of the child-care centre where I worked. Not until I began to think about the effects of engaging in critical reflection within practice did I notice how quickly I had turned my critical gaze from the (authority of the) framework to myself and my desire to regulate my practice to the framework.

I discovered too that work that requires decisions and action—as the work of an ECCE practitioner does—contains many tensions that, in some instances, permit reflection to destabilize dominant discourses and, in other instances, lead to normalization of practices and taken-for-granted truths. When an alternative discourse is loud enough to be heard in the presence of a dominant discourse, in the way that I could hear an environmental responsibility discourse in the presence of a child-centred discourse, critical reflection opens up possibilities for more ethical practices. It is when we hear no challenge to our practice, when a dominant discourse is so loud that, like traffic noise, it is not perceived, we are in danger of overlooking the effects of our choice of action.

The stated purpose of the BC Early Learning Framework is to be a tool for critical reflection by ECCE practitioners. The project participants' analysis of the pedagogical narrations with reference to the framework was intended to elicit critical reflections on their practice which they could then use to improve their future practice. Critical scrutiny of the framework itself was not an intended purpose of the project. Instead, the light of reflection was to shine on the practices revealed by the pedagogical narrations.

My experience reveals that using a curriculum framework as a tool can both challenge practices and reconfirm prejudices. My negotiations with the ELF in my practice with young children have forced me to reconsider my taken-for-granted assumptions about the process of critical reflexive practice. I mistakenly assumed that critical reflection would always reveal "best practice," making decision-making easier. In the concrete world of ECCE practice, however, I discovered that critical reflection always leads to more questions, and that decisions that are based on one's critical reflections must be seen as tentative and subject to constant revision. Thus the story we attempt to write by engaging in critical refection—just as in the practice of pedagogical narration—is never a final one.

REFERENCES

Bolton, G. (2006). Narrative writing: reflective enquiry into professional practice. *Educational Action Research, 14*(2), 203–218.

Burman, E. (2003). Narratives of "experience" and pedagogical practices. *Narrative Inquiry, 13*(2), 269–286.

Cannella, G. (1997). *Deconstructing early childhood education: Social justice & revolution.* New York: Peter Lang.

Cotton, T., & Griffiths, M. (2007). Action research, stories and practical philosophy. *Educational Action Research, 15*(4), 545–560.

Dahlberg, G., & Moss, P. (2005). *Ethics and politics in early childhood education.* New York: RoutledgeFalmer.

Dahlberg, G., Moss, P., & Pence, A. (1999). *Beyond quality in early childhood education and care: Postmodern perspectives.* London: Routledge.

Dahlberg, G., Moss, P., & Pence, A. (2007). *Beyond quality in early childhood education and care: Languages of evaluation* (2nd ed.). London: Routledge.

Davies, B., & Gannon, S. (2006). *Doing collective biography: Investigating the production of subjectivity.* Maidenhead, UK: Open University Press.

Fendler, L. (2003). Teacher reflection in a hall of mirrors: Historical influences and political reverberations. *Educational Researcher, 32,*(3), 16–25.

Foucault, M. (1972). *The archaeology of knowledge.* London: Tavistock.

Government of British Columbia. (2008). *British Columbia early learning framework.* Victoria, BC: Ministry of Education, Ministry of Health, Ministry of Children and Family Development, & British Columbia Early Learning Advisory Group.

Government of British Columbia. (2009). *Understanding the British Columbia early learning framework: From theory to practice.* Victoria, BC: Ministry of Education.

Harms, T., Cryer, D., & Clifford, R. (2003). *The infant/toddler environment rating scale* (rev. ed.). New York: Teachers College Press.

Ledwith, M. (2005). Personal narratives/political lives: Personal reflection as a tool for collective change. *Reflective Practice, 6*(2), 255–262.

MacDonald, M. (2007). Developmental theory and post-modern thinking in early childhood education. *Canadian Children, Fall,* 8–10.

MacNaughton, G. (2003). *Shaping early childhood: Learners, curriculum and context.* New York: Open University Press.

MacNaughton, G. (2005). *Doing Foucault in early childhood studies: Applying poststructural ideas.* London: Routledge.

Ryan, S., & Grieshaber, S. (2004). It's more than child development: Critical theories, research, and teaching young children. *Young Children, 59*(6), 44–52.

Scott, J. (1991). The evidence of experience. *Critical Inquiry, 17*(4), 773–797.

Smith, S. (2006). Encouraging the use of reflexivity in the writing up of qualitative research. *International Journal of Therapy and Rehabilitation, 13*(5), 209–215.

Swan, E. (2008). Let's not get too personal: Critical reflection, reflexivity and the confessional turn. *Journal of European Industrial Training, 32*(5), 385–399.

PART III

Intensities

On the one hand, multiplicities that are extensive, divisible, and molar; unifiable, totalizable, organizable; conscious or preconscious—and on the other hand, libidinal, unconscious, molecular, intensive multiplicities composed of particles that do not divide without changing in nature, and distances that do not vary without entering another multiplicity and that constantly construct and dismantle themselves in the course of their communications, as they cross over into each other at, beyond, or before a certain threshold…their quantities are intensities, differences in intensity.

Deleuze & Guattari,
A thousand plateaus: Capitalism and schizophrenia, 1987, p. 33

Is It Time to Put "Tidy Up Time" Away?: Contesting Routines and Transitions in Early Childhood Spaces

Kathleen Kummen

Young children in early childhood spaces may spend as much as half of their time engaged in daily routines such as dressing, hand washing, eating, napping, and transitions (Malenfant, 2006). "Best practices" in early childhood education imply that routines are critical for early learning (Hemmeter, Ostrosky, Artman, & Kinder, 2008). British Columbia's Early Learning Framework (Government of British Columbia, 2008) considers a predictable, dependable environment important to support a child's well-being and belonging, and DAP (developmentally appropriate practice, the seminal framework of the National Association for the Education of Young Children) recommends that teachers provide young children with an organized environment where "the schedule follows an orderly routine that provides a stable structure within which development and learning can take place" (National Association for the Education of Young Children, 2009, p. 17). Routines and transitions clearly are seen as essential components of quality early childhood education practices.

In the early childhood space, routines are predictable activities that are "generally scheduled at a fixed time and are the core of the day" (Malenfant, 2006, p. 7); they are considered requisite activities to ensure children's safety and health. Nap time and snack are examples of common early childhood routines. Transitions, in contrast, are short activities that serve to "regulate and punctuate the day" (Malenfant, 2006, p. 8). For example, following free play, children often have to tidy up the room before moving to the next activity.

This chapter uses a poststructural perspective to examine how the hegemony of child development knowledge results in the implementation of rigid routines and transitions that constrain opportunities for rich, meaningful learning in early years spaces. I explore how routines and transitions embed in early childhood practice values and beliefs that evolve into "truths" which are then used to define best practice and quality of care in early childhood education. My goal is to make visible how early childhood practice is kept hostage by such "truths," and how their continued existence as truths is maintained by those who adopt them.

To understand how a belief (such as children's need for a predictable environment) dictates practice in a field (such as early childhood education) I first explore the relationship between child development and early childhood education (ECE) and how that relationship makes an ECE discourse of routines and transitions thinkable and practicable. In the process of deconstructing this discourse, I uncover and explore other discourses—of *the known child*, *universality*, and *progress*—embedded within it. I invite readers to consider how disrupting these discourses might support them to transform their current practices to make space for new ways to be with children and families in early childhood spaces.

My context for understanding routines and transitions is that of an early childhood educator and an instructor of pre-service early childhood educators in British Columbia. I have lived both under and with routines and transitions in early years spaces, and I have observed them in my work with early childhood education students. Examples drawn from my practice and my work with students are used for illustration throughout the chapter.

o Engaging with Poststructural Thinking in Early Childhood

Poststructural thinking provides a theoretical framework to challenge theories and practices that are based on the assumption that a knowable world exists that contains absolute, universal truths (Dahlberg, Moss, & Pence, 1999, 2007). Poststructural thinkers, such as the French philosophers Michel Foucault (1926–1984) and Jacques Derrida (1930–2004), have sought to challenge and disrupt the knowledge base of many fields of study, including education and psychology. Yet, there is very little reference to Foucault, Derrida, and other poststructural thinkers in mainstream early childhood education text books (MacNaughton, 2005).

Knowledge, from a Foucauldian perspective, cannot be understood as simply technical expertise or the knowledge of common sense (McHoul & Grace, 1993). Rather, the culture, history, gender norms, language, beliefs, and practices in a community *construct* knowledge. In this way knowledge is neither neutral nor objective, but is *local* (specific to a particular time in history or a specific group of people), *partial* (always in a state of construction, thus never whole), and *situated* (an interpretation based on one's perspective, rather than objective fact or "truth"; Foucault, 1972; Hacking, 1999).

What we understand as knowledge is constituted within a *discourse*—the metaphors, images, practices, and languages that construct an understanding of a concept or object (Foucault, 1972). Discourse directs the ways we think and talk about an idea or concept (Foucault, 1972). For example, early childhood educators work within a particular discourse of daily routines and transitions that is reflected in their practice with children. This discourse organizes and frames how an educator thinks, feels, understands, and responds to daily routines and transitions in early childhood spaces. The temporal and organizational aspects of a daily routine in a childcare centre may proceed in the following manner: arrival; meeting time; free play; cleanup; snack; outside time; circle; lunch; nap time; snack; outside time; table time; dismissal. Each of these activities is constructed through a shared understanding of language, behaviours, rituals, roles, and daily schedules. In addition, each activity is understood in contrast to the others, for example, the ritual song that announces tidy up time would not be sung at snack time.

When a particular understanding (e.g., the importance of routines and transitions in early childhood spaces) is officially sanctioned as true by culturally normative knowledge (e.g., child development), it becomes a *dominant discourse*—that is, it possesses the power to inform and direct our way of understanding and being in the world (Foucault, 1972). Developmentally appropriate practice (DAP), which is based on evidence from child development researchers, asserts that young children benefit from predictable routines and transitions that provide them with specific learning opportunities (Copple & Bredekamp, 2009). Without those specific learning opportunities embedded in a set of routines and transitions, DAP assumes, children may not achieve optimal developmental outcomes. From this assumption, a consensus develops among early childhood educators that defines a "typical" or "normal" set of daily routines and transitions for early childhood spaces. According to the Early Childhood Environmental Rating Scale (ECERS; Harms, Clifford, & Cryer, 1998), for example, an environment where music and movement activities are available on a daily basis is rated as being of excellent quality. One could assume from this valuation that *not* having music or movement activities available creates an inadequate environment for children.

From my own experience, when the ECE students with whom I work encounter in their first practicum placement a centre that follows a routine that differs from the dominant discourse routine (e.g., there is no daily circle time), the students often express anxiety that their experience in the centre will not be "real" or may not provide them with experiences that will prepare them for their next practica. More than one student has frantically contacted me, terrified that she will not become an early childhood educator if the daily routine in her practicum site is void of group circle time. The students explain that "everyone knows that circle time is when you teach the children and where the children learn how to listen." Some of these students have never had any previous experience in an early childhood setting as an adult, yet they are familiar with this discourse and are very aware of the power afforded to it. MacNaughton (2005) writes that a particular knowledge of children and development has settled so firmly into the fabric of early childhood studies that its familiarity makes it just seem "right," "best," and "ethical" (p. 1).

From a poststructural perspective, this perception is troubling, for knowledge understood as a universal truth has the power to suppress or marginalize alternative discourses (Foucault, 1972). Various authors have argued that DAP's dominance in early years literature has silenced other ways of thinking about young children and their education (Cannella, 1997; Dahlberg, Moss, & Pence, 1999, 2007; MacDonald, 2007). This is not to suggest that DAP is intrinsically bad or entirely incorrect; however, its dominance has privileged one body of knowledge over others. In this way DAP operates in many early years spaces as what Foucault would call a *regime of truth*—it is a specific discourse, informed by a specific body of knowledge that has been made possible by specific historical and social conditions (Foucault, 1972).

To understand the conditions that have made it possible for DAP to function as a regime of truth with the power to define normative standards for routines and transitions in early childhood spaces, it is necessary to understand its social and historical underpinnings. Histories, Rose (1998) contends, set forth the conditions that create the divide between what can be said and what cannot be said. By disturbing a discourse's history, we are better able to understand how it was possible for what we know as a truth or reality to have been established (Rose, 1998). If, following Foucault, knowledge makes possible how we can think, write, and talk about the daily routines of an early childhood space, then it becomes necessary to understand how that knowledge—and its language—came to exist and operate within the culture of early childhood education.

Positivism and the Self-Regulating Child

Psychology's rise to prominence in the Western world is critical to understanding the existence of the discourses that dominate ECE. Psychology and its subdiscipline child development are linked to the Western world's desire to use scientific technologies to eradicate society's ills (Popkewitz, 1998; Rose, 1998). Positivist science, upon which both psychology and child development are based, assumes that scientific methods can determine universal truths—and that science and the knowledge obtained by science will allow for the development of a better world (Rose, 1998).

Writers such as Cannella (1997) and Dahlberg, Moss, and Pence (1999, 2007) describe how science has offered early childhood education a structure for understanding children through a process of comparing individual children to universal norms of development generated using scientific methods. In this process, the child becomes definable, quantifiable, and classifiable (Rose, 1998). This *pedagogical determinism* (Cannella, 1997) is most evident within the framework of DAP, which promotes the message that "true knowledge" regarding young children is knowledge that has been sanctioned by the science of child development. DAP aims to demonstrate, through scientific research, relationships between the provision of developmentally appropriate learning activities/experiences and successful outcomes for children (Copple & Bredekamp, 2009). Its teaching strategies, including the provision of predicable routines and transitions, are designed to guide children in acquiring self-regulating behaviours, which, according to the 2009 NAEYC position statement on DAP, is a long-standing goal of early childhood education (p. 7).

> Mounting research evidence confirms ... that self-regulation in young children predicts their later functioning in areas such as problem solving, planning, focused attention, and metacognition, and thus contributes to their success as learners. Moreover, helping children from difficult life circumstances to develop strong self-regulation has proven to be both feasible and influential in preparing them to succeed in school. (NAEYC, 2009, p. 7)

To make curricular decisions "with well-grounded intentionality," the NAEYC position statement continues, teachers "need to have knowledge about child development and learning in general, about the individual children in their classrooms, and about the sequences in which a domain's specific concepts and skills are learned" (p. 8). Thus DAP practices govern the behaviour of both children and educators.

Foucault (1980) linked technologies or methods designed to shape, guide, or regulate behaviour–of others or self—to the concept of *governmentality*. He argued that when liberal, democratic governments could no longer rely on physical domination to control the population, their goal became instead to create rational, productive citizens who would self-govern and conform to society's rules (Popkewitz, 1998). Developmentally appropriate practice, Popkewitz (1998) suggests, has a similar goal.

○ The Power of Words

From a poststructural perspective, words and the meanings held within them are neither neutral nor benign but powerful and political (MacNaughton, 2005). Even a word as seemingly benign as "predictable" is loaded with meaning that can be unpacked when the word is deconstructed. Jacques Derrida (as cited in MacNaughton, 2005) observed that the majority of Western languages depend on oppositions or binaries to produce their meaning. To illustrate, *predictable* can only be understood in relation to its opposite, *unpredictable*. Predictable and unpredictable "form a binary opposition in which we are offered two mutually exclusive meanings" (MacNaughton, 2005, p. 81). Significantly, Derrida argued, one of a pair of binaries is always valued more than the other, thus predictable environments are valued over unpredictable (chaotic) ones.

Similarly, a high-quality environment for young children can only be understood in comparison to a low-quality environment. A predictable daily routine, being both measurable and definable, becomes one characteristic that is used to assess quality in early learning environments. The ECERS scale, for example, in rating a program's schedule, states that an environment that is "too flexible" and lacks a dependable sequence of daily events provides an inadequate quality of environment for young children (Harms, Clifford, & Cryer, 1998, p. 42). In contrast, an environment with "smooth transitions" (e.g., materials are ready for the next activity before the current activity ends) that allows for variations based on individual needs (e.g., slow eaters may finish at their own pace) is rated as an excellent environment for young children.

This desire for measurable and definable quality necessitates strict adherence to fixed daily routines and transitions based, as we saw above, on "the sequences in which a domain's specific concepts and skills are learned" (NAEYC, 2009, p. 8). Because the sequences of child development are understood to be universal, early childhood spaces thus can be understood as sites for the modernist project to manufacture future model citizens, the epitome of the Fordist factory model whereby standardized operations lead to efficiency and quality in the mass production of desirable human beings (Fendler, 2001).

o Uncovering the Discourses Embedded in an ECE Discourse of Routines and Transitions

My memories of working within the restrictions of a rigid daily schedule are those of feeling that I was simply moving through the day as if on an assembly line, where the schedule acted as the ultimate task master. Spontaneous moments of daily living that resulted in deviation from the daily routine were fraught with anxiety. Worries over how to make up missed time or uncompleted activities were the order of the day. These anxieties were complicated by the concern that particular children would be unable to handle a change in routine and would create further disruptions to the day. More often than not, the mere thought of a possible disruption prompted strict adherence to the daily routine in order to maintain the predictability that would ensure the program's integrity.

The predictable routine as a requirement for children's successful development operates in this regard as a regime of truth, keeping the complexity of unpredictability and spontaneity in check. As one deconstructs this discourse of ECE routines and transitions, other discourses embedded within it become visible. Here, I will examine three such discourses: of the known child, universality, and progress.

The Discourse of the Known Child

As we have seen above, universal developmental norms guide educators in planning daily routines for groups of children. For example, Hast and Hollyfield (1999) write that "toddlers live so much in the moment that they have difficulty keeping track of long periods of time" (p. 36). To meet this developmental need particular to toddlers, the authors recommend providing a regular schedule to ensure that the children feel secure in their environment. Here toddlers are viewed as known subjects, and their capacities to deal with time and transitions has been predetermined. If the child can be "known objectively" (Rose, 1998), there is then the notion of a typical or "normal" child that *essentializes* our understanding of children—that is, certain characteristics of children become naturalized and normalized, "defining and fixing who and what" children are (Robinson & Diaz, 2006, p. 28).

A concept of the known child creates a "right" way of experiencing childhood that is definable and thus measurable (Fendler, 2001). A known child allows the field of early childhood education to engage in discussions of "best practice" for all children and to construct questions and develop procedures meant to measure the quality of early childhood environments (Dahlberg, Moss, & Pence, 1999,

2007). If the characteristics necessary to support the development of young children are known, it follows that these characteristics should be present in early childhood spaces.

The Discourse of Universality

Developmentally appropriate practice promotes the idea that early childhood educators should provide "x" for young children (with "x" in this case being a predictable environment) to encourage development. This view creates a universal "should" to be acted upon by a universal early childhood educator to meet a universal need of a universal child. This discourse of universality privileges the knowledge of child development over other ways of seeing or understanding children (Cannella, 1997; Fendler, 2001; MacNaughton, 2005). In this way DAP becomes the "gold standard" for achieving best practice and ensuring quality early childhood spaces. Practice that does not adhere to DAP guidelines becomes devalued.

The Discourse of Progress

Development, asserts Cannella (1997), links to the idea of progress. Both progress and development can be defined as positive, hierarchal growth towards a goal, and their implications are complex, value laden, and highly political (Cannella, 1997). To begin, their hierarchal nature creates obvious binaries: developed versus undeveloped; progression versus regression. In the context of child development, the child, at the lower end of the developmental progression, is considered primitive when compared to the adult (Burman, 2008a, 2008b). Children in an early years setting thus are seen as requiring both a predictable environment and the supervision of a mature adult to ensure their desired developmental outcome.

The concept that children, when compared to adults, are immature, lack experience, and have less knowledge, is a dominant perspective in Western culture (Cannella, 1997). This image of the child denies children's knowledge and understanding as being legitimate and worthy of consideration. Children's concept of time, for example, is considered to be immature because children measure time by the occurrence of events. As a result, children are not considered capable of participating in a discussion about routines and transitions.

○ Disrupting the ECE Discourse of Routines and Transitions

In recent years, the discourses of the known child, universality, and progress that are embedded in child development knowledge have been challenged by such writers as Cannella (1997), Fendler (2001), Dahlberg, Moss, and Pence (1999, 2007), and Burman (2008a, 2008b). Nevertheless, the latest edition of DAP (Copple & Bredekamp, 2009) suggests that ECE practice is still dependent on these concepts. Particularly troubling is the fact that the universal understanding of development is based on research conducted solely on children living in the Western world, thus disregarding the experiences of more than 90% of the world's children (Pence & Hix-Small, 2007). MacNaughton (2005) cautions early childhood educators that reproducing and acting on "these allegedly universal developmental norms [is] committing a form of violence that privileges cultural homogeneity and marginalizes cultural diversity" (p. 37).

Often these discourses position the early childhood educator as a young child's potential rescuer (Burman, 2008b). It is thought that by adhering to DAP—and providing a predictable environment for children—the educator will minimize any possible risks that may occur in unpredictable environments outside the early years setting. In early childhood practice, both unpredictability and the unexpected are viewed as abnormal. Further, in a qualitative study with ECE students, instructors, and text book authors, Langford (2007) found that students who were culturally different were seen "as less competent because (they) needed to learn the discourses of the good early childhood educators, which were assumed to be universal" (p. 350). Homogenized practices and discourses are the norm and "natural," while practices that are different sit outside the range of normal and are regarded as unnatural (Popkewitz, 1999).

Langford (2007) found that a "good" early childhood educator is seen to be one who conforms to the teachings of child development. However, in my experience as an early childhood educator, unquestioning acceptance of an ECE discourse of routines and transitions—and of the discourses embedded within it—results in the use of educational practices in an automatized fashion enacted without contextual validity. For example, as an instructor visiting a large number of early childhood spaces every year, I observe many early childhood educators striving to attain quality through adhering to DAP, not as guidelines, but as hard, fast rules. Their need to maintain a consistent and predictable routine throughout the year prevents some educators from changing that routine even when faced with compelling evidence to do so. For example, as summer approaches I often see information from the provincial Ministry of Health posted on the bulletin boards of many early childhood spaces advising against direct sun exposure between the hours of 10:00 a.m. and 4:00 p.m. Even with this warning clearly posted, many childcare centres continue to offer outside play time in playgrounds without shade during precisely these hours. In these cases, the early childhood educators' need to demonstrate quality by providing predictable, consistent routines and transitions may create more harm than good.

When the routines and transitions in an early years setting are accepted as developmentally appropriate (meaning that "normal" children are able to comply with the demands imposed by the environment), children who do not comply are often assessed as being in need of intervention or mediation (Post, Boyer, & Brett, 2006). The concern in these instances is focused on the child not having the skills to meet future demands, rather than on how the child is experiencing the present moment, and the fault is seen to lie with the child. Hemmeter, Ostrosky, Artman, and Kinder (2008) recommend individualized programming to assist children who have persistent difficulty with transitions. While I do not dispute the necessity of individual programming, I am troubled by the assumption that a need for individual programming is evidence of abnormality on the part of an individual. The notion that normal children naturally adjust to a universal set of routines and transitions that are part of the early childhood culture enables early childhood educators to maintain the social inequities and injustices that are created through the dominance of the universality and progress discourses (MacNaughton, 2005).

If child development's goal is to ensure that children become adults who are able to function within society's requirements, the implementation and regulation of consistent routines and transitions can be seen as a technology to ensure a society's future progress. The democratic classroom is a micro social setting of the larger democratic society, and in it educators create an environment that supports the ultimate goal of a liberal government: progress (Bloch & Popkewitz, 2005). What is troubling is the invisibility of the concept of governmentality within the ECE discourse of routines and transitions. The early childhood educator is being encouraged to engage in a practice that is held as neutral, universal, and in the best interest of all children. By using the technology of consistent routines and transitions, the early childhood educator takes on a political role of producing future rational and productive citizens (Fendler, 2001). In the production of future citizens, children's future lives are privileged over their present lives, for the discourse of progress is a discourse of the future and one concerned with growth. The child is seen as *becoming* a human, not as *being* a human (Lesko, 2001). Consistent routines and transitions are required not for what they offer the child in the moment, but for what they offer the future citizen.

○ Transforming Positions

In an article challenging the standardization of curriculum in early childhood education, Novinger and O'Brien (2003) contend that educators need to "resist and transform" standardization by questioning "most loudly the assumptions and outcomes of discourses that seek to regulate us" (p. 21). I would argue that this advice is valid for any practice, as all practices have the potential to restrict and control the lives of children and educators. Holding any one practice as best creates a binary in which other practices are marginalized or silenced.

If early childhood educators believe that 4-year-old children act and think in a specific way, they will bring to life those beliefs in a daily routine with transitions that are assumed to be developmentally appropriate for 4 year olds. Because the daily routine is deemed developmentally appropriate for all 4 year olds, it may remain unchanged and uncontested for successive groups of 4 year olds. By assuming that the 4-year-old child can be known as a universal subject and by adhering to the narratives of DAP, early childhood educators engage in a pedagogy that constrains or restricts practice (Cannella, 1997). To avoid reinscribing the narratives of DAP which may act as barriers to ethical practice in the classroom, educators will need to resist the hegemonic rule of child development (MacNaughton, 2005).

In *Shaping Early Childhood: Learners, Curriculum and Contexts*, Glenda MacNaughton (2003) invites the transformation of practice in early childhood education through critical reflection. A transforming perspective seeks to challenge existing practices so as to create a more just and equitable society. Critical reflection allows early childhood educators to disrupt the universality of routines and transitions as a means of achieving a predetermined developmental outcome.

Our challenge as educators is to resist turning new ideas into new discourses that operate as regimes of truth. Foucault (1972) cautioned that to construct another structure merely to image another system is to continue our participation in the present system. In the case of routines and transitions, a transforming perspective seeks not to simply replace one schedule with another, but to problematize routines and transitions to uncover the inequities and injustices enacted through them.

Lenz Taguchi (2008) writes that when "we perform pedagogical practices, we (unconsciously) theorize them into existence" (p. 61). In British Columbia this process was evident in the rise to power of the child-centred open snack routine and the subsequent decline of the traditional, community-centred snack time routine. Open snack is the practice of having snacks readily available to children during the program whenever they are hungry. Snack time (or closed snack) is when all activities cease and the children gather together to eat their snack. As a student, I was taught that communities of learners were built around such rituals as eating together; snack was seen as a group routine designed to build community and a sense of belonging. In practice, however, the transition between activity and snack time was often challenging in that not all children wanted to stop their activity to come together to eat. Some of us, who at the time were considered radical, allowed children to eat when they were hungry, thus reducing the number of routines in the program. Then as now, guidebooks for routines and transitions strongly recommended that educators pay attention to the number of routines in their program and look for ways to reduce unnecessary ones as a means of reducing young children's inappropriate behaviours (Malenfant, 2006). The practice of open snack thus evolved into a marker of quality in early childhood spaces. In the ECERS (Harms, Clifford, & Cryer, 1998), inappropriate meal/snack schedules were those that were determined by the clock and thus resulted in children being made to wait to eat even if they were hungry. A binary had been established in which snack time routines were either open or closed; open snack time was seen as an indicator of high quality while closed snack time indicated inadequate quality. In this case, the routine of an open snack was "theorized into existence" through the practices of early childhood educators (Lenz Taguchi, 2008).

I wonder what is lost for the children and adults who spend their days adhering to a set of routines and transitions constructed for them through the lens of child development? The binary of high and low quality creates either–or dilemmas for both early childhood educators and children in early years spaces (e.g., a community-centred, traditional snack versus the child-centred, open snack). What would happen if routines and transitions were situated on a continuum that was flexible and open to negotiation? What if the children and educators came together to create a way of living in the present, where the rhythm and flow of their daily life outlined their uniqueness as a community? Routines and transitions could then be enacted, remodeled, or removed as necessary to create meaning and relevance for the individuals in each early years setting.

A study by Wien and Kirby-Smith (1998) documents what happened in one early childhood space after the educators removed the clocks and watches from their program. Within the first few weeks, the program as it had originally functioned dissolved. Some of the daily activities simply disappeared as other activities expanded into longer periods of time. 'Dethroning the clock' allowed other possibilities to emerge. The authors cite one example in which the educators and children had gone for a walk and some of the children became tired and wanted to return to the centre. The original daily routine, being controlled by time, would have required the entire group to return to the centre, but educators now had a new possibility: some of the children could return with one educator while the others continued walking with the other staff. From the authors' perspective, "removing the timepiece as the decision maker for when to change activities allowed them to break open the old script for going outside and to image new possibilities" (p. 11). The authors concluded that removing clocks and watches from the program was "a catalyst for change, removing the taken-for-granted and permitting new ideas" (p. 13).

o Conclusion

In this chapter, I have problematized the practice of providing a consistent set of routines and transitions in early childhood spaces. I have made visible how early childhood educators inscribe and, in turn, reinscribe the dominant discourses of early childhood education in the context of the temporal environment. My intent was not to propose a new discourse of time in early childhood spaces, but to invite early childhood educators to critically reflect upon their practice. I do not mean to suggest that we "put tidy up time away" in a sweeping attempt to discard routines and transitions. If we tidy up routines and transitions by putting them neatly away on shelves, we will simply bring out new routines that will continue to inhibit experiential possibilities for children and educators in their daily lives within those spaces. Rather we need to disrupt tidy up time routine in order to invite messy complexity into early years spaces.

As educators, it is crucial that we move from automatized practice to *intention*, where we acknowledge the politics and values embedded in practice. With an awareness of how we unconsciously theorize practices into existence, Lenz Taguchi (2008) writes, we may "trouble our understanding" (p. 63). In this way, "deconstructive processes become part of our professionalism, as we think deeply and critically about how we state, arrange, do and analyze our pedagogical performance" (Lenz Taguchi, 2008, p. 63).

MacNaughton (2003) offers educators the choice to either "be actively involved in transformation of inequities in their work or be implicitly involved in reproducing inequities" (p. 184). In choosing the former, educators become cultural workers (Darder, 2002, as cited in MacNaughton, 2003) actively involved in constructing a more just society by challenging discrimination and making visible the effects of discrimination on learners. As educators recognize that the ECE field has privileged a very particular view of children that has resulted in practices that maintain social inequities, transformation can occur.

It is imperative that early childhood professionals, policy makers, and decision makers choose to be actively involved in transforming education, or we risk, in MacNaughton's words "remaining implicit in practices that maintain social inequities" (p. 184). I believe that early childhood educators can choose to be agents of change and, through critical reflection, resist the dominance of specific discourses around routines and transitions. At the same time I acknowledge that the concept of individual or group agency is problematic from a poststructural perspective. Early childhood educators themselves are both positioned in society and maintain their position through education's dominant discourses. The scope of this chapter does not allow for a meaningful discussion of this issue; nevertheless, it needs to be raised.

Given that many early childhood educators work in environments that lack the infrastructure to support critical reflection of practice, some educators may see the task as insurmountable. To address this issue, it is imperative that research continue to examine and document the impact of providing educators with opportunities to engage in critical reflection. Projects like the Investigating Quality (IQ) Project (Pence & Pacini-Ketchabaw, 2006) have the potential to provide the evidence needed to bring forth policy changes and create early learning environments that support educators' critical thinking. Training institutions for early childhood educators might also examine how critical reflection is incorporated within their daily practice.

As early childhood educators we need to understand why we practice as we do and to be aware of the discursive genealogy that underlies our beliefs. This awareness has the potential to bring about a powerful and provocative process of discovery and change. Unreflective acceptance of dominant discourses creates barriers to openness, possibility, and change. Entering into a process of deconstruction through dialogue, collaboration, and a willingness to welcome diverse perspectives can bring about unexpected possibilities for being with children in early education spaces. By adopting a deconstructive approach to the ECE discourse of routines and transitions, early childhood educators have an opportunity to resist developmental, predictable, and linear narratives of practice. Instead, routines and transitions can be understood as unique, culturally determined, fluid components of the complex and unpredictable everyday lived experiences of children and educators in early childhood spaces.

Perhaps the philosopher Levinas can inspire each of us to consider our responsibility to the "Other" in our interactions with children. For Levinas, the "Other" is always unknowable and incomprehensible. Maybe if we approach each child, each group of children, as an unknown entity, we will be inspired to discover the infinite possibilities that exist for the temporal organization of early childhood spaces.

REFERENCES

Bloch M., & Popkewitz, T. (2005). Constructing the parent, teacher and child: Discourses in development. In L. Soto (Ed.), *The politics of early childhood education* (pp. 6–32). New York: Peter Lang.

Burman, E. (2008a). *Deconstructing developmental psychology* (2nd ed.). London: Routledge.

Burman, E. (2008b). *Developments: Child, image, nation*. London: Routledge.

Cannella, G. (1997). *Deconstructing early childhood education: Social justice & revolution*. New York: Peter Lang.

Copple, C., & Bredekamp, S. (2009) *Developmentally appropriate practice in early childhood programs* (3rd ed.). Washington, DC: National Association for the Education of Young Children.

Dahlberg, G., Moss, P., & Pence, A. (1999). *Beyond quality in early childhood education and care: Postmodern perspectives*. London: Routledge.

Dahlberg, G., Moss, P., & Pence, A. (2007). *Beyond quality in early childhood education and care: Languages of evaluation* (2nd ed.). London: Routledge.

Government of British Columbia. (2008). *British Columbia early learning framework*. Victoria, BC: Ministry of Education, Ministry of Health, Ministry of Children and Family Development, & British Columbia Early Learning Advisory Group.

Fendler, L. (2001). Educating the flexible soul. In K. Hultqvist & G. Dahlberg (Eds.), *Governing the child in the new millennium* (pp. 119–142). London: Routledge.

Foucault, M. (1972). *The archaeology of knowledge*. London: Tavistock.

Foucault, M. (1980). *Power/knowledge: Selected interviews and other writings 1972–1977*. New York: Pantheon.

Hacking, I. (1999). *The social construction of what?* Cambridge, MA: Harvard University Press.

Hast, F., & Hollyfield, A. (1999). *Infant and toddler experiences*. St. Paul, MN: Redleaf Press.

Harms, T., Clifford, R., & Cryer, D. (1998). *Early childhood environment rating scale: Revised edition*. New York: Teachers College Press.

Hemmeter, M., Ostrosky, M., Artman, K., & Kinder, K. (2008). Planning transitions to prevent challenging behaviour. *Young Children, 63*(3), 18–25.

Langford, R. (2007). Who is a good early childhood educator? A critical study of differences within a universal professional identity in early childhood education preparation programs. *Journal of Early Childhood Teacher Education, 28*(4), 333–352.

Lenz Taguchi, H. (2008) Deconstructing and transgressing the theory. In S. Farquhar & P. Fitzsimons (Eds.), *Philosophy of early childhood education: Transforming narratives* (pp. 52–67). Oxford, UK: Blackwell.

Lesko, N. (2001) Time matters in adolescence. In K. Hultqvist & G. Dahlberg (Eds.), *Governing the child in the new millennium* (pp. 35–67). London: Routledge.

MacDonald, M. (2007). Developmental theory and post-modern thinking in early childhood education. *Canadian Children, Fall*, 8–10.

MacNaughton, G. (2003). *Shaping early childhood: Learners, curriculum and contexts*. Maidenhead, UK: Open University Press.

MacNaughton, G. (2005). *Doing Foucault in early childhood studies: Applying poststructural ideas.* London: Routledge.

Malenfant, N. (2006). *Routines and transitions: A guide for early childhood professionals.* St. Paul, MN: Redleaf Press.

McHoul, A., & Grace, W. (1993). *A Foucault primer: Discourse, power and the subject.* Melbourne, Australia: Melbourne University Press.

National Association for the Education of Young Children (NAEYC). (2009). *Position statement: Developmentally appropriate practice in early childhood programs serving children from birth through eight years.* Retrieved October 31, 2009, from http://www.naeyc.org/

Novinger, S., & O'Brien, L. (2003). Beyond "boring, meaningless shit" in the academy: Early childhood teacher educators under the regulatory gaze. *Contemporary Issues in Early Childhood, 4*(1), 3–31.

Pence, A., & Hix-Small, H. (2007). Global children in the shadow of the global child. *International Journal of Educational Policy, Research and Practice, 8*(1), 83–100.

Pence, A., & Pacini-Ketchabaw, V. (2006). The Investigating Quality (IQ) Project: Challenges and possibilities for Canada. *Interaction, Fall,* 11–13.

Popkewitz, T. (1998). Dewey, Vygotsky, and the social administration of the individual: Constructivist pedagogy as systems of ideas in historical spaces. [Electronic Version]. *American Educational Research Journal, 35*(4), 535–570.

Popkewitz, T. (1999). A social epistemology of education research. In T. Popkewitz & L. Fendler (Eds.), *Critical theories in education: Changing terrains of knowledge and politics* (pp. 17–37). New York: Rutledge

Post, Y., Boyer, W., & Brett, L. (2006). A historical examination of self-regulation: Helping children now and in the future. [Electronic Version]. *Early Childhood Education Journal, 34*(1), 5–14.

Robinson, K., & Diaz, C. (2006). *Diversity and difference in early childhood education.* London: Open University Press.

Rose, N. (1998). *Inventing ourselves: Psychology, power and personhood.* New York: Cambridge University Press.

Wien, C., & Kirby-Smith, S. (1998). Untiming the curriculum: A case study of removing clocks from the program. *Young Children, 53*(5), 8–13.

CHAPTER SEVEN

○ Art Encounters: Movements in the Visual Arts and Early Childhood Education

Sylvia Kind

As a visual artist and educator I am interested in the connections and collaborations between contemporary art and early childhood education. The movement between the two fields deeply interests me and shapes much of my work—both as an educator and as an artist. I have my feet (and my heart) in both places, and it is the journeying within and between them that provokes my thinking and shapes my practices.

For the past 2 years I have been working as an *atelierista* in an early childhood centre. Like many others inspired by the pre-primary schools in Reggio Emilia, Italy, the staff of the Children's Centre has made a commitment to taking children's artistic explorations seriously. In this centre the arts are not superfluous additions, teacher-directed projects, or even idealized examples of children's inner worlds or creativity. Instead they are seen as integral aspects of children's daily inquiries, explorations, and learning. This has made it a wonderful place to work. I have had opportunities to try out ideas and to be involved in explorations I have never been privileged to before. Yet, strangely enough, this is not what has brought me the most satisfaction. Like a work of art in progress, the work has been imperfect, marked by struggle and, at times, resistance. The work has been slow, often challenging and unsettling. Yet these are the rhythms of artistic practice. As Ken Lum, a Canadian conceptual artist, insisted while speaking on a panel during the 2004 Vancouver Art Gallery-University of British Columbia Summer Teacher Institute, "Art is hard."

It is a commonly held misconception that art should be easy—that an artwork emerges effortlessly in a singular moment of inspiration or that an artist knows the work in advance and an idea comes into an artist's mind fully formed. There often is a large difference between an artist's idea and the realization of that idea in paint, fibre, or clay. The process of working through an idea is not straightforward as if the materials merely illustrate a mental image; rather there is a dynamic interaction of thought and image, and both are shaped in the process of creating. Shaun McNiff (2008), for example, writes:

> Artistic inquiry, whether it is within the context of research or an individual person's creative expression, typically starts with the realization that you cannot define the final outcome when you are planning to do the work …. In the creative process, the most meaningful insights often come by surprise, unexpectedly, and even against the will of the creator. (p. 40)

Art also relies on failures, mistakes, and disjunctures (Kind, 2007). As Alain Toumayayan (2004) describes, artistic inspiration is a "consequence of failure… an accomplishment which exceeds one's powers of conception, planning and execution" (p. 93). Thus to create is to step into the unknown with improvisation at the heart of the endeavour. Failure, struggle, uncertainty, and not knowing the outcomes in advance may be difficult concepts for education to embrace, yet these are essential elements of artistic practice. For example, William Kentridge (quoted in Stobart, 1998), a South African artist, describes his approach:

> Arriving at an image is a process, not a frozen moment. Drawing for me is about fluidity. There may be a vague sense of what you're going to draw, but things occur that may modify, consolidate or shed doubt on what you know. So drawing is a testing of ideas; a slow motion version of thought. It does not arrive instantly like a photograph. The uncertain and imprecise way of constructing a drawing is sometimes a model of how to construct meaning. What ends in clarity does not begin that way. (p. 105)

Kentridge creates animated films that are constructed from layers of charcoal drawings that have been altered by erasing and redrawing. Each drawing holds traces of earlier marks. In this process he draws attention to the passages of time. His drawings then are never "pure" or "innocent" but marked in their historicity, carrying traces of what has gone before. Kentridge also works with concepts and questions as the material and substance of his art. He explains: "I work with what's in the air, which is to say a mixture of personal questions and broader social questions" (in Stobart, 1998, p. 105). In *Drawing the Passing*, a documentary that highlights his work, he describes, "it is in the activity of drawing ... that new ideas throw themselves forward ... often it's the actual physical process of repeating and repeating a drawing that releases a new way of thinking" (Wulf, 1999). In this way his work is intuitive, gestural, and emergent—a fluid and complex interaction of body, movement, charcoal, camera, time, thought, questions, idea, and process: much more than the physicality of charcoal images drawn on a page.

Thus an artist might begin with a partially formed concept and, through marks, gestures, colours, textures, fibres, and the act of creating, ideas are set in motion. The process is a dynamic, creative, *productive*, or generative one as the art takes shape through movement, rhythm, intuition, reflection, constant judgments and considerations (see also Dewey, 1934). It is not a linear process from conception to image or form; rather it has turns and re-turns, stops and starts, resistances and uncertainties. It may involve a measure of chaos and disruption; it inevitably involves tension and struggles. Struggle, uncertainty, and not knowing are crucial, and are often necessary productive events—that is, they produce something so that something new comes into being through the difficulty (McNiff, 1998). This is not, however, a privileging of process over product or a division of the two as separate entities. Both are entangled in their meanings and interactions—that new knowledge, understandings, or conceptualizations are produced is as important as the journey one takes in getting there. Both are in resonance with and part of each other (see also Dewey, 1934).

My work as an atelierista has taken shape through these rhythms of creative difficulty. Through these rhythms there has been an active shaping and becoming of the early childhood space, movements in the educators' pedagogical views and in the daily curriculum. It has been an early childhood space becoming, ideas in the making, and curriculum shaped as a journey into the unknown—in this way it has been a large creative project. This chapter takes up these ideas and enters into the movements between visual art practices, the languages and meanings of art, and early childhood education. It presents a view of curriculum as a journey of learning and improvisation and an image of curriculum that "comes into form as art does" (Pinar, Reynolds, Slattery, & Taubman, 1995, p. 567).

○ Visual Arts Inquiry

Over the past 2 years my role as an atelierista has taken shape in similar ways to an artist-in-residence and artist-consultant. One of my primary interests has been to work alongside the educators at the Children's Centre in order to more deeply understand children's artistic languages—that is, how to read, interpret, respond to, enrich, problematize, and *encounter* the visual processes and artistic engagements of children. One of my aims has been to open up conventional and developmental readings of children's artistic processes in order to imagine them in their complexity and to wonder, along with the children, about the possible worlds and interrogations their works propose. In early childhood too often what children do is taken literally: a scribble indicating an imperfect rendering of a representational drawing or a graphic image of a figure a literal rendering of self. I have also been particularly interested in concepts of studio practice as research and how the visual arts can be a language for inquiry for children and adults.

Engaging in the visual arts as a means of exploring ideas, developing concepts, posing questions—that is, using art as a language for inquiry—has been a familiar idea in my own artistic practice, dissertation research, and ongoing investigations. In early childhood contexts, however, this is most often an unfamiliar frame. Within Canadian early childhood contexts the visual arts often find their meaning within the scope of children's development. Processes such as painting, working with clay, and drawing are seen as activities that contribute to children's social, physical, emotional, and creative development. It is not unusual to see signs posted in art areas emphasizing the value of the arts in these terms. A typical sign may indicate that when children work with art materials they are "creating, expressing themselves, exploring a variety of media, building self esteem, experimenting with colour, using language, taking risks, using big and small muscles, and having fun" (text paraphrased from a sign in a local childcare centre).

Thus whether a project is structured, teacher-directed, open-ended, or exploratory, the visual arts are most often seen as an individual or private affair, as recreation, as *self*-expression, or as necessary to an individual child's sensory or creative development. While movements have been made towards thinking of children's artistic explorations as languages (e.g., Pelo, 2007), even centres that view the arts in this way typically have thin understandings of art and artistic practices. There may be an interest and desire to engage with the arts as a visual language, yet without a depth of conceptual understanding too often the visual arts are viewed as literal representations of self, experience, or knowledge.

While I have been very interested in understanding young children's processes (i.e., how children use visual media to explore ideas) and in helping to create an environment that facilitates and supports the use of these languages, I have primarily been interested in figuring out how to develop a shared language. So the focus is not just on children's inquiries but also on adults' perceptions and ways of seeing and listening as well. While I'm hesitant to sound as if I am romanticizing young children's processes, there is an incredible richness, variation, and eclecticism in what young children do. In many ways educators limit this richness or provoke a narrowing of experience by what we think, what we expect, and the frames we use to interpret children's artistic explorations. If the tendency is to see only what is in our field of vision, then the imperative is to expand our vision and learn to see that which lies beyond the familiar. Thus my aim has been to work with educators and children, to provoke, open up understandings, challenge assumptions, and develop other ways of thinking about children's artistic and creative processes—to disrupt the commonplace and the taken for granted and to engage with the visual arts in provocative and dynamic ways.

○ Art as Provocation

In a recent art exhibit, *Shift: Working through Repetition and Difference*, held at the Richmond Art Gallery, I installed a trail of 1000 hand-felted pod-like forms on the gallery floor (Figure 1). I made the forms by wrapping stones with wool, felting and releasing them. I created over a thousand of these "openings"—each felted object was a response to particular questions and wonderings, each one an opening into possibility and a gesture of hope. This trail of felted "stones" meandered through the exhibit space, went up to the large floor-length window, and extended beyond as the line of pod-like sculptures continued outdoors down a grassy slope. As the trail went through the window the installation interrupted boundaries of inside and outside, gallery and recreation space; in doing this it explored passages and movements. At times when I was present in the gallery, I watched how the work invited touch. Visitors would bend and touch the forms; children, tempted to step into and even sit in the trail, were reminded to take care and move away; and I would frequently see small groups crouched beside the trail speaking quietly and gently reaching fingers to feel the pieces. The trail invited interaction and seemed to call out and ask for participation.

At the beginning of my work as an atelierista I brought this piece into the Children's Centre. I wanted to respond to the invitation of the work and give it

Figure 1. One thousand hand-felted pod-like forms on the Richmond Art Gallery floor.

time and space to be touched and lived with—to respond to the unspoken requests of the children in the gallery and to see what would happen. I was also very interested in how the early childhood space could be, or become, a creative and generative space—not just a space that held or contained moments of creativity, but a space that itself was inherently creative. I was curious: What would, or could, art do? What effects could art have? What would an encounter with this artwork be like? What would happen and how could this artwork be a creative agent of change? How could it provoke other understandings and engagements with art?

So one morning, as educators and children entered the centre, they were met with an installation of these forms trailing through the rooms and onto the common adjoining deck. The educators had been somewhat prepared for this and were expecting an artistic "surprise" to greet them in the morning, although no one really could have anticipated this particular installation or the events that were set in motion. Over 1000 small, soft, white, hollow, stone-like felt shapes graced the floor and curved and meandered as a pathway through the centre (Figure 2). Some pods hung from the windows; others that were on the ground were reflected in floor-length mirrors. The space was transformed.

As the centre opened in the morning, most children responded eagerly. The first children to arrive stopped to look, touch, and step into the trail. They grouped the "stones" into large pools and jumped into them, gathered the forms in baskets, invented lively games, put them on fingers and toes, and created many meanings and possibilities for the pieces (Figure 3). Over the course of the morning, the trail was spread throughout the rooms, scattered into corners, and reinvented in multiple ways. The children moved from room to room with the pods, follow-

Figure 2. Over 1000 small, soft, white, hollow, stone-like felt shapes gracing the floor of the Children's Center.

ing the spread of the forms. Little space was left free of the pods, making it difficult to move around and avoid them. They were everywhere. The day's plans had been dramatically interrupted and little sense of the familiar order remained.

In this centre, as is typical in early childhood practices inspired by the philosophies of Reggio Emilia, the educators in their daily interactions with children were committed to following the children's interests and lines of thought. Yet in this context, attending to children's meanings and engagements was very challenging. It was difficult to figure out what the children were asking them to attend to. And how could the educators listen and attend to something that was beyond the scope of the familiar and beyond their own imaginations? To that which appeared disruptive, chaotic, and intrusive? When there was no language, perception, or understanding what meanings could be constructed from such an experience? This was not art in a familiar sense or an encounter with recognizable processes. It was not an event that was containable, manageable, or easily understood. And in the absence of other frames for making meaning, for the most part the event was initially read as chaos and as disrespect for the children's space. While several educators and parents joined in and spent most of the morning in conversations and explorations with the pods and many lovely moments and interactions occurred, several of the teachers found it a very difficult morning as they didn't have a framework to respond. It left them unsettled, uncertain, and even anxious. In many ways it brought the educators face to face with the limits of their understanding. Some watched and others distanced themselves as the event interrupted their space, the sense of predictability, and the known and familiar.

In the days that followed, this disorientation and encounter prompted many questions and exchanges about art, learning spaces, images of the teacher, and inquiry in early childhood. The event interrupted dominant understandings of educator and caregiver–child relationships and early childhood spaces and brought in a new and strange language of what the possibilities of art might be. It provoked other ways of thinking about the visual arts and was the beginning of many conversations together of ways of attending to and encountering art. Three years later the event still provokes discussion. Yet in spite of the differing viewpoints and with the memory of the disruption still lingering, there is a keen appreciation for the disorientation of the event. Art is not easy, it is not always calm and nice and pretty. It can be messy, disruptive, and unsettling. It works with the excesses, in the openings and ruptures (Springgay, 2008). It pushes boundaries and it has the potential to disorder, transform, and bring in the unthought and unimagined (Kind, 2006).

Perhaps in early childhood centres this kind of experience is not something we might deliberately seek or incite, yet it is important to broaden the scope of

Figure 3. Children inventing games and spending time with the felt pods.

artistic practice and perception, to enter into encounters and dialogues with art, and to disrupt the habitual and taken for granted. I understand the tensions and difficulty the event presented for many of the educators and for the impossible situation it provoked as discourses of care, regulation, and safety conflicted (and even collided) with the invitation of art. Nevertheless, the event's resonances have been rich and vibrant and continue to echo throughout the centre. Much of my work since that day would not have been possible had it not been for this event's disturbance.

A key change since that day has been a shift in the educators' conceptual frameworks and understandings of visual art and the beginning of juxtaposing our thinking about the arts and children's engagements with artistic processes alongside contemporary artists and their processes and investigations. We began to discuss different contemporary artists with the goal of attending to the questions, suggestions, and invitations of art. It has not been an exploration into what an artist does as in copying their forms and images, but an engagement with their ways of thinking and with the provocation of contemporary art practices.

For instance, discussing artists such as Andy Goldsworthy, Ellis Gallagher, Richard Long, Aileen M. Stackhouse, and Jim Dine brought in concepts such as impermanence, time, and place. We considered art as an event, as momentary, site specific, and relational, and we began to think about art as gesture, ritual, movement, trace, and memory. These were things that had resonances with these artists' processes and with the felt-pod event. They shaped how we talked about art and what was made possible for children—not as if the children and educators were doing similar things to the artists, but as an invitation to engage with particular artistic processes and ways of conceptualizing art so that adults' understandings and children's experiences in the visual arts could be contextualized within the frame of contemporary art. It was an effort to develop a language of inquiry that reverberated with art and artists, a language that moved beyond modernist and developmental perspectives and opened to resonances with studio art practices, contemporary art, and the work of artists.

o Art as a Language

Thinking about children's visual representations and artistic explorations as languages is a concept that holds many possibilities. Paintings and drawings, for example, may be seen as visual constructions and representations of children's thoughts, ideas, and theories. This is an important move away from thinking about children's visual processes as individual creative self-expression or the production of a particular product toward thinking about them as processes for investigation, expression, meaning making, and communication.

One very significant contribution to the field of early childhood has been Loris Malaguzzi's concept of *the hundred languages of children* (see Edwards, Gandini, & Forman, 1998). *The hundred languages of children* highlights the richness and variety of children's expressive and communicative languages and ways of constructing meaning and emphasizes that the arts are an essential and creative way of researching and learning. Lela Gandini (Gandini, Hill, Cadwell, & Schwall, 2005) elaborates on this idea:

> Drawing, painting (and the use of all languages) are experiences and explorations of life, of the senses, and of meanings. They are expressions of urgency, desires, reassurance, research, hypothesis, readjustments, constructions, and inventions. They follow a logic of exchange, and of sharing. They produce solidarity, communication with oneself, with things, and with others. They offer interpretations and intelligence about the events that take place around us. (p. 9)

While the Reggio Emilia pre-primary schools and the circulating *The Hundred Languages of Children* and *The Wonder of Learning* exhibits have brought this issue to our attention and beautifully emphasize children's creative competency and inquiries, these are not new ideas. Artists have long understood and worked with the idea of art as a language and the concept of art as research. These ideas have also been taken up very seriously in graduate research programs in universities, acknowledging that the arts and artistic practices are the foundation for important research methodologies (see, for example, Knowles & Cole, 2008; Springgay, Irwin, Leggo, Gouzouasis, & Grauer, 2008). That the processes of creating art can generate new perceptions, knowledge, and understandings is a particular way of thinking about visual art (McNiff, 1998; Sullivan, 2005) so that art, in its processes and productions, is not just a representation of an already formed idea, but an act of inquiry and investigation: a provocation and a question.

The difficulty in fully engaging with and developing these ideas in early childhood contexts is that children's art, for the most part, is still languaged by a modernist discourse of elements and principles of design (colour, shape, line, texture, etc.), individual skill development, or exploratory play. Children first must understand the sensory properties of the materials, master skills and tools, and then use these skills for representational and communicative purposes. That a foundation of skills is needed first before art becomes a tool for thinking and inquiry and individual competency is the foundation for dialogue with others.

> Through encounters with a wide range of media and materials, children explore the sensuousness and beauty of color, texture, movement, lines, and space …. As children become more comfortable and skillful with these media, they are able to use them to communicate their understandings, emotions, and questions. Their fluency in a range of art "languages" in turn, opens new possibilities for collaboration and dialogue, for taking new perspectives, and for deepening their relationships with each other. (Pelo, 2007, p. 1)

Of course within developmental framings this makes sense. And while it is generally true that children (and artists) become more fluent with practice and familiarity with the medium, it is not necessarily a linear progression from experimentation to communication. Even very young children's marks can be an investigative process and an act of research. Entering into a serious engagement with art as a language for inquiry means thinking of children's earliest marks, explorations, and art encounters as intentional, investigative, relational, communicative, and conversational acts (see Matthews, 2003)—as gestures, sounds, movements that are *inherently relational* and interactive. So that children's artistic languages, even their early efforts, might be understood as explorations in interrogating spaces and investigating relationships, and as social processes of making meaning and as generative acts. This requires learning to see what children do, not as decontextualized or simplified skills, techniques, or experiences, but as moments of questioning and complexity of thought. In essence, coming to deeper understandings of how art might be a language for inquiry and research.

o The Nature of the Language

As I have previously mentioned, for the most part, the "language of art" in early childhood tends to be described as stable and predictable: Children develop an artistic language through a progression of skills enabling them to more efficiently articulate inner worlds, theories, and ideas, and a medium is chosen for how well it represents one's ideas as if ideas are already known in advance. In this way artistic languages are viewed as skill based and as representations of experience or perception, as if children's ideas exist already and the trick is to help them find the "right" language to represent their thoughts. Or as if different languages (painting, drawing, construction, etc.) can represent different aspects of experience. This view is supported, for example, by authors such as Silver (2001), who emphasizes that art is language in that it can take the place of words. A drawing, for instance, according to Silver, can access emotional and cognitive processes and can bypass the need for words. She writes that drawings circumvent young children's language deficiencies and become a linguistic parallel so that one can say in drawing what one can't effectively communicate in words. In this way a drawing replaces spoken or written language and is a direct representation of a mental image or concept.

Hagberg (1995) elaborates on this further:

> If one conceives of language in mentalist terms, whereby meaning is a mental phenomenon only contingently associated with a particular physical sign or specific utterance, one is then led, through the fundamentally influential analogy between language and art, to a number of further assumptions concerning artistic meaning. One such assumption would define the meaning of an artwork as an entity originating in the mind of the artist, a mental object whose existence we infer through the physical work itself. Another assumption, proceeding from the behaviorist conception of language which gives priority to the material over the mental, results in a competing conception of artistic meaning: the artist discovers the work's meaning in the materials of the medium rather than by infusing the materials with significance through the embodiment of artistic intention. (p. 2)

In this way mental meaning and its outward expression or representation are connected in a one-to-one correspondence. This gives an illusion of a direct and simple correspondence between thinking and saying or thinking and creating—between thought and image. It also gives the illusion that an artwork merely *illustrates* the artist's concepts or ideas, or that the work's meaning is found *in* the materials. This orientation is common for instance, in describing materials as languages. Recycled and found objects, clay, and wire are often referred to as languages in these mentalist or behaviorist terms as if the materials embody ideas or illustrate coherent mental images and concepts. Thinking with objects and thinking in a medium are generally much more complex than this.

Sullivan (2005), for example, describes how artists think in a medium. The art materials don't just feel or act differently or have different properties and produce different kinds of forms and images, they also provoke different ways of thinking as the artist engages and works with them. My camera, for instance, is not just a tool for recording information, but evokes a particular way of thinking, processing ideas, and making meaning, which is profoundly different from the way I work with wool, dyes, found objects, or drawing. In drawing the human figure or in using my camera to create a particular image of a person, the subject may be similar yet engagement with the different media and processes constructs unique perceptions and ways of thinking through the subject. The meaning is not in the technologies, materials, or processes, rather they invite interactions, evoke certain possibilities, frame ways of seeing, and give particular structure to the ideas being explored.

While children's visual processes may have their own rhythms, time frames, and contexts there is much we can learn from contemporary art and its semiotic and postmodern structures. For example, a semiotic view considers that perception and understanding are shaped *in the use of* these languages. As Atkinson (2002) describes, "signs such as words and images shape our perception and understanding of experience" (pp. 18–19). This view is in contrast to the notion that first we have experiences and then we find the right words, images, or artistic languages to express or represent those experiences. Atkinson writes:

> Words and images are not labels we attach to reveal prior ideas, events, experiences, or perceptions, rather these semiotic orders actually create our conceptions of reality and therefore, the conceptual framework through which reality is made accessible. This suggests that conscious experience and thought is a construction built out of signs and that our lives are largely lived within and according to different sign systems that we inherit and develop. (p. 19)

Thus, meaning is not fixed *in* specific materials, images, processes, or artworks; rather meanings are generated in their use and in their interaction. This also means that how we think about visual art processes and visual art media shapes what is possible. For example, if we think of clay as a sculptural material that is used for making objects, then it suggests certain engagements. We may set out individual clay slabs or balls on the table and give directions or support in how to create particular objects. We might talk about form, texture, structure, and balance. We may subtly or directly encourage individual sculptural objects. What we think clay is for shapes our experience with it, and the language we use to talk about the experience constructs particular meanings.

If, on the other hand, we think about movement, place, impermanence, and relationality then we may consider the possibility of moving towards and away from the clay, attending to the relationship of clay to its surroundings, and inviting interaction with others. These concepts give structure to and shape the investigations with the medium. And so we may set the clay out in other ways, for instance, as a big block in the centre of a large mat on the floor, as several blocks stacked so they echo a child's height, in a space with several overhead projectors so there is a complex play of shadow, bodies, movement, and constructions. This doesn't just invite different interactions but also shapes what and how we see and the meanings we construct of the experience. As Dahlberg, Moss, and Pence (1999) write, "The language we use shapes and directs our way of looking at and understanding the world, and the way we name different phenomena and objects becomes a form of convention" (p. 31).

What if we thought not of materials and processes but of encounters and negotiations? We might see a young child sitting on a large slab of clay on a mat and begin to imagine how the clay becomes a medium for negotiating power and strength. The child presses into the clay, working her hands and feet and body into the dense clay. As she presses in, the clay resists, it doesn't bend easily. In its resistance the clay speaks back—in its strength, density, weight, heaviness it is a force to be struggled with. In this sense clay also has a voice and a presence. It is not a medium that one does something to as an instrument for an artist's purpose, but a medium for negotiating and interacting with. The clay becomes a partner in the creative process, an object of encounter rather than a medium for representing thought.

◦ Art Encounters

Within contemporary art contexts, visual art is meant to have a presence, provoke thought, unsettle assumptions, pose questions, and interrogate ideas. As Sullivan (2005) writes, "visual arts knowledge is transformative…[it is] recursive and constantly undergoes change as new experiences 'talk back' through the process and progress of making art" (p. 100). The language of art is resonant with more than just the artist's voice and intention, and it is unsettling and provoking. This is also echoed by Jake Chapman (quoted in Field, 2003), talking about his art in an interview with *Time Out London*:

> The job of a work of art is to raise questions about its terms and conditions …. That's what we do. We present the viewer with a puzzle. We put an injunction on speedy consumption, by refusing to offer a straightforward aesthetic experience. And to defend the integrity of the work, we produce a bit of turbulence that makes it more than a simple sip—of art. (para. 1)

Entering into a work of art requires the viewer's active engagement, as meanings are constituted collectively in relation to and between others so that art production and critique take place in a social, relational, and interactive space (see also Rose, 2001). Therefore, meanings are not just constructed in the acts of creating, but are also displaced, ruptured, and contested. Nicolas Bourriaud (2002) enlarges this idea as he emphasizes *art as an encounter*. In this way he describes art as relational and as a "set of artistic practices which take as their theoretical and practical point of departure the whole of human relations and their social context, rather than as an independent and private space" (pp. 112–113). Therefore visual expressions, meanings, and exchanges are not objective, stable, or even primarily individual. Meaning is not held *within* a work of art, *in* the artist's intention or idea, or *in* the materials used, but in the active exchange and co-construction of meaning, which may also be site specific and may change in relation to time, space, and place.

Meanings of children's works may also change when located in different times and contexts (Kind, 2006). Thus entering into art as an *encounter* situates art as an interactive event, an engagement with the world. This means conceptualizing art, and children's artistic engagements and productions, not primarily as self-expressive, individual, interior, or private experiences, even though they may exhibit and invite these qualities, but as a complex, conceptual, inventive, shared, participatory, and investigative encounter.

O'Sullivan (2006) describes the nature of this encounter and how it is radically different from art as representation:

> An object of an encounter is fundamentally different from an object of recognition. With the latter our knowledges, beliefs and values are reconfirmed. We, and the world we inhabit, are reconfirmed as that which we already understood our world and ourselves to be. An object of recognition is then precisely a *re*presentation of something already in place. With such a non-encounter our habitual way of being and acting in the world is reaffirmed and reinforced, and as a consequence no thought takes place. Indeed we might say that *re*presentation precisely stymies thought. With a genuine encounter, however, the contrary is the case. Our typical ways of being in the world are challenged, our systems of knowledge disrupted. We are forced to thought. The encounter then operates as a rupture in our habitual modes of being and thus in our habitual subjectivities. It produces a cut, a crack. However, this is not the end of the story, for the rupturing encounter also contains a moment of affirmation, the affirmation of a new world, in fact a way of seeing and thinking this world differently. This is the creative moment of the encounter that obliges us to think otherwise. (p. 1)

Therefore, *art as a state of encounter* considers that meanings are constituted in the relation between things and in moments of disruption of previously held ideas.

○ Thinking through Encounters

In thinking through encounters and the concept of art as an encounter, it is help-ful to consider how an encounter might be conceptualized. The philosophies of Emmanuel Levinas have challenged the certainty of knowledge and education's "will to know" (Dahlberg & Moss, 2005, p. 77). Levinas challenges our reliance on technical practice and normative thinking and opens the possibility of an encounter which goes beyond understanding.

Contrary to the popular belief that we must know the good in order to do it, Levinas (2003) posits that all beliefs are a result of the face-to-face relationship. In this face-to-face relationship with the other, we experience a moral demand prior to knowledge, and based on this demand we come to knowledge about how we should act. Much of education tends toward the initial positioning—that if we learn about teaching methods then we should be able to apply these to or inte-grate these in our teaching practices. If we learn about children, appropriate devel-opmental practices, and principles of caring then we should know how to act with children. Or if we learn about art materials, interesting art activities, and how to help children use visual means to explore ideas then we should know how to facil-itate children's artistic and visual languages. That is, knowledge of the "good" comes first, then comes the application of it.

This is not to say that these are not important things to know, however, Levinas asks us to consider knowledge as an ethical question (Todd, 2001b). Rather than learning about something, we learn alongside, through, and from it and con-sider the relations and conditions that are necessary in order for knowledge to be possible. And what is necessary is an orientation of receptivity and radical open-ness, that is, an openness to something completely new, unthought, and "totally other beyond the self" (Todd, 2001b, p. 68), an ethical relation to difference, and susceptibility to alterity. This requires decentering self and centering alterity. It asks: "What can I learn from the other?" "How can I respond to the other's demand? "What can I do for the other" (Todd, 2001a)? This responsibility is not something one can learn as knowledge or curriculum content; rather it comes into being through one's response to the other and the face-to-face moral demand. Learning from and learning through means being changed by the other.

An encounter, then, requires this kind of receptive susceptibility. Rather than knowing the meaning ahead of time, or understanding a work within predeter-mined frameworks, the encounter is marked by a question. According to Massumi (1993), meaning is constituted in the encounter between forces; it is an event, a dynamic process with forces acting on one another in a reciprocal and transfor-mative relationship. This means not looking at what art is, but at what it does, or

its effects. This resonates with Deleuze's assertion that the predisposition of art
is the *production* of affects and percepts:

> What we *can* acknowledge is that art is not about knowledge, conveying "meanings"
> or providing information. Art is not just an ornament or style used to make data more
> palatable or consumable. Art may well have meanings or messages but what makes it
> *art* is not its content but its *affect*, the sensible force or style through which it produces
> content. (Colebrook, 2002, pp. 24–25)

This summer, for instance, while visiting Scotland during the Edinburgh Art
Festival, I had the opportunity to experience an exhibit of Eileen M. Stackhouse's
drawings. Her exhibit *How Long Is Now?* was an evolving 28-day installation in
the Granton Gallery, a former lighthouse factory. Her site-specific drawings, conceptualized as a responsive conversation with the surroundings, investigated perception of the present moment (Sierra Metro, 2009). As I entered the gallery I
was met with a room alive with drawings. There were large panels strung up and
draped from cords hanging from the ceiling, drawn gestures marked on walls and
floors, and folded drawings stuffed in corners, torn in small remnants in ordered
piles on the floor, and bits stuck to windows. Soft spotlights cast a warm glow
and highlighted the hanging sheets of translucent graphite drawings as they gently moved in a breeze generated by large freestanding fans. It was the final day of
the exhibit, the artist had finished her work in the gallery, yet it was evident that
I had stepped into the midst of something still breathing.

Stackhouse's work marked the doing and undoing of drawing, drawing as a
process, as an artifact, as a moment, and movement. It carried with it the trace of
time, yet not fixed as if in the past, but present in its movements and rhythms so
that the installation was still in motion. The artist wasn't present yet I could feel
her gestures and bodied movements in the drawn lines and torn fragments, her
drawings *enacting* her curiosities and questionings.

I spent several hours there walking around and in the midst of the drawings,
taking photos, sometimes sitting and just watching, all the while presented with
questions: What is this? What am I to think? What really is (a) drawing? I could
sense my own drawings and the textures of graphite and charcoal and the sounds
as they marked the paper. I remembered the struggles of working an idea out on
paper, the meeting of materials, image, and thought, and the deep satisfaction of
rendering something anew. I recalled the smells, the dust, and the residue on my
hands and clothes, the chalky traces implicating and marking me along with the
paper. When I left I carried these wonderings with me and they still resonate
through my work in the centre. The meaning of these drawings—not in the gallery or in the paper or materials, or even contained in the installation or artist's
intentions, but becoming understood as the *experience* of the exhibit—meets my

work with children. It was an installation that set questions in motion and opened possibilities of meaning and of thinking of drawing as a living, breathing *place*. Stackhouse writes about her own process:

> My intention is to create environments that allow experimentation and questioning, which permit a continual making and unmaking, a marking and erasing, a tracing and plotting of our perceptions and realities. I believe the experience of making is not fully understood until some time after the art exists and that hindsight is a pivotal part of the imaginative process. (Sierra Metro, 2009, para. 4)

In this way art becomes a meeting place. It brings thought, place, time, materials, image, and form into conversation. In its process of materializing and in its form it provokes, opens to questions, and produces an effect. O'Sullivan (2006) elaborates on the process and form of art:

> In fact "art" might be the name for both of these encounters, a meeting, or collision, between two fields of force, transitory but ultimately transformative. Both of these encounters are precisely at the moment of production. The encounter, between participant and art work, is a productive, albeit in a different sense, as that between artist and material. "Meaning" might then be thought of as this productive "event," this "moment" of meeting, ungraspable in its moment of occurrence, but real in its effects. (p. 21)

In this way we can think of art as a rupture and displacement. "Art is like a 'cut'; it shakes us out of our habitual modes of being and puts other conditions into play" (O'Sullivan, 2006, p. 125). Thus, as Colebrook describes, language (and the language of art) is creative. It creates concepts. And "a concept does not just add another word to a language; it transforms the whole shape of a language" (2002, p. 17). Concepts such as impermanence, encounter, or relationality aren't just ideas, perceptions, or vocabulary added to existing structures, or even alternative ways of reading an interaction; they fundamentally change the modes, possibilities, and compositions of artistic engagements. From a Deleuzian perspective, this means thinking about art as a possible world, folded, enfolded, and unfolding.

○ **Continual Unfoldings**

As I close this chapter, I return to the initial encounter with the trail of felt pods. To have the effect it did, this moment could not have been otherwise. It could not have been fully explained or anticipated beforehand. It was the surprise, the difficulty of this *encounter* that has made, and continues to make, my work possible. Since that day we have had many other encounters with the pods. While none have been quite so disruptive and generative as the first event, each encounter still unfolds other meanings and effects. Yet the meaning and possibility is not in the felt pods or in the interaction with them, but in their effects and the resonances that still play out in the centre. That day has left many other traces and a persuasive invitation to see art as an event, a situation, and an encounter. This displaces (and continues to displace) the process/product binary and the developmental, skill based, and self-expressive or exploratory perspectives. The pod event has also made space for many other encounters with painting, charcoal, dance and mark making, clay, and sculpture, a space and time of dwelling with, responding and listening to, and stepping in the midst of the processes, productions, and meanings of art.

Rupture and affirmation are two moments of the same encounter, two moments that only seem opposed if considered in the abstract, outside of actual experience. Art, in breaking one world and creating another, brings these two moments into conjunction. Art then is the name of the object of the encounter, but also the name of the encounter itself, and indeed that which is produced by the encounter. Art is this complex event that brings about the possibility of something new (O'Sullivan, 2006). The invitation then, is to think beyond representation and to imagine art as a place of encounter—to find ourselves, as Deleuze might say, as forced to thought.

REFERENCES

Atkinson, D. (2002). *Art in education: Identity and practice*. London: Kluwer.

Bourriaud, N. (2002). *Relational aesthetics* (S. Pleasance & F. Woods with M. Copeland, Trans.). Paris: Les Presse Du Reel. (Original work published 1998)

Colebrook, C. (2002). *Gilles Deleuze*. New York: Routledge.

Dahlberg, G., & Moss, P. (2005). *Ethics and politics in early childhood education*. New York: RoutledgeFalmer.

Dahlberg, G., Moss, P., & Pence, A. R. (1999). *Beyond quality in early childhood education and care: Postmodern perspectives*. London: Falmer.

Dewey, J. (1934). *Art as experience*. New York: Berkley Group.

Edwards, C., Gandini, L., & Forman, G. (1998). *The hundred languages of children. The Reggio Emilia approach: Advanced reflections*. Cambridge, UK: Cambridge University Press.

Field, C. (2003). *Jack & Dinos Chapman: A retrospective at the Saatchi Gallery*. Retrieved December 19, 2009, from http://www.culture24.org.uk/art/art18306

Gandini, L., Hill, L., Cadwell, L., & Schwall, C. (Eds.). (2005). *In the spirit of the studio: Learning from the atelier of Reggio Emilia*. New York: Teachers College Press.

Hagberg, G. L. (1995). *Art as language: Wittgenstein, meaning, and aesthetic theory*. Ithaca, NY: Cornell University Press.

Kind, S. (2006). *Of stones and silences: Storying the trace of the other in the autobiographical and textile text of art/teaching*. Unpublished doctoral dissertation, University of British Columbia, Vancouver, British Columbia.

Kind, S. (2007). In open spaces. In L. F. Darling, A. Clarke, & G. Erickson (Eds.), *Collective improvisation in a teacher education community* (pp. 67–74). Dordrecht, the Netherlands: Springer.

Knowles, J. G., & Cole, A. L. (Eds.). (2008). *Handbook of the arts in qualitative research*. Thousand Oaks, CA: Sage.

Levinas, E. (2003). *Totality and infinity: An essay on exteriority* (A. Lingis, Trans.). Pittsburgh, PA: Duquesne University Press. (Original work published in 1969)

Massumi, B. (1993). *A user's guide to capitalism and schizophrenia: Deviations from Deleuze and Guattari*. Cambridge, MA: MIT Press.

Matthews, J. (2003). *Drawing and painting: Children and visual representation* (2nd ed.). Thousand Oaks, CA: Sage.

McNiff, S. (1998). *Art-based research*. London: Jessica-Kingsley.

McNiff, S. (2008). Art-based research. In J. G. Knowles & A. L. Cole (Eds.), *Handbook of the arts in qualitative research* (pp. 29–40). Thousand Oaks, CA: Sage.

O'Sullivan, S. (2006). *Art encounters Deleuze and Guattari: Thought beyond representation*. New York: Palgrave Macmillan.

Pelo, A. (2007). *The language of art: Inquiry-based studio practices in early childhood settings*. St. Paul, MN: Redleaf Press.

Pinar, W., Reynolds, W., Slattery, P., & Taubman, P. (1995). *Understanding curriculum*. New York: Peter Lang.

Rose, G. (2001). *Visual methodologies*. Thousand Oaks, CA: Sage.

Sierra Metro. (2009). *Aileen M. Stackhouse: How long is now?* Retrieved December 19, 2009, from http://www.sierrametro.com/page10.htm

Silver, R. (2001). *Art as language: Access to emotions and cognitive skills through drawings*. Philadelphia: Routledge.

Springgay, S. (2008). *Body knowledge and curriculum: Pedagogies of touch in youth and visual culture*. New York: Peter Lang.

Springgay, S., Irwin, R. L., Leggo, C., Gouzouasis, P., & Grauer, K. (Eds.). (2008). *Being with a/r/tography*. Rotterdam, the Netherlands: Sense.

Stobart, J. (1998). *Drawing matters*. London: A&C Black.

Sullivan, G. (2005). *Art practice as research: Inquiry in the visual arts*. Thousand Oaks, CA: Sage.

Todd, S. (2001a). Guilt, suffering and responsibility. *Journal of Philosophy of Education, 35*(4), 597–614.

Todd, S. (2001b). On not knowing the other, or learning from Levinas. *Philosophy of Education, 2001*, 67–74.

Toumayayan, A. P. (2004). *Encountering the other: The artwork and the problem of difference in Blanchot and Levinas*. Pittsburg, PA: Duquesne University Press.

Wulf, R. (Director). (1999). *William Kentridge: Drawing the passing* [Video]. Johannesburg, South Africa: David Krut Publishing.

....

CHAPTER EIGHT

A Curriculum for Social Change: Experimenting with Politics of Action or Imperceptibility

....

Veronica Pacini-Ketchabaw *with* Fikile Nxumalo

Difference and diversity have become important topics in contemporary early childhood education discussions. The early childhood field has been preoccupied with diversity, asking, for example, *How do we encourage young children to appreciate cultural diversity? How do we welcome cultural differences in early childhood education classrooms?* These issues have become particularly relevant in recent early childhood curricula/frameworks in which early childhood educators are encouraged to work with young children on issues of diversity in their classrooms. In the *British Columbia Early Learning Framework*, for example, early childhood educators are encouraged to create environments where children can

- ☐ begin to recognize discrimination and inequity and respond appropriately
- ☐ learn to appreciate and celebrate diversity
- ☐ understand that all persons have value; accept and welcome individual differences. (Government of British Columbia, 2008, p. 33)

While these goals are worthy of consideration as part of a societal project towards social justice, they are embedded within an identity-focused paradigm that is based on recognition from others. I argue that social justice needs to be conceptualized as a practice rather than as a transcendent solution; therefore early childhood education cannot maintain its developmental, identity-focused approaches. My intention is not to dismiss these goals as unimportant or wrong, but I want to move beyond them to rethink the project of social transformation in early childhood education and engage with a new kind of politics. As Grosz (2002) proposes,

> we need to begin with different working assumptions, which may cover some of the same issues as those conceived by identity politics, without however, resorting to the language and assumptions governing recognition. In space of the desire for recognition, the emptiness of a solipsistic existence, the annihilation of identity without the other, the relation of desperate dependence on the other for the stability of one's being, we could place an account of subjectivity, identity, or agency at the mercy of forces, energies, practices, which produce altogether different understandings of both politics and identity. (p. 468)

This chapter is an encounter between posthumanist theories and the early childhood field's preoccupation with diversity. Particularly, I experiment with thoughts on different/ciation (Bignall, 2007), corporeality (Grosz, 1993, 2002), and the materiality of race (Saldanha, 2006) to think about social change in early childhood education. Through this exploration, I briefly conceptualize a pedagogy of action or imperceptibility (Grosz, 2002) for early childhood education. A pedagogy of action entails a different kind of engagement with the goals noted above, an engagement that looks very different to what we might think these goals entail. "What we need," Moulard-Leonard (2005) suggests, "is a metaphysics, a new ontology, a novel way of establishing the possibility of a different kind of experience, hence a different approach to knowledge" (p. 232). This approach might move us away from well-intentioned ethical theories of moral values to new understandings of ethics.

A specific goal of this chapter is to reflect on the conceptual tools that might be necessary to develop a pedagogy of action in early childhood education that can help us to create spaces for social justice. The conceptual tools I outline here are informed by the positive and productive philosophy (and politics) of Gilles Deleuze and Felix Guattari and borrow specifically from scholars who have employed their concepts, such as Elizabeth Grosz, Simone Bignall, and Arun Saldanha. Rather briefly, a positive and productive political philosophy is "a somewhat restless manner of engagement that seeks to contribute to the calling-forth of different worlds but knows that it is not a simple matter to escape this one, that the elaboration of concepts and collectives...requires a degree of 'betrayal' if politics is to resist cliché and closure and remain open to the inadmissible" (Buchanan & Thoburn, 2008, p. 6).

Following this political philosophy requires a particular view of children and early childhood education spaces that might alarm and dishearten some, as it moves us away from the innocent image of young children that is assumed in developmental knowledge. Briefly, as MacNaughton and Davis (2009), Taylor (2007), and Lenz Taguchi (2006) note, early childhood spaces are gendered, racialized, ethnically marked spaces in which certain categories already count more or are more privileged than others. Young children are aware of human differences "because they embody them" and they are also knowledgeable that "these differences do not all attract and enjoy the same status and authority" (Taylor, 2008, p. 199; also see MacNaughton, 2000; Pacini-Ketchabaw & Berikoff, 2008).

Many early childhood education scholars (e.g., Lenz Taguchi, 2006; MacNaughton, 2000; Taylor, 2007, 2008) have written about diversity and topics such as racialization, gender, and sexuality. It is the dialogue these scholars have begun that I join in this chapter. One important contribution these scholars have made is their challenge of developmental explanations of gender, class, sexuality, and racialization. They have acknowledged the invisibility of political pasts, presents, and futures in the fight towards social justice. For example, MacNaughton and Davis (2009) argue that "young children's ability and desire to use 'race'-color to sort, classify, compare, and assign status to people is a direct result of the politicizing of skin tone in a specific country or nation state at a specific point and over time" (p. 29).

Borrowing from poststructural feminist theorists, an additional contribution made by the literature that challenges developmental explanations of gender, race, and sexuality in young children has been how we think about young children's identity (as hinted above). Poststructural feminist theorists and practitioners have rethought developmental psychology's views of children's identity as fixed, stable, and rational. Poststructuralists argue

> that the processes of being and becoming are full of tensions, as children gain access to competing discourses of gender, "race," and class and negotiate possibilities for themselves as gendered, "racialized," and classed beings. Amongst this, children attempt to clarify which forms of becoming are possible and desirable. In this process, children identify with particular ways of thinking and being, and resist, reject, or "disidentify" with others. (MacNaughton & Davis, 2009, p. 36)

Postcolonial scholars have also provided useful critical lenses for understanding the histories and continuing influences of colonialism, imperialism, and neocapitalist ideologies in early childhood education (Soto & Swadener, 2002; Viruru & Cannella, 2004). These scholars argue against colonial, oppressive, and exclusionary understandings and practices of early childhood education. They have been influential in questioning the taken-for-granted globalization of developmental theories that reflect the colonial pattern of the minority world, "helping" the majority world to understand children (see also Pence & Hix-Small, 2007; Viruru, 2001). Indigenous scholars have also been influential in rethinking the exclusionary and oppressive nature of normative colonial discourses on Indigenous communities around the world. Linda Tuhiwai Smith's important contribution, *Decolonizing Methodologies: Research and Indigenous Peoples* (1999), for example, has been used to think about the invisibility and silencing of Indigenous knowledges (Ritchie, 2007).

Overall, if we can put it in one sentence, what this body of work has placed attention to is the role of language and discourse in creating social injustices. The introduction of language and discourse in analyses of the workings of social injustices has made the field differently aware of the politics of early childhood education and brings us closer to creating spaces for engaging in social justice (Dahlberg, Moss, & Pence, 2007). My intention in this chapter is not to repeat and/or dismiss this literature, but rather to continue the tremendous contributions this body of work has made towards transforming early childhood education ideas related to social justice.

Before highlighting some important conceptual movements embedded within the idea of a pedagogy of action, I present two moments of practice collected through my ongoing research with early childhood educators in British Columbia and note some highlights of this research (see also Pence & Pacini-Ketchabaw, 2010). These encounters were the provocations that allowed me to begin exploring the concepts and ideas I introduce in the latter part of the chapter.

○ A Participatory Action Research Project with Early Childhood Educators

I draw from my experience of working with early childhood educators for the last 5 years in two large participatory action research projects in British Columbia, Canada. The primary goal of the projects is to engage with early childhood educators in discussions related to practices that produce crises or disrupt business as usual in the early childhood classroom. Together with educators, we engage in the ongoing process of deconstruction and reconstruction of our early childhood practices using poststructural, feminist, posthumanist, postcolonial, and anti-racist theoretical locations (also see Dahlberg, Moss, & Pence, 2007; Lenz Taguchi, 2009; MacNaughton, 2005).

Since the beginning of the projects, the participating educators have been collecting moments of practice in their centres using journal writing, photography, and video and audio recording (following the practice of pedagogical documentation, see Dahlberg et al., 2007; or pedagogical narrations, see Chapter 4). The moments of practice are shared with the project group. During our meetings, we critically reflect together on each educator's documentations and make visible how we might work with postfoundational theories. For the purposes of this chapter, I detail two pedagogical narrations and use them to capture the ways in which social justice comes to matter in the classroom.

Before presenting the moments of practice, a few words may be helpful as to the ways in which I think of pedagogical narrations. Following Lenz Taguchi (2008), the moments of practice below "temporarily 'capture' an intra-active event that has happened, and in its materialisation it becomes a territory for further intra-activity and processes of new learning" (p. 8). Pedagogical narrations "can be understood as a *materialising apparatus of knowing* that produces different kinds of knowledge, as phenomena…a *material-discursive apparatus*…that offers constraints on what is produced as knowledge and produces exclusions, depending on both the limits of our discursive understandings, and the limits and constraints of the material realities involved" (p. 9).

Encounter One: Who Is Included/Excluded?

This encounter was related by a teacher (Christine) who had never paid attention to issues of racialization until they were discussed in a meeting with other educators. The encounter took place in a preschool on the grounds of a large university; many of the children in the preschool were of Asian descent.

At the lunch table, a child says to Christine: "I'm not going to kindergarten at U-Climb because Mommy says there are too many Chinese people there." Another child adds to the conversation: "No Korean children…."

Following this discussion, the two children at the lunch table were playing outside with three others. The following conversation took place when another preschool friend attempted to join them:

Sam: You can't play—you're not Korean.
Allie: That is not very nice—we're all friends and you have to play with everyone.
Sam: OK, you have to know the password, but it's a Korean word and you don't know it.

Encounter Two: Becoming a Princess, a Musketeer, Rapunzel…

This series of encounters was related by Thandi, an educator who runs a family childcare centre. Thandi's youngest daughter, Andile, had recently drawn a picture of herself with long blond hair (Figure 1). Thandi was particularly surprised about this spontaneous drawing in which Andile did not colour in the face with brown as she had always done before when drawing herself. Thandi had always seen her daughter as being proud of her biracial ethnic identity (Swazi-Filipina or Asian/African). In her practice, Thandi had been mindful of nurturing a sense of belonging as well as addressing equity issues such as challenging ethnic, gender, and racial stereotypes and discussing experiences with exclusion from play.

Here is a dialogue between Thandi and Andile after the drawing was done.

Andile: I have really long, long hair.
Thandi: Long hair?
Andile: Ya—really long. I'm wearing my tiara. My clips are in.

Figure 1. Andile's recently drawn picture of herself.

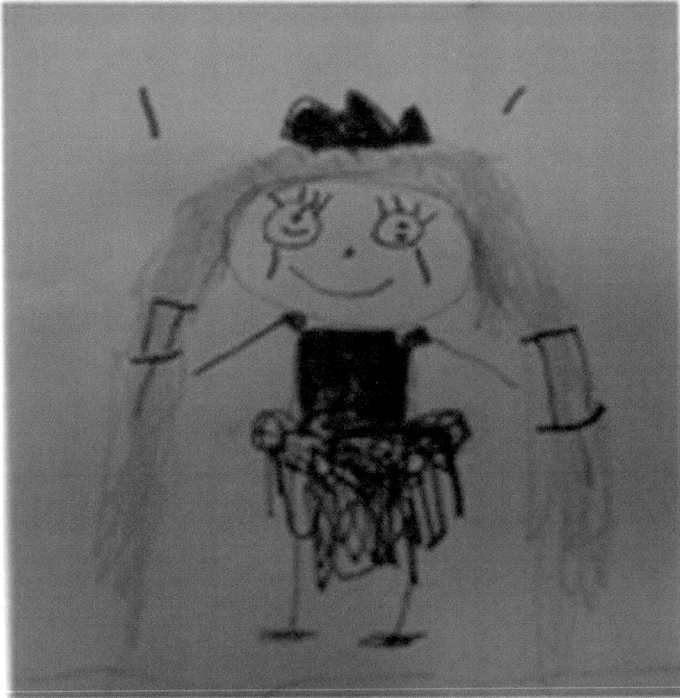

Thandi then decided to engage the children in a critical dialogue about racial and gender identities. She was interested in exploring "other" possibilities for the children to see themselves and especially to begin to challenge marginalizing ideas related to both gender and race identities. Through this exploration, Thandi wanted to avoid a didactic approach and was wary that focusing on differences could somehow reinforce black/white and girl/boy binaries. She felt the children could benefit from more exploration around the construction of identities. In wanting to engage with the idea of building on the children's voices and perspectives, Thandi prepared an activity that she hoped would invite the children to explore, and perhaps question, their views and representations of themselves and others in a social context.

She set up some mirrors at a table with drawing paper and black pencil crayons at each seat. She didn't give the children any specific instructions and waited to see how their interests would be provoked. The children engaged with the mirrors and studied themselves, making playful expressions and telling each other about their facial features as they explored their similarities and differences (Figure 2).

Figure 2. Children with the mirrors studying themselves and making playful expressions.

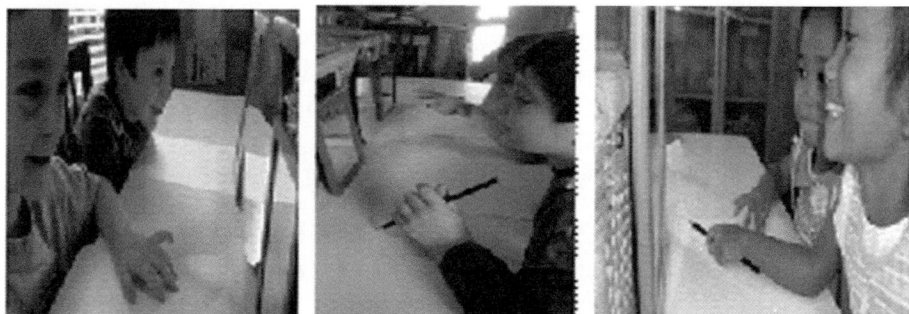

Simon: I have a lot of freckles on my cheeks! I have about four on my nose.
Nosizwe: I don't have any; I have beauty marks by my chin and eyes.
Simon: What's a beauty mark?
Nosizwe: It's blackish—it's a beauty spot.
Simon: If you just think about getting freckles, you'll get them, you know.
Mark: [smiling broadly] Me have a lot of hair!
Simon: I have sticking down hair on my face.
Andile: Mine is in my pom-pom [ponytail].

Nosizwe: (laughs) I have a triangle-shaped tooth and a line on my face!

Andile: Why does everyone have a line on their face?

Nosizwe: Well you can't see it sometimes; it's showing where blood is going in your face.

Simon: Yeah—I have lines of blood going down in my arms.

After some time spent studying their faces, including making playful expressions, the children started to draw (Figure 3). The first drawing is the one done by Andile .

Figure 3. Drawings by children at Thandi's childcare centre.

Here are some of Thandi's initial reflections after this activity,

I did not discern anything in their conversation that indicated negative attitudes about their identities.....In retrospect perhaps Nosizwe's reference to beauty spots could have been used as an entry point to negotiate different perspectives on the (gendered?) meanings of external "beauty." From my initial view, she had used the term in a positive way in reference to herself but did not exclude others. I was also struck by her association of something she described as "blackish" with beauty and thought perhaps this could be interpreted as a positive view of her racial identities. In wondering why a direct discussion of their racial differences did not come up in their narratives, I thought perhaps the children were simply more interested in exploring what they viewed as their most interesting and/or individual distinctive features, possibly influenced by the available materials, as I provided only a black pencil with which to draw.

Following this episode, Thandi was still unclear whether the positive identity attitude that she perceived from the children in the mirror activity was an indication of self-views and/or whether the meanings in their drawings were constructed by the particular social context, such as by unspoken influences of older siblings on the younger. Therefore, to gain more insight, she revisited some of Andile's past drawings with her and listened to her interpretations. Here are Andile's narratives of each drawing (Figures 4a-d).

Drawing 1 (Figure 4a): "It's me being a musketeer—I have a sword. I'm pretending it's a wand. I swing it, that's how the bad guys just fall down."

Drawing 2 (Figure 4b): "I am spinning on one leg and I made my arms go out—I like dancing in the living room."

Drawing 3 (Figure 4c): "It's me laughing. I have a pink line on my face. I got a tiara from the store." This drawing was made soon after the previous drawing exercise where the children had discussed the "lines" (veins) in their faces.

Drawing 4 (Figure 4d): "I'm being Rapunzel jumping on the bed! I made the hair fancy."

In her reflections, Thandi wrote:

> It is interesting that in re-visiting Andile's picture with blonde hair she gave it new meanings by placing herself in an imagined Rapunzel princess storyline. However, I remain unclear about the extent to which I can make inferences about Andile's self-view based on her drawings and her shifting interpretations. How significant are these representations to her self-view if they are understood as contextual and imaginative representations of identity? I think her drawings and interpretations bring meanings and show influences that could be seen as maintaining socially shaped (through popular culture?) power relationships. This could negatively influence her self-view. On the other hand some meanings could be seen to disturb gendered (and racialized?) socio-cultural influences, such as in her (agentic?) imaginative representation of herself as a brown-skinned, curly-haired, wand-swinging musketeer. I am hoping that sharing the documentation and learning more about the construction of identities will help me to understand how I can begin to ethically challenge those meanings that could be seen as constraining children's self-views, particularly given (the paradox of?) children's agency in negotiating identity.

Figure 4a. Andile's drawing of herself.

Figure 4b. Andile's drawing of herself.

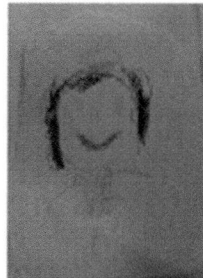

Figure 4c. Andile's drawing of herself.

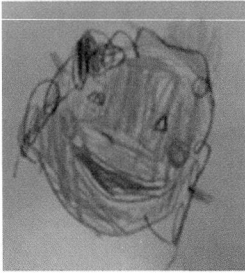

Figure 4d. Andile's drawing of herself.

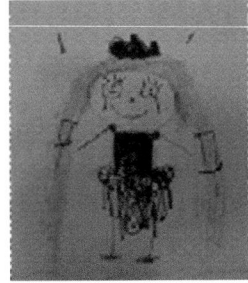

○ Binaries and New Futures

What becomes clear in these encounters, particularly the first, is the presence of dichotomies that underpin current early childhood education approaches to social justice (e.g., categories of racialization; same-different). These dichotomies, Grosz (1993) contends, are "deeply implicated in regimes of oppression" (p. 169). Furthermore, within these binaries we encounter prevailing centrism, unity, identity: boy, girl, Korean, Chinese, biracial, male, female, body, mind. From a Deleuzian perspective, the dichotomies and centrisms that characterize the actual realities depicted in these examples become problematized, rejected, or displaced.

Deleuze and Guattari explore the displacement of binaries through new understandings of the world and consequently of subjects, bodies, materiality, and difference. Grosz (1993) eloquently summarizes their project:

> They seek to position metaphysical identities and theoretical models in a context which renders them merely effects or surface phenomena within a broader or differently conceived ontology or metaphysics. The systems of thought based on the centrality of the subject and the coherence of signification…are no longer privileged or casual terms, but effects or consequences of processes of sedimentation, the congealing or coagulation of processes, interrelations or "machines" of disparate components, functioning in provisional alignment with each other to form a working ensemble. (p. 169)

We can see in the first encounter that centrisms and binaries were not necessarily treated as effects of processes of sedimentation, but rather the differences between Chinese and Korean identities were privileged. In the second encounter the centrality of the subject is not displaced either. Thandi tries to understand the effects of racialization as she is faced with Andile's drawings. However, biracial identity is still central to her project. I will elaborate on these ideas later on in the chapter.

These new understandings of the world, described above by Grosz, are productive—they produce change that never becomes static or fixed:

> "Production" consists in those processes which create linkages between fragments, fragments of bodies and fragments of objects; and "machines" are heterogeneous disparate, discontinuous assemblages of fragments brought together in conjunctions... or severed through disjunctions and breaks, a concept not unlike a complex form of "bricolage." (Grosz, 1993, p. 173)

Deleuze's philosophy makes dichotomous thoughts become dissonant—hard to understand, a cacophony, a discordant and meaningless mixture of sounds. To develop a productive philosophy, Saldanha (2006) says, we need a *machinic* politics: "A machinic geography of bodies asks what immanent connections they forge with things and places, how they work, travel, fight, write, love—how these bodies become viscous, slow down, get into certain habits, into certain collectivities" (p. 19).

Following this philosophy, we are provoked to engage in a pedagogy that is always trying to understand what racialization, gender, and sexuality are capable of, discovering their potentialities, sensing them "hiding around" us, finding out how we can make them produce alternative assemblages (Saldanha, 2006). In this kind of pedagogy, we are not trying to find the meaning of children's dialogues, children's own productions (e.g., a drawing), children's play; different ways of interpreting them; or whether children are inherently racist/sexist or not. Instead, we must ask what the child's dialogue or drawing does and "how it connects with other things" so that we can begin to create new connections (Grosz, 1993, p. 173). For example, in Thandi's documentation, we are to ask what Andile's drawing does, what kinds of effects it produces. The drawing produced new worlds for Thandi, worlds that she had not imagined before. Another question this example raises is what new worlds were created for Andile, who became different through the creation of this drawing. Although Thandi's documentation does not engage with these questions, they are nonetheless questions that a pedagogy of action provokes for educators to consider.

○ The Problem of Politics of Identity and Recognition: Toward a Different Pedagogy

A common approach to engaging with practice moments like those described above is to practice a politics of identity or recognition with children. A politics of identity or recognition "inscribes the other onto and as the subject, and the subject as the other's counterpart" (Grosz, 2002, p. 466). If we are to follow a project of recognition that assumes fixed identities, what we might do in these moments is to reinforce entities and situate the subject (children) at the centre of our solutions (and this might be what took place in some instances in the encounters above). We tell children to accept other children who are different from themselves, that we need to include Chinese children, that deep down what is important is that we are all human beings, to be proud of their own cultural identity, and so on. What these responses do is to maintain fixed identities in which inequalities are produced, and submit marginalized identities to the recognition and valuation of others (often those who occupy dominant positions). Grosz (2002) cautions us, however, that "oppression cannot simply be resolved into failed, unsuccessful, or unaffirmed identities, identities lagging for want of recognition" (p. 468).

Instead of a politics of recognition based on identity, Grosz proposes to engage in a politics of action or imperceptibility in which identity is rethought. She writes: "The more dynamic and affirming representation is to understand identity in terms of practice: one is what one does, the history of what one has done constitutes one's character: and what one can or will do as that which is unpredictable and open" (p. 468). A politics of action "functions as a mode of rendering the subject the backdrop to a play of forces which are themselves what constitute the ever shifting and uncontrollable terrain of politics and identities" (p. 470). We move towards rethinking the concept of the subject in terms of force:, "forces act through subjects, objects, material and social worlds without distinction, producing relations of inequality and differentiation, which themselves produce ever-realigning relations of intensity or force" (Grosz, 2002, p. 469).

The concept of force then is paramount in a politics of action or imperceptibility. Force, as described by Deleuze and Guattari, encompasses complex and heterogeneous characteristics and activities, which Grosz (2002) summarizes in the following way:

- ☐ Force is always both specific and a multiplicity…and is that which both establishes and severs connections between things and relations.
- ☐ Force is always engaged in becoming. It is never stationary. It has a history and a duration. Force does not seek intentions, goals, or purposes, but simply expansion and magnification.
- ☐ Force is always a relation of intensity and thus of magnitude, a relation of more or less, never ceasing, never depleting itself.
- ☐ It is differences in the quantity of forces that produce differences in quality.

◻ Force is always contestatory: each force seeks its own expansion in its own way and time, but this inevitably places forces in relations of hostility and competition with each other, where forces seek to subdue each other, to subvert or convert each other, where the stronger seeks to overcome the weaker.

◻ Force is that which produces competition and struggle between forces functioning in the same sphere and level, but is also that which produces relations of alignment and cooperation between forces. (pp. 468–469)

In politics of imperceptibility, pedagogical work does not entail liberating/recognizing/celebrating the identities that are marginalized in the classroom, but rendering "more mobile, fluid and transformable the means by which [subjects in the classroom are] produced and represented" (p. 471). In other words, pedagogical work involves producing "a future in which forces align in ways fundamentally different from the past and present" (p. 471). This is a pedagogy that requires us to move and transform "the alignment of forces that constitute [marginalized] 'identities' and 'positions'" (p. 471).

The question to ask in relation to the encounters described above moves us away from pondering how we can make children understand concepts of inclusion and sameness, and towards understanding the forces and intensities that come together in the encounters: How can the forces and intensities that came together in these particular moments be rearranged to create new movements and new arrangements? How can we slow down the forces that create binaries and centricisms and take them somewhere else where different arrangements would be intensified (Lenz Taguchi, 2009)? This is a productive and affirmative critique that holds the possibility of recognizing moments of escape from binaries or centricisms and generating new possibilities for flight (Skott-Myhre, 2008).

We can, for example, read Andile's drawing as a moment in which she is escaping the striated spaces of biracial identity. She is generating new possibilities to what we define as Swazi-Filipina. New possibilities were opened not only during the making of the drawing, but also when Thandi and Andile revisited it. The mirror activity also generates new possibilities for the children, not necessarily the results that Thandi had anticipated, but possibilities that transformed everyone and everything involved. The mirrors activate new forces in the investigation of identities that magnify new becomings in the children. All of a sudden, the children become interested in the materiality of their bodies, what bodies are capable of doing and becoming. It appears as if the children are interested in producing a stuttering in the concept of identities and self-views, moving away from Thandi's goal of creating positive cultural self-views among the children.

○ Difference-in-Itself: From Diversity to Different/ciation

An important concept that underlies both the learning goals stated in this chapter's introduction (*British Columbia Early Learning Framework*) and the moments of practice described above is that of difference. In particular, the goals depict difference in the form of "different from." From a Deleuzian perspective, this conceptualization of difference is problematic and requires some unpacking. This specific understanding of difference is embedded in what I have identified above as a politics of identity and recognition.

> Difference is represented negatively, as the opposing class in a binary relation which is negative by virtue of its lack in relation to a standard. Difference thus becomes thought of as a state of being which is measurable by degrees of inequality or disadvantage, and the "solution" necessarily becomes the elimination of inequality or disadvantage by the reduction of degrees of difference. Difference is treated as a problem and proposed solutions aim to reduce difference by creating unity as a basis for equality. (Bignall, 2007, p. 197)

When difference is understood from a negative perspective, pedagogical work will then move towards creating social transformation in a progressive approach towards an ideal solution: "The ideal functions as a transcendent, final cause of social action, which draws history inexorably towards completion, and society towards agreement and unity" (Bignall, 2007, p. 198). From this perspective, we already know what social equity should look like in early childhood education, and the pedagogical work entails moving towards that stated ideal, towards a process of unification or equalization.

In contrast to negative notions of difference, or what Deleuze calls *difference in degree*, Deleuze proposes a positive notion of difference (*difference-in-itself*) that might be very useful in early childhood education as we attempt to create social justice in our classrooms. This is a creative difference that "is *internal* to a body as it transforms over time" (Bignall, 2007, p. 202). While a negative understanding of difference pays attention to how "bodies differ from *each other*," a positive notion of difference highlights how "bodies constantly differ from *themselves* in the process of their becoming" (p. 202). This is a *difference in kind*, a difference through which bodies constantly change in a qualitative manner and reassemble themselves to become other, to be combined differently. This positive difference is referred to as differen*c*iation (Bignall, 2007).

Deleuze proposes another related concept: differen*t*iation. While differen*c*iation involves the process of becoming something else or of transforming bodies, differen*t*iation "is the decomposition of these actual bodies back into the virtual and elementary conditions of their formation," involving a critical process of tracing back the way in which bodies had emerged (Bignall, 2007, p. 203). As explained above through the idea of a politics of action or imperceptibility, what is important is that new assemblages can then emerge as constituting elements of bodies create new connections or as assemblages are composed with different elements. Differen/iation questions the taken-for-granted nature of actual configurations of our realities.

Then, putting these two complex concepts together, Deleuze refers to "different/ciation" which involves "agents associating elements and forming relationships to produce a complex reality, while simultaneously remaining mindful that this established reality might always be recombined in alternative ways" (Bignall, 2007, p. 203). Like Bignall, I argue that the notion of different/ciation is a useful one for transforming pedagogical encounters and creating new futures of social justice. Bignall (2007) writes:

> Deleuze's concept of different/ciation translates into critical practice as the problematization of the actual or the given. The constructive aim of different/ciation is then to make possible an alternative process of actualization, in which systemic inequity or select privilege would no longer be produced. Different/ciation encourages the becoming of the actual, a shift in the way actual bodies currently relate, that they might transform to produce an alternative, more cohesive complex organization. (p. 204)

Bignall (2007) argues that practicing from a concept of different/ciation involves "a shift from a politics that criticizes lack or disadvantage, to a politics that criticizes the genealogy of presence or advantage; from unity organized at the level of the solution in the form of ideal identity, to a unity organized at the level of the problem, now conceived as the actual present; and finally, to a critical practice that is immanent to the process of transformation itself" (p. 207).

In the first encounter above, we are to criticize the forces that bring together the identities of Chineseness and Koreanness, how they have actualized, through what processes. In the dialogue, unity is presented as an ideal (e.g., "We are all friends and you have to play with everyone") at the level of the solution. Bignall (2007) argues that this unity is somewhat precarious as unity is only possible when various ways of being Chinese and Korean are excluded. It also presents both Chinese and Korean groups as creating disruption and divisiveness to the ideal unity. If instead we look at unity at the level of the problem and not the solution, only the problem is universal: positioning Chinese and Koreans against each other as well as against the Canadian national identity. The solution then needs to be diverse (and not work towards unity) and attempt to continually dismantle the problem of unity within the identities of Chinese and Korean. We then come back to the question posed above: How can the forces and intensities that came together to create Chineseness and Koreanness in these particular moments be rearranged to create new movements and new arrangements?

In the second encounter, we see how Andile—and later all the children, through the mirror activity—are invited to explore their identities. We also see that they find this exploration too limiting. As Olsson (2009) might describe it, there are leakages in the activity. The children propose a different direction— they explore the "lines" in their faces. The mirror transforms them, so that when they look at their image in the mirror something totally new has already happened. They make possible, as Bignall would argue, an alternative actualization of the activity. Identity becomes somewhat unrecognizable, even to Thandi as she reflects back and says *"I did not discern anything in their conversation that indicated negative attitudes of external beauty."* A pedagogy of action would propose that we latch onto children's desires and explorations and be open to the unpredictability this might bring, rather than closing off possibilities if what we predicted will happen does not take place. In some ways this is what Thandi was after here. She did not find what she was looking for, so she continued to explore new possibilities.

Before moving forward into other areas of analysis, a few words are needed about the children's drawings. We cannot take these drawings as representing a reality, or representing children's understandings of difference and identity. Rather we are to look at these drawings as constructing new realities and new meanings that might not have been possible until now (see Chapter 7). Our task in a pedagogy of action is to think of the children's drawings as an actualization of "what was in the air" at the moment in which the drawings were produced. This is how we can begin to think about children's identities—never final, always shifting, and always becoming different. In the words of Deleuze and Guattari, "this text [or image] constitutes an assemblage and must be read as such; in this text there are "lines of articulation or segmentarity, strata and territories; but also lines of flight, movements of deterritorialization and destratification" (Deleuze & Guattari, 1987, p. 3).

o Bodies and Social Justice

As I noted in the introduction, early childhood education has responded to the systemic (rather than individual) realities of social injustices by analyzing the ways in which language and discourse work to create conditions of inequality. Recently, however, early childhood scholars have made us aware of what we have lost by focusing only on language and discourse (see Olsson, 2009; Lenz Taguchi, 2009) and displacing materiality because of the tendency for it to be essentialized. Lenz Taguchi (2009), for example, argues that it is necessary to bring the material back to discussions of social justice in early childhood education curriculum, but a few words of caution are in place. Returning the material to discussions of social justice requires conceptualizations of materiality that allow us to move beyond the binaries of mind/body, interior/exterior, subject/object, and nature/culture (Grosz, 1993).

Bodies are key to discussions of materiality and social justice. The two encounters described above illustrate the important role that discourses and the materiality of bodies play in early childhood education. Bodies are always present, affecting and being affected, interacting with other bodies and becoming other. So, how can we move beyond the binary mind/body and the essentializing aspects of modern theories of the body? Bodies, according to Deleuze and Guattari, are not defined by what they are, but by what they can do, what they are capable of. Elizabeth Grosz (1993) says:

> The body is regarded neither as a locus for a conscious subject nor as an organically determined object; instead…the body is analysed and assessed more in terms of what it can do, the things it can perform, the linkages it establishes, the transformations it undergoes and the machinic connections it forms with other bodies, what it can link with, how it can proliferate its capacities—a rare, affirmative understanding of the body. (p. 171)

Bodies are conceptualized as flows, energies, discontinuous processes, and intensities in constant flux, forming connections with other bodies (human and non-human, animate and inanimate) and social practices. Springgay (2008) notes:

> The notion of an embodied subject is central to my understanding of living in the world as difference. I take the concept of the body to be a flow of energies and surface intensities; a complex interplay of social and affective forces. This is a shift away from the psychoanalytic idea of the body as a map of semiotic inscriptions and culturally enforced codes, towards an understanding of the embodied subject as becoming, as enfleshed. (p. 1)

These ideas highlight the relationality of bodies, always connecting to many other bodies, always changing and shifting their connections in an immanent process.

Bringing Back the Materiality of "Race"

The above discussion of bodies, as well as the importance of bodies in the context of the encounters described above, opens windows onto new discussions of "race" and racialization. Specifically, it opens up discussions and arguments around the materiality of race. As I have been elaborating in this chapter, we need to be able to generate discussions that include the materiality of bodies, therefore we need new ways to theorize the materiality of race.

With the discursive turn, race has been conceptualized as a matter of language and mental categories primarily through the argument that "race" is a social construction (Saldanha, 2006). Saldanha suggests that this approach to racial transcendence, although justified for many reasons, could be rethought using Deleuze's material ontological theories, allowing us to move beyond the reductionist and positivist aspects of previous theories of materiality. He argues that:

> the insistence on the natural stability of "races" has been integral to empire, genocide, and eugenics, and continues to be evoked to justify racial hierarchies and antagonisms. But why are nature and biology, just like the body and matter in general, assumed to be static and deterministic? What if the cultural and biological dimensions of race are *both* inherently dynamic? Race is like everything else, much *more* than a social construction. Race is impure from the start. (p. 15)

Saldanha (2006) proposes to engage in theorizing "the heterogeneous [and complex] materiality of the social" that involves rethinking biology as fixed and given to think of it instead as "the science of *life*: of movement and unpredictability at every level" (p. 16). This rethinking moves away from the idea that racial hierarchy is "natural" and therefore unavoidable (p. 17): "Human phenotypes can be understood as continuous and multifaceted, not discrete or linear; as much products of isolation as of migration and miscegenation" (p. 17).

To bring the complex materiality of the social back to discussions of racism without falling into the essentializing nature of most biological theories of race, Saldanha argues, we need to move beyond the idea of race as a taxonomic ordering, "a logic of solids and grids" (p. 19). Instead, race needs to be "conceived as a chain of contingency, in which the connections between its constituent components are not given, but are made viscous through local attractions" (p. 18). He argues that a nonessentialist understanding of race challenges the binary of self/ other and, as I described above, sees bodies as emergent.

Following Deleuze and Guattari, Saldanha (2006) conceptualizes race as a machinic assemblage—an *event* that "cannot be transcended, only understood and rearranged" (Saldanha, 2006, p. 9). Race as an event constitutes "an assemblage of things, phenotypes and practices which is made, remade, revised and reformed in the constant flux (and occasional showcase event) comprising daily life" (Smith, 2009, p. 500). Saldanha writes:

> A machinic geography of phenotype...studies how certain bodies stick to certain spaces, how they are chained by hunger, cold, darkness, mud, poverty, crime, glances

full of envy and anxiety. The segregation between colonist and colonized is the *apparently* binary result of many nitty-gritty material processes which, when analysed, render it a lot less binary. This also means that race is devious in inventing new ways of chaining bodies. Race is creative, constantly morphing….Deleuze and Guattari might say that what defines race is not rigidity or inevitability, but its "lines of flight." (2006, p. 20)

What becomes important in practice is to understand how race works, "how economic, cultural, phenotypical and other disparities open those bodies to certain kinds of interactions and transformations" (Saldanha, 2006, p. 500). Saldanha proposes that we not work towards erasing or transcending race in our practice. Instead, we need to engage in understanding what race (or gender or sexuality) "*is* and *can be*, in as many variations as possible" (Hames-Garcia, 2008, p. 330). We need to think creatively about what race can be instead of trying to make it go away from our classrooms. Understanding what race can be allows us to work towards making race work differently. What new elements can race be linked to and, as a result, transformed into something new? What kinds of encounters are possible?

The encounters I described in this chapter are powerful instances of race as event. In the first scenario, race is what *emerges* when bodies come together with other bodies, with tables in the classroom, with the food the children are eating, the smells from the food, and so on. The language that children use *charges* phenotype in this moment. There are phenotype differences before the exclamation "No Korean children." What this exclamation does is to "circumscribe what [phenotype] is capable of doing in particular spaces (such as in the playground or at the lunch table). The memories of colonization that are carried around by bodies also charge the situation, as do the memories of conversations in the playground and conversations with families.

Race emerges and works differently in the second encounter, and different possibilities come into view. Here we can see how phenotype matters. Thandi sees Andile's drawing as not matching how she knows Andile's phenotype. Phenotype in this example is capable of raising suspicions for Thandi, of activating fears, desires, and stereotypes. But as Saldanha (2006) notes, it is not that phenotype "*mechanically* invokes histories and geographies of race, but within a racialised regime of vision, phenotype does always matter somehow—to experience, imagination, and belonging, to interaction and the allocation of bodies" (p. 11). The embodiment of race is real in this example; it matters for what happens in the classroom next. The drawing itself also activates and charges phenotype. Following the drawing, Andile's phenotype "demands active management," "is alive," connects her to histories of racialization and colonialism (Saldanha, 2006, p. 12). In the mirror activity, phenotype is activated differently. Race emerges through the activation of different forces, creating a different assemblage from the one assembled before. The mirrors, the reflection back from the mirror, the black pencil, the proximity of the children's bodies around the table, children's different phenotypes, the light that comes into the room, what children say at that moment, and other human and non-human things charge phenotype differently. This is the machinic assemblage Saldanha (2006) refers to, in which its entities are not "perfectly knowable cause-effect sequences" but can be understood "as bundles of virtual capacities" (p. 19).

If, then, we view race as a machinic assemblage, in practice we are to be "prepared for the unpreparable" because "phenotype connects in infinite ways" (p. 19)—as we can see in the second example. Race and racism always creep up and we need to understand how, rather than making race go away. Saldanha (2006) notes: "Race is always creative, constantly morphing, now disguised as sexual desire, now as *la mission civilatrice*, all the while weaving new elements in its wake" (p. 20). In the series of encounters that Thandi relates, we can see how race is subtle, not necessarily rigid, how it morphs and takes up different lines of flight. Therefore, we need more than one solution (e.g., unity or equality) to racism. We need many different ways to make racism stutter.

o Closing Thoughts

The chapter has explored possibilities for engaging in a different kind of pedagogy for social justice that works against binaries and closed identities and that follows what Lenz Taguchi (2009) refers to as an ethics of immanence and potentialities. Such an ethics addresses life in "an affirmative, evolutionary and creative way, in that it always looks for the virtual possibilities and potentialities" in the event, and does not necessarily look for what is lacking in the moment or how to work towards reaching predefined goals (p. 176). Lenz Taguchi suggests that we investigate how different forces and intensities become productive: "We should try to make ourselves aware of what happens in the events of the present and look for what *might* be possible, what emerges, and what *can* become" (p. 177). We should ask "what it is we *can* do *here and now* to affect something or someone in a different way in line with an affirmative thinking of unknown potentialities, rather than what we *should* do in line with the transcendent idea of a higher value to be strived for" (p. 176). This ethics requires a pedagogy for social justice, perhaps a pedagogy of action and imperceptibility, that does not necessarily consist of solving a conflict between groups or individuals through recognition of marginalized groups or unity between groups. A curriculum for social justice, Grosz (2002) would argue, requires instead a struggle to mobilize and realign the forces that create marginalized identities, transforming them until they are unrecognizable.

REFERENCES

Bignall, S. (2007). Indigenous peoples and a Deleuzian theory of practice. In A. Hickey-Moody & P. Malins (Eds.), *Deleuzian encounters: Studies in contemporary social issues* (pp. 197–211). Basingstoke, UK: Palgrave Macmillan.

Buchanan, I., & Thoburn, N. (2008). Introduction: Deleuze and politics. In I. Buchanan & N. Thoburn (Eds.), *Deleuze and politics* (pp. 1–12). Edinburgh, UK: Edinburgh University Press.

Dahlberg, G., Moss, P., & Pence, A. R. (2007). *Beyond quality in early childhood education and care: Languages of evaluation.* London: Taylor & Francis.

Deleuze, G., & Guattari, F. L. (1987). *A thousand plateaus: Capitalism and schizophrenia.* Minneapolis, MN: University of Minnesota Press.

Government of British Columbia. (2008). *British Columbia early learning framework.* Victoria, BC: Ministry of Education, Ministry of Health, Ministry of Children and Family Development, & British Columbia Early Learning Advisory Group.

Grosz, E. (1993). A thousand tiny sexes: Feminism and rhizomatics. *Topoi, 12,* 167–179.

Grosz, E. (2002). A politics of imperceptibility: A response to "Anti-racism, multiculturalism and the ethics of identification." *Philosophy & Social Criticism, 28*(4), 463–472.

Hames-Garcia, M. (2008). How real is race? In S Alaimo & S. Hekman (Eds.), *Material feminisms* (pp. 308–339). Bloomington, IN: Indiana University Press.

Lenz Taguchi, H. (2006). Reconceptualizing early childhood education: Challenging taken for-granted ideas. In J. Einarsdottir & J. Wagner (Eds.), *Nordic childhoods and early education: Philosophy, research, policy and practice in Denmark, Finland, Iceland, Norway and Sweden* (pp. 257–287). Greenwich, CT: Information Age.

Lenz Taguchi, H. (2008, September). *Doing justice in early childhood education? Justice to whom and to what?* Paper presented at the European Early Childhood Education Research Association Conference, Stavanger, Norway.

Lenz Taguchi, H. (2009). *Going beyond the theory/practice divide in early childhood education: Introducing an intra-active pedagogy.* New York: Routledge.

MacNaughton, G. (2000). *Rethinking gender in early childhood education.* London: Paul Chapman.

MacNaughton, G. (2005). *Doing Foucault in early childhood studies: Applying poststructural ideas.* New York: Routledge.

MacNaughton, G., & Davis, K. (Eds.). (2009). *"Race" and early childhood education: An international approach to identity, politics, and pedagogy.* New York: Palgrave Macmillan.

Moulard-Leonard, V. (2005). Revolutionary becomings: Negritude's anti-humanist humanism. *Human Studies, 28*(3), 231–249.

Olsson, L. (2009). *Movement and experimentation in young children's learning: Deleuze and Guattari in early childhood education.* New York: Routledge.

Pacini-Ketchabaw, V., & Berikoff, A. (2008). The politics of difference and diversity: From young children's violence to creative power expressions. *Contemporary Issues in Early Childhood, 9*(3), 256–264.

Pence, A., & Hix-Small, H. (2007). Global Children in the Shadow of the Global Child, *International Journal of Educational Policy, Research, and Practice, 8*(1), 83–100.

Pence, A., & Pacini-Ketchabaw, V. (2010). Investigating Quality Project: Opening possibilities in early childhood care and education policies and practices in Canada. In N. Yelland (Ed.), *Contemporary perspectives on early childhood education* (pp. 121–140). Maidenhead, UK: Open University Press.

Ritchie, J. (Ed.) (2007). Seeking pathways beyond colonialization [Special issue]. *Childrenz Issues, 11*(1).

Saldanha, A. (2006). Re-ontologising race: The machinic geography of phenotype. *Environment and Planning D: Society and Space, 24,* 9–24.

Skott-Myhre, H. (2008). *Youth and subculture as creative force: Creating new spaces for radical youth work.* Toronto, ON: University of Toronto Press.

Smith, L. T. (1999). *Decolonizing methodologies: Research and Indigenous peoples.* Otago, New Zealand: University of Otago Press.

Smith, S. (2009). Author meets critics: a set of reviews and response. Introduction [Review of the book *Psychedelic white: Goa trance and the viscosity of race,* by A. Saldanha]. *Social & Cultural Geography, 10*(4), 499–501.

Soto, L. D., & Swadener, B. B. (2002). Toward liberatory early childhood theory, research and praxis: Decolonizing a field. *Contemporary Issues in Early Childhood, 3*(1), 38–66.

Springgay, S. (2008). *Body knowledge and curriculum: Pedagogies of touch in youth and visual culture.* New York: Peter Lang.

Taylor, A. (2007). Playing with difference: The cultural politics of childhood belonging. *The International Journal of Diversity in Organisations, Communities and Nations, 7*(3), 143–149.

Taylor, A. (2008). Taking account of childhood excess: "Bringing the elsewhere home." In B. Davies (Ed.), *Judith Butler in conversation: Analyzing the texts and talk of everyday life* (pp. 195–216). New York: Routledge.

Viruru, R. (2001). *Decolonizing early childhood education: An Indian perspective.* New Delhi: Sage.

Viruru, R., & Cannella, G. (2004). *Childhood and postcolonization: Power, education, and contemporary practice.* London: RoutledgeFalmer.

CHAPTER NINE

○ Disrupting Colonial Power through Literacy: A Story about Creating Inuttitut-Language Children's Books

Mary Caroline Rowan

Indigenous stories, Archibald (2008) believes, "are at the core of our cultures" (p. 139). Stories ignite the imagination, offer cautions, reveal histories, detail cultural knowledge, clarify family connections, articulate sacred beliefs, complicate understandings, expose scandals, record daily life, support us in understanding who and why and where we are, and stimulate us to dream of new challenges. Thomas King (2003) asserts that telling Native stories gives Indigenous peoples a place at the table and positions them to challenge hegemonic assumptions.

This chapter is about using stories to disrupt colonial discourses. It describes how the Nunavik Educators' Bookmaking Workshop produced 19 Inuttitut children's books as part of the Atuasilaurluuk (let's read together) project. The project and the workshop were conceived to promote and preserve the Inuttitut language and Inuit culture through the publication of children's books written and illustrated by Nunavimiut (people of Nunavik). This work was grounded in a depth of importance accorded during an Elders' conference in Akulivik, Nunavik, in August 2000. The Elders stated:

> We believe that children have the right to childcare that is culturally and linguistically appropriate, incorporating the values and traditions of their parents and community.

During that conference, the Elders passed a resolution mandating Avataq Cultural Institute to develop culturally appropriate Inuttitut-language materials for Inuit babies, toddlers, and preschoolers. The dream is that these children's books will provide the foundation for an emerging Inuttitut children's literature.

This chapter briefly describes the geographical and cultural context for the Nunavik Educators' Bookmaking Workshop and explores some ideas integral to the project. I examine the content of three of the books and consider the possibilities the books present both to preserve and promote Inuttitut language and Inuit culture and to provide a conduit to explore contemporary and historical meanings in Nunavik life. The imprint of colonialism in contemporary Inuit life is made visible through dialogue with the books, leading me to consider the possibilities of bookmaking as a way to disrupt colonial discourses.

○ Inuit Culture and Inuttitut Language in Nunavik

Nunavik occupies 563,515 square kilometres—the top third of the province of Québec, Canada. It has a population of about 9200 Inuit who live in 15 communities along the shores of Hudson's Bay, Hudson Straight, and Ungava Bay. The Indigenous language is Inuttitut.

Inuit culture has been severely challenged by colonization and the introduction of the wage economy. Fifty years ago, most Inuit in Nunavik lived as hunters and gatherers in small camps situated along the shores and bays connected to the waters of the Arctic Ocean. Extended family groups lived together. Elders were highly respected and children were cared for by the collective, with older siblings assuming many childrearing roles. The imposition of Euro-Western schooling dramatically altered Inuit life, culture, and power structures. When Inuit children were placed in government-run schools in the late 1940s,

> this marked the first time in Inuit history that children had been segregated from the rest of their society. Learning was taken out of the realm of the family and placed in an isolated setting. Since most of the families still lived in isolated camps across the north, children were airlifted to the schools at the administrative centres where they usually spent the winter. Schooling no longer consisted of teaching children how to survive in a hunting society. The courses for study were similar to those offered in southern Canada. Curriculum was based on an urban industrialized lifestyle that was entirely foreign to Inuit children. Moreover instruction took place in English under the guidance of non-Inuit teachers. (Department of Indian Affairs and Northern Development, 1990, p. 56)

Families felt powerless and disoriented by the absence of their children. Eventually many families moved from camps to town, both to be reunited and live with their children and on the promise of federally funded health, education, and housing programs. Where previously families were responsible for all aspects of life, including health, education, and justice, the government took over. With the imposition of the colonial structure came colonial language and culture. These changes disrupted family relationships, undermined the traditional role of the Elder, and interrupted the intergenerational transmission of Inuit knowledge.

Like other Indigenous languages, Inuttitut is in a perilous state. According to Taylor and Wright (2003), "the stark reality is that indigenous languages of Aboriginal people have all but disappeared in Canada, the United States, and indeed around the world" (p. 3). Of 83 known, distinct Aboriginal languages in Canada, Inuttitut is one of only three that are considered to be healthy (Taylor & Wright, 2003). In Nunavik, Inuttitut appears to be strong and vital. Approximately 97% of Inuit in the region report Inuttitut as their mother tongue (Duhaime, 2008, p. 53) and 85% of families speak the language at home. Yet Taylor and Wright, who conducted a multi-year study in Nunavik on language and education, provide four main reasons why every effort must be made to support and protect the Inuttitut language in Nunavik.

First, people speak and understand Inuttitut better than they can write it. Taylor and Wright suggest that "literacy skills will need to be improved if Inuttitut is to achieve status that will allow it to compete with mainstream languages" (p. 5). Second, English is the lingua franca that connects French, Inuttitut, and English language speakers. This reality leads to a pattern of increased fluency in English at the expense of ability in Inuttitut. The phenomenon, which Taylor and Wright refer to as *subtractive bilingualism* (p. 7), can be extremely detrimental to the frequency with which Inuttitut is spoken, as evidenced by statistics from Canada's other three Inuit regions: Nunavut reports that 83% of those whose mother tongue is Inuttitut speak the language; Nunatsiavut reports 23%; and the Inuvialuit region reports only 14% (Duhaime, 2008). A third undermining factor is location: People speak Inuttitut on the land and at home, but are speaking it less at work. For a language to remain strong it must be spoken at the work place, yet people in Nunavik are increasingly conducting their business in English and French. Finally, the prevalence of English in the media is pervasive. By far the majority of television programs are in English. Some Inuttitut language information is available on the Internet, but most searches result in English language information. Taylor and Wright conclude that "dramatic steps will need to be taken to protect the strength of Inuttitut, or it will become extinct as has happened to so many Native languages" (p. 8).

Crago, Annahatak, and Ningiurvik (1993) have written about social changes in Nunavik related to the introduction of formal education. These include the disappearance of *aquasiit* (special songs created uniquely and specifically for each Inuk child) and a diminishment in the use of *nilliujuusiq* (affectionate, nonsensical baby talk) and *piarainjausiitt* (specialized baby talk). In their study, which examined two sets of older and young mothers in two communities, they found that older women used a specialized vocabulary with babies up to about 3½ years of age. In contrast, young mothers "expressed disdain for this specialized vocabulary" (p. 213). According to the older women, young Inuit children were not expected to participate in adult conversations. Children were expected to eat quietly, listen carefully, comprehend meanings, and follow directions. As the authors explain, "the early comprehension of directives is part of a process of acquiring cultural membership, of becoming an appropriate Inuk who knows how to learn by looking and listening" (p. 214). Inuit parents in the past did not ask questions of children or practice Euro-Western "please and thank you" protocols. The work of Crago et al. (1993) shows how almost 20 years ago communication patterns were changing and intimate ways of relating with children were starting to shift as the younger mothers seemed to be "adapting their childrearing practices in view of the rapid social and cultural changes" (p. 219). This may be seen as a process of redefinition—"the social construction of a new identity" (Crago et al., 1993, p. 219).

Graham H. Smith (2000), writing about the Māori, explains how Indigenous culture and knowledge have been compromised through colonization. He writes:

> For Māori the history of colonization has been extremely painful: Not only has it caused loss and change of culture, but it has also brought about systemic cultural denigration and undermined the validity and legitimacy of Māori knowledge and culture. The consequences of this process go beyond the assimilation of culture and reach also into the loss of the mana (integrity, self-esteem, dignity) of a people. That is Māori culture, language, and values became regarded as not simply different, but inferior. (p. 59)

Smith's depiction of pain, loss, and destruction to Māori culture and integrity is transferable to other Indigenous groups, including Inuit. The effects of colonization in Nunavik include low literacy rates and levels of formal education; reliance on social support; family violence and child abuse; poor nutrition; high suicide rates; shorter lives; alcoholism; and drug addiction. These problems are based in racism, social injustice, and poverty and compounded by issues related to shaken confidence in Inuit systems and families (Inuit Tapirisat of Canada, 2001).

○ Disrupting Colonial Discourses through Literacy

Linda Tuhiwai Smith (1999) writes about the "globalization of knowledge" and how "Western culture constantly reaffirms the West's view of itself as the centre of legitimate knowledge, the arbiter of what counts as knowledge and the source of 'civilized' knowledge" (p. 63). Decolonizing, according to Smith, was once "viewed as the formal process of handing over instruments of government [but] is now recognized as a long-term process involving the bureaucratic, cultural, linguistic and psychological divesting of colonial power" (as cited in Iseke-Barnes, 2008, p. 123). Postcolonial discourse provides "a new consciousness and a conceptual framework that challenges and deconstructs structural inequality, and resists relations of domination" (Weenie, 2008, p. 549). It sets out to dismantle hidden meanings and messages of colonialism and reconfigures the landscape in a way that prioritizes Indigenous voices (Rau, 2007, p. 34).

For the purposes of this chapter, I understand postcolonial discourse to entail making visible ways in which colonial structures disintegrate Indigenous knowledges and ways of being. Its aim is to elucidate actions and activities which have the potential to make accessible Indigenous knowledges—in this case Inuit knowledges through the creation of Inuttitut language children's books.

Children develop language and literacy by communicating thoughts in a variety of ways, including by "experiencing stories of their own culture" (Government of British Columbia, 2008, p. 29). Children's "personal, social and literate identities are co-constructed in their interactions with others and by the expectations ... held by others" (Government of New Brunswick, 2007, p. 30). Literacy is important because it provides a means to construct identities and because it enables the development of reading and writing skills that facilitate access to information. In Nunavik, literacy is important as a means to protect, promote, support, and sustain the Inuttitut language and fortify Inuit culture.

Stories are a powerful way to come to know about how people make meaning in their lives. In *The World of Tivi Etok: The Life and Art of an Inuit Elder*, Jobie Weetaluktuk (2008) shares stories of life in 1930s Nunavik: Tivi Etok's first fish, first feast, first rifle; his experiences of spirituality, starvation, and marriage. Here's a sample from the section "Getting Lost and Found":

> I used to get lost even when I still had a dog team. I was younger then, and thought I knew more than my dogs. I know exactly why I got lost. In low visibility I thought I knew the way and would start commanding the dogs which direction to go. "Turn, turn," I would command insistently. When they were reluctant to obey, I commanded them all the more. I was the master, after all. Then we would get lost. I just commanded the dogs some more, hoping to find a landmark I could identify. When we were hopelessly lost I would then shut up and just let the dogs figure it out. Eventually

they would bring me home. They knew the way. They could smell the trail even when it was covered by windblown snow. (Weetaluktuk, 2008, p. 198)

Tivi's story reveals meaning and relevance based in Inuit knowledge. It enables us to imagine life in Nunavik in the early 20th century. The goal of the Atuasilaurluuk bookmaking project was to create for young children new stories and story lines based on Inuit communities, drawing on local knowledge, and told in the Inuttitut language. Paulo Freire's thinking was motivational in planning for the project. Freire is known for his work in critical literacy and his belief that literacy education provides a way for people to see inequities and to negotiate for social justice (Viruru, 2006). As Ada and Campoy (2004) articulate, "literacy can advance the critical consciousness that leads to speaking one's personal and social truth" (p. 14).

o "Let's Tell a Story"

Unikkaangualaurtaa ("Let's Tell a Story"; Avataq Cultural Institute, 2006) was the first book published in the effort to meet the Elders' stated objective of creating culturally meaningful materials for young Inuit children. The research for the *Unikkaangualaurtaa* manual took place entirely in Inuttitut and was the collaboration of a unilingual Elder, Elisapee Inukpuk, and a bilingual teacher, Stephanie Pov. The team visited 14 Nunavik communities and met with Elders, educators, parents, and children. The book itself is a collection of 26 stories told by Nunavimiut, each accompanied by a song, craft, and game. Inuit educators and program administrators have celebrated this curriculum guide for meeting an important need for Inuttitut language and culturally appropriate Inuit resources. The volume, which has been reprinted twice, is also available in English and French and has been distributed to Aboriginal Head Start sites throughout Canada. As important as this book has been to the goal of developing culturally appropriate Inuttitut language materials for young children, it was not enough.

In the spring of 2006, Kativik Regional Government (KRG) invited Avataq Cultural Institute (ACI), a nonprofit organization whose mission is to preserve, protect, and promote Inuit culture and the Inuttitut language, to develop a set of Inuttitut language books for young children (0–5 years) in child care. ACI contracted my consulting company, Tagataga, Inc., to coordinate the bookmaking project, with funding from the KRG. I have been working on projects related to developing, designing, and delivering licensed childcare services in Inuit communities since 1987, when I was living in Iqaluit, Nunavut, and sought Inuttitut language and Inuit culturally meaningful daycare programs for my children.[1]

Ritchie and Rau (2007) write about getting beyond clothing, songs, and symbols—what Whyte (1982, cited in Ball & Pence, 2006, p. 5) refers to as the "beads and feathers" approach to developing curriculum. Writing about early childhood education in Māori programs, Ritchie and Rau encourage curriculum developers to move "much further to include deeper signifiers such as culturally specific patterns of interaction and emotion, philosophical conceptions and childrearing practices" (p. 107). Getting deeper, to get at Inuit knowledge and find ways to produce that knowledge in programs for young Inuit children, has been a driving force of my work. Would the books present an opportunity to investigate Inuit ways of being and becoming? Could the bookmaking project help to uncover and reaffirm Inuit knowledge by telling stories about Inuit ways of knowing and being? Could we, by making Inuttitut language books for young children and sharing the stories in the childcare centres throughout the region, position Inuttitut as a serious and potentially enduring language? Could bookmaking provide a way of "getting deep"?

Few books are available in Nunavik for children to pick up and read. Many of the story books originating from publishing houses in North America, Great Britain, and Europe show pictures and tell stories depicting the dominant discourse of the colonizer such as the cute little bunny, the domesticated doggie, trees, princes and palaces, tall city buildings, farms, highways, white-skinned nuclear families—stories that employ visual references far removed from, and written in languages foreign to, the Arctic context of the young Inuit child. I have wondered how these stories and images interfere with and disrupt the grounding of Inuit knowledge.

Roberts and Crawford (2008) argue that literature "serves as a point of reference so children can better understand their life experiences" (p. 13). The goal in developing the Atuasilaurluuk bookmaking project was to create a base of Inuttitut children's literature that could serve as a meaningful reference point for young children 5 years of age or younger. Inuit authors and illustrators from Nunavik would create these books. The stories would be linguistically rich and based on the life experiences of young children living in Canada's north. The illustrations would be beautiful, stimulating, and intriguing.

o A Bookmaking Workshop for Early Childhood Educators

The idea of involving early childhood educators in the bookmaking project and developing a workshop for them came together when I read Alma Flor Ada and F. Isabel Campoy's (2004) *Authors in the Classroom: A Transformative Education*

Process. Ada and Campoy base their work in "a synthesis of theoretical principles from various disciplines" (p. 11) including constructivist theory, feminist theory, aesthetics, critical theory, multiculturalism, anti-bias education, critical pedagogy, and bilingual education. These theories resonated closely with my work in Nunavik; Ada and Campoy employed words that articulated issues of concern and described ideas that were forming in my mind. For example, the transformative education model sees home and community knowledge as integral parts of students' lives and as valuable sources of knowledge. The authors articulate the benefits of teachers as writers: When teachers write and share the process, Ada and Campoy state, they "offer a valuable model.... The more empowered teachers feel the more able they will be to help their students become empowered" (2004, p. 32).

I joined with Stephanie Pov, the educational program counselor for Kativik Regional Government Child Care who was identified as the KRG project representative, to prepare for the bookmaking workshop. In planning the Nunavik Educators' Bookmaking Workshop, our hope was that the educators would produce books in which young children in the childcare centres could see themselves, in their own world, in their own community. The idea was that children's cultural identities would be strengthened by creating stories that featured local language and realities. In our workshop the educators would create Inuttitut language stories—which we anticipated would provide story lines consistent with local Inuit practices. Making local stories available has great potential for affirming Inuit knowledge and ways; this is particularly valuable for young children growing up in communities struggling with imposed Western educational, health, and social systems and compromised Indigenous cultural value systems.

Educators in Nunavik have been making their own books for years. They have taken the stories from *Unikkaangualaurtaa* and made little books, and they have fabricated their own stories including wonderful touch and feel books using seal skin, caribou skin, shells, bone, and other materials from the land as well as body books featuring Inuit children and Inuttitut language text. Educators have also taken English-/French-language books and pasted Inuttitut language labels over the script. We wanted to go much deeper. Weenie (2008) describes Aboriginal curriculum as a way of including content that makes up "our embodied way of knowing" (p. 552). She sees in curriculum a way to "speak/write our way into existence" (Davies, 2000, as cited in Weenie p. 552), and we did too. The project specifically set out to provide opportunities for early childhood educators to connect their cultural knowledge with their work and to create opportunities to see themselves as capable, competent, and creative. We saw curriculum as a way to address inequities and rectify problems related to disadvantage, through the production of local stories and the recognition of educators' knowledge. We hoped that Inuit educators in our workshop would feel creative, comfortable, and agentic.

During the initial planning meeting, Stephanie and I set out the following project principles:

- ❑ We value Inuit children and the opportunities that picture books create.
- ❑ We value Inuttitut language in the childcare centre. The books will be in Inuttitut.
- ❑ We value Nunavik-based knowledge. We'll use Nunavik resources.
- ❑ We value Inuit culture and knowledge. Our books are in Inuttitut and about Inuit.

The Nunavik Educators' Bookmaking Workshop involved 30 hours of training spread over 5 days. In October 2008, 15 early childhood educators and 2 pedagogical counselors from 9 Nunavik communities assembled in Salluit along with the writer-in-residence and the 2 facilitators (Stephanie Pov and myself). The training took place in Inuttitut and English. The writing was all done in Inuttitut. The goal was that each participant would create a children's story book in Inuttitut. The workshop began with an activity where the educators shared their own handmade materials. It continued with a session in which they rewrote old Inuit legends into language appropriate for young children and one in which they created poetry using items collected from the land. It concluded with the production of an Inuttitut language story, ready for publication.

Stephanie and I developed 10 main objectives as the basis for the learning cycles; a selection of key objectives is considered below with examples of how they were enacted in the workshop and discussion of their significance.

1. *To share examples of homemade books that people have made at their own centres.* The participants brought with them an array of homemade books and presented them to the group. These included a ringed book with photos of the children from the centre; photocopied pencil-coloured Bible stories with Inuttitut text; a picture book about Inuit clothing including *kamiks* (sealskin boots); a tactile book featuring a sealskin cutout of a seal; a body part book complete with labelling in syllabics and a "handbook" where the pages were cutouts in the shape of a hand laminated on brightly coloured paper. These books represented the majority of the available Inuttitut-language children's literature in the region.

   Ada and Campoy (2004) write that "the process of transformative pedagogy relies on reawakening and connecting with the inherent desire to learn, creating loving and caring relationships and environments that strengthen the arts" (p. 14). As the educators shared their homemade books with their peers I wondered if this process of transformation was taking place.

2. *To examine commercial books and determine what makes for a "good Inuttitut-language children's book."* We brought over a hundred books to the session, including Inuttitut-language books from Nunavik, Nunavut, and Greenland; a range of classics from the English-language tradition of children's literature, such as Bill Martin's *Brown Bear, What Do You See?* and Eric Carle's *The Very Hungry Caterpillar*; a collection of commercially available books about Inuit and the Arctic; soft tactile books for babies; and stubby, hard, small-hand-sized board books for toddlers.

Books transmit cultural norms and understandings; many commercially available books are inaccurate, offensive, and objectifying of Indigenous peoples (Roberts, Deans, & Holland, 2005; Taylor & Patterson, 2001). Iseke-Barnes and Danard (2007, cited in Iseke-Barnes, 2009b) write: "Stereotypes of Indigenous peoples, which have been promoted around the world, are maintained to support the beliefs and biases of Western society and exercise control" (p. 30). Thus our selection of sample books was careful and critical. Our intent was to create an opportunity for the educators to reflect on the qualities of books they liked. We wanted to prepare them to create their own books from their own experiences about their own communities, with a considered opinion of what makes a "good Inuttitut-language children's book." One quality of a "good book" we identified was that it represent Inuit children. Ada and Campoy (2004) write: "Because schools emphasize the value of books, it is the school's responsibility to ensure the students' families and communities are fully represented in these books, that they are inclusive, rather than exclusionary" (p. 33).

A second "good book" quality delineated in the project principles was that it be written in Inuttitut. McIvor (2005) writes:

> Knowing the language of one's ancestors greatly contributes to a sense of belonging and a connectedness to one's primary group and offers stability for coping with adult responsibilities later in life. Furthermore, by immersing children in Indigenous language, a negative impact on self-identity and self-image can be reversed. This is an important strategy to develop resiliency in Aboriginal children who may face racism and other disadvantages of being Aboriginal in a colonial society. (p. 6)

Weenie (2008) suggests that decolonization takes place through the process of speaking Indigenous languages. She explains that syntax and word order are "indicative of a different way of seeing and experiencing the world" (p. 554). In the Nunavik Educators' Bookmaking Workshop we wanted the educators to conceive the ideas of their books in Inuttitut, to discuss the structure of their speech and the expressions of the characters in Inuttitut. We wanted to support educators in creating stories that originated within Inuit spaces and incorporated Inuit views. We thought that one way to do this was through the Inuttitut language.

3. *To meet, listen, and work with a published Nunavik-based author.* Emily Tooloogak Novalinga (who passed away suddenly in October 2009) was a successful, published, Nunavik-based Inuk children's author and poet. Emily came to support the educators' artistic development and took part in the workshop as the writer-in-residence. She provided inspiration and literary expertise. While in Salluit, Emily read from her book *L'écho du Nord* (Novalinga, 2005). She wrote and illustrated a new book, *Foggy These Days,* based on the legend of the Kuuttaaq River (Novalinga, 2008). She participated in the educators' workshops, made a wonderful action poem, read her poetry on the local radio, visited Inuttitut language classes at both the high school and elementary schools, and was the featured author at a special community event held at the library. After the Salluit session was over, Emily told me about her dream to travel around Nunavik sharing her stories.

Emily provided a powerful role model. She shared herself as an author and poet, as a thinker, as an Inuk woman. She presented the possibility for the educators to see themselves as writers. She did this through her own authorship and enthusiasm for story telling and story sharing. When Emily presented her stories, the room drew still and we engaged with her, as she enchanted us with words that stimulated visual images and with soundscapes created by her body and voice. Emily opened the door to the educators seeing themselves as authors because she spoke in Inuttitut and drew on culturally meaningful images and references from within the Nunavik region. Weenie (2008) explains how seeing ourselves as we are is a source of strength. Davies (2000) speaks of subjects "who take up the act of authorship, of speaking and writing in ways that are disruptive of current discourses, that invent and break old bonds, that create new subject positions" (p. 66). Davies provides a poststructuralist definition of agency as a sense of oneself as one who can go beyond the given meaning in any one discourse and forge something new, through a combination of previously unrelated discourses, through the invention of words and concepts that capture a shift in consciousness that is beginning to occur, or through imagining not what is, but what might be (p. 67).

4. *To make a childhood memory story.* Eileen Hughes (2007), who writes about her work with the Chevak people in Alaska, explains how the "people in Chevak struggle between preserving their cultural values and traditions and integrating Western beliefs" (p. 48). Hughes emphasizes "the importance of looking at traditions and history to create a starting place for change that focuses on discerning the meaning of childhood particular to the cultural context" (p. 48). Childhood memory stories are the tool Hughes has used to encourage educators to consider their values and beliefs about children and childhood, and we used them, too.

We provided the educators with thick acrylic paints and vellum paper and invited them to "make a picture of a memory from your childhood, which you can use to tell a story." The participants painted pictures of themselves in many ways, including walking on the land in the summer, berry picking, sitting on a sled pulled by dogs, camping, ice fishing, and playing with friends. Once the paintings were completed, the educators told their stories and reflected on the values portrayed in their words and art. The educators spoke about the importance of family, the power of doing physical activities outdoors, the grounding of Inuit culture in nature. The idea was that through this process, the educators would link their personal stories and Inuit values, and would see the potential for weaving Inuit values into culturally meaningful story sharing and activities in the playroom. Greenwood and Fraser (2005) write: "Our children deserve to have opportunities to both understand indigenous knowledges and to develop a firm foundation of who they are" (p. 43). Our intent was that the childhood memory activity would be a part of a foundation-building process.

5. *To retell an Inuit legend in our own words.* Inuit legends keep history alive. They preserve Inuit viewpoints and record Inuit knowledge. Some Inuit legends provide advice about how to behave. For example. the legend about the Qallupilluit—sea monsters who dwell beneath the cracks in the ice—serves to caution those who love the excitement of jumping from ice pan to ice pan to watch out.

While discussing the direction education should take in Nunavik during the mid-1970s, participants at a meeting in Puvirnituq provided this advice:

> It is a necessity for Inuit children to learn the Inuit tradition first...because once a person forgets his thinking he would seem to be nowhere. Such a person wouldn't feel at home anywhere, like a lost child (Comité pédagogique, pp. 5–6). (Quoted in Stairs & Bernhard, 2002, p. 312)

As Weenie (2008) writes, "despite centuries of colonialism and oppression, language and culture remain as veritable sources of knowledge that reinforce and validate Aboriginal identity" (p. 555). One's own language and culture ground the structure of one's thinking.

We thought that if we invited the educators to read Inuit legends contained in the *Unikkaangualaurtaa* manual and retell them using their own words, we would encourage them to expand their base of Inuit knowledge, reference familiar images (Inuit legends), and start writing from within Inuit visual and cultural referencing. Foucault, a French poststructuralist thinker, talks about knowledge and power and the silencing of local or alternative knowledges (Madigan, 1992, p. 269). In the legend writing session we set out to see, hear, write, share, and celebrate local Inuit knowledge. To do so we invited Maaji Putulik, the pedagogical counselor from Tasiurvik Child Care Centre in Inukjuak, to facilitate the session. Maaji has created a booklet in which she retells the legend of the woman who adopted a caterpillar (Putulik, 2008), using photos of people from the community, including a respected Elder, dressed in traditional caribou clothing. That afternoon, each participant created a story for children based on an Inuit legend.

6. *To make a poem/song.* This session began with the educators collecting five items from the land. McIvor (2005) writes: "The link of the language to the land is unmistakable. Indigenous languages are intertwined with nature" (p. 6). "The important relationship between Indigenous land and Indigenous life," Iseke-Barnes (2008) writes, "recognizes the importance of this relationship to the well being of Indigenous peoples and the interrelationships of land, water, plants and animals as all our relations" (p. 140). We wanted to create an opportunity for the educators to link the land and words. By using materials from the land and word images of poetry, we thought we could support the writing process during the workshop. What we did not anticipate was how the poetry challenge might provide a vehicle for some of the participants to access deep and sometimes painful thoughts. One participant, in particular, recalled through her poetry the tragic death of her child.

> Inutsuta
> We as the Inuit people
> We humans all have a life,
> Just as the lovely flowers,
> Our life can be a long one,
> Or it can be a short life,
> We are all owners of a heart,

Some hearts are hard,
As if they were made of stone,
Some hearts are soft,
As if they were warmth itself,
Even then, we are all destined to die,
We all are eventually to be put into the earth,
We therefore should grab the roots of those who precede us,
That we may enjoy a good life.
(Ainalik, 2008, as translated from the original Inuttitut by Weetaluktuk, 2008)

For many in the group the poetry afternoon was deeply meaningful and emotional. This process provided a path for educators to see themselves as authors and to be seen by their peers and colleagues as authors. Yet the process gave more: It supported educators in validating and being validated by their work, their thoughts, and their writing. Davies (2000) writes: "Authorship needs to be reconceptualized as authority, with emphasis on authorship, the capacity to speak, write and be heard, to have voice, to articulate meanings from within the collective discourses and beyond them. This capacity does not have to stem from the essence of the person in question but from the positions available to them within the discourses through which they take up their being" (p. 68).

7. *To write a story, create the art, and prepare the story and art for publication.* The workshop's end goal was that each participant would write the text and have the art needed for a children's picture story book. By 16:00 on Friday afternoon a total of 19 books were made that drew on images and language of the community. The books are about Inuit and Inuit life, people, places, and things as told by the educators. When my colleague Stephanie Pov and I were reading through a draft version of the collection, Stephanie repeated the refrain, "I love these books because the Inuttitut language in them is perfect for the community of the writer." I consistently replied, "I love these books because they are full of familiar images—including children playing, the typical three-bedroom municipal house, and people dressed in parkas and kamiks." Best of all, the educators liked their books. When I e-mailed one of the directors with the question "How did the educators like the books?" the response was, "they were thrilled, practically to tears." During a telephone conversation, one of the educator/writers asked, "Do you think I could make my own book now, without you and Stephanie?"

Each book followed a basic format with a cover featuring a strong image from the art, the title of the book and name of the author, an inside cover page including all of the standard copyright and publication information, and a dedication page. The dedications were made to sons and daughters, classes of children, and, in two cases, to all the children of Nunavik. On the inside back cover a listing of each of the 19 books is presented (see Table 1). The back cover presents a picture of the author and her biography. The books are glossy, bright, and beautiful. In all a total of 100 copies of each book were printed. Every one of the 70-plus playrooms in Nunavik Child Care Centres was presented with a boxed set.

Table 1. Books

Author	Community	Title
Sarah Ainalik	Ivujivik	*Bumblebee*
Jeannie Angatuk	Quartaq	*Inuit Knowledge*
Gaina Angiyou	Puvirnituq	*Inuit Then and Now*
Elisapee Angma	Kuujjuaq	*Dora Always Wants to Do Something*
Saniliayuk Baron	Kaniqsualujuaq	*Inuit World of Colours*
Anna Eetook	Kangirsuk	*Mermaid*
Annie Hubloo Etok	Kangiqsualujuaq	*Northern Lights*
Timmiak Kakayuk	Salluit	*You're So Lovable*
Elizabeth Nassak	Kangirsuk	*Atungakkuuk Travels around the World*
Diana Nastapoka	Inukjuak	*Let's Play Outside*
Annie Novalinga	Puvirnituq	*Weather*
Emily Novalinga	Puvirnituq	*Foggy These Days*
Louisa Paningayak	Ivujivik	*Child Development*
Jeannie Partridge	Kuujjuaq	*Can You Count? I Can Count*
Maaji Putulik	Inukjuak	*Across the Breadth of the Peninsula*
Annie Puttayuk	Quartaq	*Caribou*
Rita Sala	Umiujaq	*Dod, Dog What Can You See?*
Rita Sala	Umiujaq	*Colours*
Levina Taqulik	Kangirsuk	*Annie's Ulu*

○ In Dialogue with the Books

In this section I closely examine three of the books to explore ways in which these stories connect with the main themes of this chapter, including Inuttitut language, Inuit culture, identity, literacy, curriculum, and colonial and postcolonial discourses.

Annie's Ulu

Annie's Ulu is the story of a little girl who was always eating junk food, so she decided to have arctic char. She goes to the community freezer, gets a char, and brings it home. She leaves the char to thaw on the floor, but it is too frozen. She asks herself, "How am I going to cut the char? I need an ulu." There were not any ulus at her house so she went to her grandmother's place. Annie borrowed an ulu from her grandmother, returned home, cut up the char, and ate it. The next day was Annie's birthday. She opened the present from her father and she got an ulu. She was so excited to receive an ulu that she said, "I will try my best to eat Inuk country food instead of junk food" (Taqulik, 2008).

Annie's Ulu is about a young Inuk girl in the 21st century, in the context of her community where she can walk to her grandmother's house, get a fish from the freezer, and use an *ulu* (a woman's knife) to eat a frozen fish. Roberts et al. (2005) compiled a list of guidelines for teachers choosing books with "American Indian characters and settings." It includes presenting American Indians authentically and respectfully; seeking images and stories that are authentic to time, place, and culture; and depicting American Indians in everyday tasks of living (p. 3). The criteria on this list seem to be highly transferable to Indigenous peoples broadly, including Inuit, and are, I suggest, represented in *Annie's Ulu*.

Annie's story is local and specific to Nunavik, and when told and retold around the region will resonate with children and families. It will do this because the story incorporates and documents ways that are familiar to Nunavimiut. First, Annie walks to her grandmother's house by herself. In most Nunavik communities, young Inuit children can safely walk from one family member's home to another. In fact children and adults travel with fluidity, often on foot, from grandma's to sister's to uncle's and so on. Second, Annie gets a fish from the freezer. Many communities in Nunavik have a community freezer. Often the door is not locked. Local hunters stock the shelves with locally available food, and community members who don't hunt, or who need food, are encouraged to help themselves to frozen fish, caribou, ptarmigan—whatever food is in season and available. Third, the story documents young Annie manipulating a knife with care and responsibility as she uses the ulu to cut her fish. Young Inuit children learn how to handle tools, including knives. Fourth, Annie eats her frozen fish on the floor. Inuit eat frozen food placed upon cardboard on the floor. Taqulik's story validates Inuit ways.

Annie's Ulu could be about a real little girl. The book gives the reader an idea about life in an Inuit community in Nunavik. This book makes visible and recognizes Inuit ways. It provides a validation of community activities in Nunavik through words and pictures. Iseke-Barnes (2009a) writes: "Through story telling, we can acknowledge indigenous knowledges, histories and stories, reconnect with indigenous agency and resistance in community activities, and focus upon cultural vitalization and self-determination" (p. 78). Taqulik's story can help to displace the omnipresent and culturally inconsistent story line of the colonizer by making the Nunavik-based story and cultural images available to young children and those who read to them.

Figure 1. From the cover of *Annie's Ulu* (Taqulik, 2008).

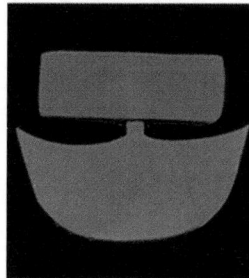

Taqulik's story prompts me to wonder, Why was Annie alone? Was her mother at work? Did she not have any siblings? Does the picture of Annie alone stand as a marker of societal change? My experience in Inuit camps involves eating with lots of people—and rarely, if ever, alone. Why is the birthday such a cherished part of the story for me, and furthermore how does the birthday represent colonial values embedded in the contemporary discourse? In my middle-class culture, birthday parties are important. Every year on May 17th my mom organized big parties to celebrate my birth. On the special day my invited guests came to my home wearing party dresses with shiny shoes and bearing gifts wrapped in colourful paper. During the party we played games and ate cake. As a young white teacher working in the Inuit community of Inukjuak on Hudson's Bay, one way in which I integrated my culture into the classroom was through celebrating the birthdays of my students. The birthday chart, noting each student's name and birthday, was a featured item in the room. At the time, in the early 1980s, birthdays were occasionally celebrated in Inuit homes. My husband, who grew up in Inukjuak in the 1960s and 1970s, told me, "We never celebrated birthdays. I never knew my birthday until I started going to school."

I cite these examples to demonstrate how, on reflection, Taqulik's book can be used to make visible practices of the dominant society as they become embedded in contemporary life. Taqulik's text makes available for discussion markers of colonialism, such as the birthday. This text provides the opportunity to consider how birthdays have become seamlessly embedded in contemporary Inuit life and stimulates the potential for postcolonial discourses.

MacNaughton (2005) implores her readers to "challenge the privilege to define meaning that comes from 'whiteness'" (p. 177). The Nunavik educator books, such as *Annie's Ulu*, place Inuit children in the story as decision makers and community members with caring relationships, disrupting the dominant white colonial discourse and creating opportunities for Inuit children to take up subject positions and make meaning with references that come from within their geographical, historical, and linguistic Arctic world. Most young children in my home city of Montréal would not walk back and forth from home to home, access a community freezer, use a sharp knife unattended, or eat frozen food on the floor. MacNaughton asks us to "act for change in the 'racial' politics and imagery of all that we do with children so that the privilege of 'whiteness' is undermined through early childhood education rather than strengthened in the daily living experiences of our communities" (p. 178). The Nunavik educators' books undermine the privilege of 'whiteness' by telling stories about Inuit, written in Inuttitut, with images from the community.

Across the Breadth of the Peninsula

The cover of Maaji Putulik's book *Across the Breadth of the Peninsula* (2008) is a map of Nunavik. The text of the story goes as follows:

> A long time ago Inuit used to cross the breadth of the peninsula in Nunavik from Ungava to Hudson Bay, back and forth. When my grandmother was still a baby her mother carried her on her back and she crossed the breadth with her family and relatives. Later, when my grandmother lived near Tasiujaq and a group decided to cross the breadth my grandmother followed them. My grandparents came back from the other side leaving their family in the Hudson Straight. Now 25 years have passed, we have transportation now with planes and ski-doos and we can learn more about our family in Nunavik. Back then Inuit didn't stay in the same place; they used to move a lot by qajaq, dog sled and walking. (Putulik, 2008)

Figure 2. From the cover of *Across the Breadth of the Peninsula* **(Putulik, 2008).**

Many history texts have been written that represent the interests and viewpoints of the colonizer and the oppressor. Putulik presents a piece of Nunavik history from the perspective of someone within the region. Smith (1999) suggests that it is important to know history as "part of the critical pedagogy of decolonization" (p. 34). Putulik's story gives Nunavik readers a historical story as told by a voice from within the region, from within an Inuit cultural, historical, and linguistic perspective.

Iseke-Barnes (2009b) talks about the importance of stories and enumerates Darling's three principles for choosing cultural stories: enhance appreciation and respect of culture; increase student's historical and geographical knowledge base; and familiarize students with language and dialects of a culture. Putulik's (2008) book provides a map for geographical referencing and tells about a part of Nunavik history based on the map. The text moves from the past to the present and the book is in Inuttitut. In my opinion Putulik's book meets all of Darling's principles. I think that when Inuit educators of young children create books for children in their community, the chances are high that those books will be culturally appropriate. Smith (1999) explains how Indigenous ways of knowing were "excluded and marginalized" under colonialism (p. 68): "Reclaiming a voice in this context has also been about reclaiming, reconnecting and reordering those ways of knowing which were submerged, hidden and driven underground" (p. 69).

Caribou

Annie Puttayuk's (2008) book *Caribou* includes eight pictures with text:

- People go hunting for caribou.
- They cut caribou into pieces.
- Inuit eat caribou boiled, frozen, dried, and fried.
- Inuit make clothing from caribou skin; we make caribou skin parkas, kamiks, mittens, and snow pants.
- When the caribou are hungry, they eat grass.
- Caribou go swimming when they don't like mosquitoes.
- Caribou crouch to hide when they are tired.
- Inuit kill caribou for food and clothing.

Iseke-Barnes (2009b) argues: "By privileging some aspects of the story and dismissing others, authors and their publishers decide which parts of a culture are admissible into the dominant mainstream cultural representations" (p. 32). The caribou story provides text and images that resonate with Inuit children and are not available in the commercial market. Puttayuk's (2008) story is important because it talks about caribou hunting and the importance of caribou in Inuit life.

Figure 3. From the cover of *Caribou* (Puttayuk, 2008).

Almost every Inuit family in Nunavik goes or has gone caribou hunting. Butchering caribou with care and speed is an essential skill. The hunter who provides food for family and friends is a respected and valuable community member; people in Nunavik remember starvation. Caribou is an important source of food and clothing. Caribou skins, are cleaned, dried, tanned, processed, and sewn. The seamstress who provides clothing for family and friends is a respected and valuable community member; people in the Arctic wear their homemade caribou skin clothing with pride. Inuit live in relationship with caribou.

Will this book provide a script for children in the childcare centre to act out? Certainly the story resonates with community-specific meanings. Shooting caribou with guns for food and clothing is an important part of 21st-century Inuit life made visible by Puttayuk's story.

o Conclusion

The story of the Nunavik Educators' Bookmaking Workshop is one about the Inuttitut language, Inuit culture, literacy, curriculum, identity, and colonial discourses. Through the bookmaking project the Nunavik educators spoke, wrote, drew, were published, took up positions as authors and artists, and are now seeking ways to continue the process. I am left with questions: What will the educators say about what these stories mean to them? How might these stories be used to think about Inuit culture and to enter into postcolonial discourses?

I am excited by the possibilities that the bookmaking workshop has created. By publishing 19 new Inuttitut language books for young children, their educators, and their families we have found an important way to position Inuttitut as a serious language in the childcare centres of Nunavik. The process has helped to uncover and reaffirm Inuit knowledge by telling stories about Inuit ways of knowing and doing, as demonstrated in *Across the Breadth of the Peninsula* and *Caribou*. In *Annie's Ulu,* Taqulik (2008) provides an avenue for getting deeper to examine contemporary meanings grounded in Inuit ways and to make visible the imprint of colonialism in contemporary Inuit life.

I suggest that the 19 Inuttitut language children's books created through the workshop disrupt colonial discourses by providing literature in an Indigenous language, Inuttitut. By making available subject positions based in Inuit knowledge and by offering stories—pictures and words—the books enable the reader to dream, imagine, envision possibilities, reflect on what was, and consider what could be as an Inuttitut-speaking Inuk in Nunavik.

ENDNOTES

1   I am a white woman married to an Inuk man from Inukjuak, Nunavik. We have three Inuit children.

REFERENCES

Ada, A. F., & Campoy, F. I. (2004). *Authors in the classroom: A transformative education process.* Boston: Pearson.

Ainalik, S. (2008). Inutsuta. Unpublished poem.

Archibald, J. (2008). *Indigenous storywork: Educating the heart, mind, body and spirit.* Vancouver, BC: University of British Columbia Press.

Avataq Cultural Institute. (2006). *Unikkaangualaurtaa. Let's tell a story: A collection of 26 stories and songs from Nunavik, with activities for young children.* Montréal: Author.

Ball, J., & Pence, A. (2006). *Supporting Indigenous children's development: Community-university partnerships.* Vancouver, BC: University of British Columbia Press.

Crago, M. B., Annahatak, B., & Ningiuruvik, L. (1993). Changing patterns of language socialization in Inuit homes. *Anthropology & Education Quarterly, 24*(3), 205–223.

Davies, B. (2000). *A body of writing 1990–1999.* New York: Altamira Press.

Department of Indian Affairs and Northern Development. (1990). *Inuit.* Ottawa: Minister of Supply and Services Canada.

Duhaime, G. (2008). Socio-economic profile of Nunavik, 2008 edition. Canadian Research Chair in Comparative Aboriginal Condition: Québec. Retrieved January 3, 2010, from http://www.chaireconditionautochtone.fss.ulaval.ca/extranet/doc/159.pdf

Government of British Columbia. (2008). *British Columbia early learning framework.* Victoria, BC: Ministry of Health, Ministry of Children and Family Development, & Early Learning Advisory Group.

Government of New Brunswick. (2007, May). Communication and literacies. In Government of New Brunswick (Ed.), *Early learning and child care: Curriculum framework for New Brunswick* (pp. 30–33). Fredericton, NB: Author.

Greenwood, M., & Fraser, T. N. (2005). Ways of knowing and being—Indigenous early childhood care and education. *Research Connections Canada, 13*, 41–58.

Hughes, E. (2007). Linking past to present to create an image of the child. *Theory into Practice, 46*(1), 48–56.

Inuit Tapirisat of Canada. (2001). Inuit early childhood development issues discussion paper. Ottawa, ON: Author.

Iseke-Barnes, J. (2008). Pedagogies for decolonizing. *Canadian Journal of Native Education, 31*(1), 123–148.

Iseke-Barnes, J. (2009a). Grandmothers of the Métis nation. *Native Studies Review, 18*(2), 69–104.

Iseke-Barnes, J. (2009b). Unsettling fictions: Disrupting popular discourses and trickster tales in books for children. *Journal of the Canadian Association for Curriculum Studies, 7*(1), 24–57.

King, T. (2003). *The truth about stories: A Native narrative*. Toronto, ON: House of Anansi Press.

MacNaughton, G. (2005). *Doing Foucault in early childhood studies: Applying poststructural ideas*. New York: Routledge.

Madigan, S. (1992). The application of Michel Foucault's philosophy in the problem externalizing discourse of Michael White. *Journal of Family Therapy, 14*, 265–279.

McIvor, O. (2005). The contribution of indigenous heritage language immersion programs to healthy early childhood development. *Research Connections Canada, 12*, 5–20.

Novalinga, E. T. (2005). *L'écho du nord*. Québec, QC: Les Éditions du Minuit.

Novalinga, E. T. (2008). *Foggy these days*. Montréal: Avataq Cultural Institute.

Puttayuk, A. (2008). *Caribou*. Montréal: Avataq Cultural Institute.

Putulik, M. (2008). *Across the breadth of the peninsula*. Montréal: Avataq Cultural Institute.

Rau, C. (2007). Shifting paradigms: Māori women at the interface of Te Tiriti (treat)-based early childhood education in Aotearoa. *Childrenz Issues, 11*(1), 33–36.

Ritchie, J. & Rau, C. (2007). Mā wai ngā hua? "Participation" in early childhood in Aotearoa/ New Zealand. *International Journal of Educational Policy, Research, & Practice: Reconceptualizing Childhood Studies, 8*(1), 101–116.

Roberts, L. C., Dean, E., & Holland, M. (2005, November). Contemporary American Indian cultures in children's picture books. *Beyond the Journal, Young Children on the Web*, 1–6.

Roberts, S. K., & Crawford, P. (2008). Literature to help children cope with family stressors. *Young Children, 63*(5), 12–17.

Smith, G. H. (2000). Maori education: Revolution and transformative action. *Canadian Journal of Native Education, 24*(1), 57–72.

Smith, L. T. (1999). *Decolonizing methodologies: Research and Indigenous peoples*. Dunedin, NZ: University of Otago Press.

Stairs, A., & Bernhard, J. (2002). Considerations for evaluating "good care" in Canadian Aboriginal early childhood settings. *McGill Journal of Education, 37*(3), 309–330.

Taqulik, L.(2008). *Annie's ulu*. Montréal: Avataq Cultural Institute.

Taylor, D. M., & Wright, S. C. (2003). Do Aboriginal students benefit from education in their heritage language? Results from a ten-year program of research in Nunavik. *Canadian Journal of Native Studies, 23*(1), 1–24.

Taylor, R. H., & Patterson, L. (2000). Getting the "Indian" out of the cupboard: Using information literacy to promote critical thinking. *Teacher Librarian, 28*(2), 1–8.

Viruru, R. (2006). Postcolonial perspectives on childhood and literacy. In N. Hall, J. Larson, & J. Marsh (Eds.), *Handbook of early childhood literacy* (pp. 13–21). Thousand Oaks, CA: Sage.

Weenie, A. (2008). Curricular theorizing from the periphery. *Curriculum Inquiry, 38*(5), 545–557.

Weetaluktuk, J. (2008). *The world of Tivi Etok: The life and art of an Inuit Elder*. Québec, QC: Éditions MultiMondes.

CHAPTER TEN

Families and Pedagogical Narration: Disrupting Traditional Understandings of Family Involvement

Laurie Kocher *with* Paul Cabaj, David Chapman, Nancy Chapman, Carmen Ryujin, *and* Elizabeth Wooding

The importance of family–educator partnerships has long been emphasized within the field of early childhood education. Partnership, though, is an amorphous term that does not always make explicit either the nature or the unresolved terrain of family–educator relationships. In practice, family–educator relationships are often strained and are not always meaningful (MacNaughton & Hughes, 2003).

What do families and educators want from partnership? In my experience as a kindergarten educator, families[1] and teachers both have expressed that they want more opportunities to connect and to work together on behalf of the children. They want to talk to each other, but they find that many obstacles hinder satisfying conversations. They want to support each other, but they find it difficult to articulate this support in meaningful ways. In our conversations together, families and educators express as important values involvement, direct communication, trust, respect, emphasis on common goals—all of which are the building blocks of communities. The meanings that families and educators attach to their encounters might be characterized as a search for reinforcement that their individual contribution to this child is important, that their trust is not misplaced, and that they and their opinions are respected.

What can happen when an educator adopts a mission to include all families in the educational process? What can happen when opportunities are created for sustained family involvement? Can these efforts disrupt the restrictive parent and educator roles that are imprinted on the culture of educational spaces for young children?

The case presented here offers an opportunity to examine family–educator relations in the context of an attempt to shift traditional patterns and provide new venues for family involvement in the classroom community. Inspired by the world-renowned Reggio Emilia programs, over the course of this particular year in my kindergarten room I developed collaborative structures and invited families to contribute to class activities as valued participants and decision makers. I believed we had the potential not only to increase family involvement in the life of the school but to upset the power imbalance that impedes family–educator relationships. At the conclusion of our year together, families were asked to think about their experience and contribute their thoughts to inform this chapter. The events and topics included here are ones they identified as being significant or memorable in terms of creating community, connecting with one another, and building home–school alliances. In particular, I explore how the practice of sharing pedagogical narrations profoundly influenced the nature and quality of relationships between families, children, and teachers.

Scrutinizing family–educator relationships may be uncomfortable, possibly because it challenges the embedded authority of traditional relationships by suggesting that parents and teachers exist (or should) on a level playing field. This chapter begins by examining some of the factors that inhibit meaningful family–educator relationships. From there I propose alternate perspectives that disrupt traditional understandings of these relationships, and describe strategies that I undertook with families to forge new understandings. At the heart of these efforts is engagement with the practice of sharing pedagogical narrations.

○ Distant and Unequal: Family–Educator Relationships

Studies of family–educator relationships in early childhood settings have tended to see educators and families as separate entities (Haseloff, 1990; Henry, 1996; Shpancer, 1998). Critics argue that the relatively narrow focus in these studies on elements perceived to be discrete contributing factors to parent–teacher relations (e.g., rates of parent–teacher contact, teachers' perceptions of parents' competence as caregivers, or parents' satisfaction with the program provided by the childcare setting) has tended to obscure the complexity of these relationships. As Shpancer

(1998) points out, for example, it is not the day-to-day contact rates between families and educators that are important but the responsiveness of their relationships.

Notions of appropriate relationships between families and educators are shaped by deep-seated, enduring social and institutional beliefs and practices. These include our own experiences of school (Hargreaves, 1997); images of schooling popularized in the media (Dehli, 1995); policies that define parents' roles in their children's schooling (Crozier, 1998; Whitty, Power, & Halpin, 1998); cultural beliefs (Bourdieu, 1977; Ogbu, 1993); and notions of teacher professionalism that are grounded in the idea of "teacher-as-expert" (Epstein, 1995). Many of these influences have created symbolic and actual separation between families and educators in relation to care and education. Robust relationships require commitments and conditions that allow emotional understanding to occur between individuals. Yet a great deal of the history, culture, and organization of teaching makes achieving such understanding difficult or impossible.

To begin, public schools in North America have traditionally offered few opportunities for educators and family members to meet. Interactions tend to be largely school- or centre-based: volunteering, fund-raising, attending school events. Additionally, teachers of young children are often expected to be firm yet caring with children and emotionally detached, in control, or calm when interacting with families (Grumet, 1988; Hargreaves & Goodson, 1996). By and large, the educator is seen as responsible for learning about and adapting to whatever particular family "limitation" is exhibited or to find a way to "manage" the parent successfully (Thorne, 1993). The teacher retains authority, and the parent remains in a client position. One real tension that many educators experience is their sense that personal relationships with, and moral obligations to, children and their families are constantly overridden by a spirit of contractualism (Nias, 1999). The paradox is that educators are expected to remain professionally distant while at the same time demonstrating emotional involvement through caring (Grumet, 1988).

In a review of early childhood texts and policy documents, Hughes and MacNaughton (2003) conclude that the discourses contained therein primarily position parents as "others," preventing the creation of equitable family–educator relationships. Their literature review reveals that problems arise from a constant "othering" of parental knowledge by educators. Parental knowledge of the child is subordinated to professional knowledge in the following ways:

- ☐ Parental knowledge is seen to be inadequate. Parents are viewed as ignorant about what and how to teach their children. Parent involvement programs are designed to rectify this.

- Parental knowledge is seen to be supplementary. Parents' knowledge of their child does not complement educators' professional knowledge, but merely supplements it.
- Parental knowledge is seen to be unimportant. Parents' voices are absent from much of the literature about parent involvement.

(Hughes & MacNaughton, 2003)

Education privileges professional knowledge by placing it in binary relationship with parental knowledge (e.g., Moore & Klass, 1995). Professional knowledge of the child is assumed to be scientific and developmental, objective, norm-referenced, and applicable to all children. In contrast, parental knowledge of the child is understood to be anecdotal, subjective, individualized, and applicable to specific children (Hughes & MacNaughton, 2003).

Family–educator relationships, too, have been framed by juxtaposing binaries. For example, educators can be defined as professionals by drawing sharp distinctions between them and parents. Binary relationships may be mutually defining but are seldom relationships between equals; typically they create an "other" who is subordinate. Research that documents the importance of mutual respect and "social trust" in educational settings (e.g., Bryk & Schneider, 2002; Payne & Kaba, 2001) is a recent development.

The emblems and interactions that comprise educational culture are embedded in relations of status and power: in the authority relationships of the classroom (Waller, 1932); between principals and teachers (Grumet, 1988); in the micropolitics of teachers' careers (Blase & Anderson, 1995); in patterns of surveillance between parents and teachers (Crozier, 1998); in the home knowledge sanctioned by the school that connects or disconnects children and their family cultures from the social curriculum (Hargreaves, Earl, & Ryan, 1996); and in the ideologies of professional status and identity that educators often use to distance themselves from families (Hargreaves, 1997). In short, culture and power are inseparable components of school life.

Very few studies document any process of families and educators talking together about their relationship. Those that do (Birrell et al., 1998; Coahran, Kay, Kay, & Fitzgerald, 1999; Harner & Davis, 1991) suggest that personal interaction—beyond the usual venues of parent–teacher conferences, classroom newsletters, and open houses—will be key to truly moving families and educators beyond stereotypes and into authentic relationships. Many aspects of educational and care settings can be redesigned to be more inclusive of family participation. School cultures can be changed. Power can be shared (Comer, 1996; Delpit, 1995; Epstein, Coates, Salinas, Sanders, & Simon, 1997).

○ **In Search of a Learning Community**

Prescriptions for increasing family involvement in the educational setting often are limited to sending home more frequent newsletters, providing workshops so that families can help children with homework more effectively, creating positions for families on councils, and encouraging educators to contact families more frequently (and with occasional good news). While such measures do create more interactions between the centre or school and the home, they also keep family members in the role of visitors. Such activities do not provide families with a real voice that contributes to what Fine (1993) calls a "democratic, critical, lively public sphere within public education" (p. 708).

In the critical task of creating educational environments that sustain the communication indicative of democratic communities, families are not typically presented as part of the equation (see, e.g., Apple & Beane, 1995; Hemmings, 2000; Kahne, 1996; Soder, 1996). Miretzky (2002), however, finds that the values teachers and parents express as important to their collaboration include investment in the school community, direct and honest communication, trust, mutual respect, and mutual goals, all of which reflect the "communication requirements" of democratic communities. Families and educators may routinely frame the meanings of their encounters in terms of the children they have in common, but it appears that what they look for from each other is connected to what they need for themselves as people who share a community.

Educators who adopt a position of collaborative community building and seek to create equitable and inclusive relationships with families must challenge the knowledge–power links that currently underpin them (Hughes & MacNaughton, 2003). Practices that support this position include giving families a real voice without feeling that doing so threatens their professional identity; negotiating shared meanings and understandings about who children are and how they should be treated; and ensuring they have sufficient time to interact with parents face to face (Hughes & MacNaughton, 2003).

If educators are to perform those practices successfully, they will need to see themselves not as experts marshalling (scientific) facts about children, but as collaborators with families and the wider community in the task of building shared understandings of who children are and what they are capable of. Such partnerships stress shared power as opposed to the expert–learner relationship—where the educator is the expert and the family member is the learner—that once was advocated in the field. The overarching goal of these co-constructed relationships is to create a learning environment for children that supports family involvement, provides families with social support, and promotes family empowerment (Lopez, Kreider, & Caspe, 2004).

○ Building Alliances with Families

As a classroom educator, I have been particularly inspired by the educators of Reggio Emilia, Italy, and of Hilltop Children's Centre, a Reggio-influenced program in Seattle. In these early childhood programs, family involvement is envisioned as a system of interactions and relationships that is based on a strong collaboration among educators, families, and children. The continuous work and attitude of exchange, sharing, communication, and elaborating together about the experiences that are part of daily life in the schools and the infant–toddler centres supports the growth of interest and curiosity on the part of families.

The partnership that is established between educators and families in these centres provides a fertile context for conversation. Family members' voices are continuously put in relationship with everything that takes place in the centres. Different organizational forms of participation enable families to make essential contributions to initiatives, projects, experiences, and activities. Together families, educators, and children all become part of a community of learners.

Relationships are also created and supported through a continuous documentation of the work that is carried out in the centres. Pedagogical documentation (also known as learning stories in New Zealand and pedagogical narration in British Columbia) has developed into a fine art in the Reggio Emilia children's programs. The practice is based on educators' detailed observations of children's activities and conversations, supported by photographs and video recordings. This documentation is used as research data by the educators to consider the children's theories about their work, to plan for supporting future work, and to publicly share the learning of both the children and their educators. Pedagogical documentation makes learning visible and contributes to an image of a competent child who is full of potential. Sharing this documentation with families offers the possibility and opportunity for parents and others to feel part of the learning process. Carlina Rinaldi (1998) writes:

> Documentation provides an extraordinary opportunity for parents, as it gives them the possibility to know not only what their child is doing, but also how and why, to see not only the products but also the processes. Therefore, parents become aware of the meaning that the child gives to what he or she does, and the shared meanings that children have with other children. It is an opportunity for parents to see that part of the life of their child that is often invisible. Furthermore, documentation offers the possibility for parents to share their awareness, to value discussion and exchanges

with the teachers and among their group, helping them to become aware of their role and identity as parents. (pp. 121–122)

In recent years I have found myself asking: Would it be possible to disrupt the traditional logic of home–school relations through deliberate family involvement strategies? I believe that if I truly value family participation and partnership with families, then I must attempt, in the words of Cagliari and Guidici (2001), to "create spaces, contexts, and times when all subjects—children, teachers, and parents—can find opportunities to speak and be listened to" (p. 136). To this end, I am committed both to the practice of pedagogical narration and to building alliances with families. I want open-hearted relationships that nourish our community and move us beyond the formal roles of teacher and parent. Reggio educator Paolo Cagliari (2002) expresses this idea beautifully: "In the *alliances* between parents and teachers, we have the opportunity to be close to the children."

○ Inviting Families over the Threshold

Like many educators, I have felt protective of the classroom as my personal, professional space—a place where I create a particular culture, a particular ambience, an aesthetic classroom that reflects me. Echoing the sentiment of Ann Pelo (Hilliard & Pelo, 2001), an educator at Hilltop Children's Centre, I was called to recognize that teachers are typically expected to "check their families at the door" (p. 49). Yet I also recognized that families care passionately and deeply about their children. While I extolled an "open door" policy, parents were not a true presence in my classroom. Clearly, I was somehow holding families at a distance.

It was eye-opening to start honestly asking what I was going to do differently. When I've worked with student teachers in the past as a teacher educator, I have encouraged them to look carefully at the educational environments they found themselves in, reading both the written and the unwritten messages in the "text" of the space. I had never as a classroom teacher, however, considered how families would read the text of "my" space. Was it a welcoming space? How could I invite families over the threshold and draw them in?

Creating a Welcoming, Engaging Environment

Creating beautiful environments that engage children, and are calm, organized, full of natural materials and devoid of plastic has long been an interest of mine. But a good look at my classroom made me realize there were no places for adults to comfortably sit. I brought in some soft seating, Tiffany-style lamps, and some lovely artwork in an effort to create a more family-friendly, home-like environment that would be conducive to inviting people in. I encouraged families to contribute plants, objets d'art, and framed photos of themselves in whatever configuration their family took. I wanted to create a space that reflected the personalities and the cultures of the families represented by the children in my class, to send a message of welcome, and to include families in creating this space.

Helping Families Connect to Each Other

Reggio educators believe that orchestrating gatherings throughout the school year gives families a sense of the strong community that they are part of creating. Strozzi (2001) makes a significant point that describes the intentionality of these efforts: "the school is not a place for anonymous users, but for people who live a portion of their lives together" (p. 64).

With this idea in mind, I invited family members to launch the school year off site in a ceramics gallery where, over food and drink (because intimacy develops through sharing food), we painted little ceramic tea mugs that would remain in the classroom as a surprise for the children. All caregivers and parents were encouraged to come, and when one of the fathers told me that dads would only come if there was beer, we provided beer—and the dads came. Conversation revolved around getting to know one another and recalling favourite childhood memories. Through this conversation we were able to tease out some common themes of childhood (love of the outdoors; long, uninterrupted periods of play; the importance of friendships; and so on). We drew upon these recollections to brainstorm our hopes and wishes for the children of this class—and then wrote these dreams on tiny slips of paper and placed them in a Chinese wishing pot. The notion of the wishing pot is that a wish or intention that is recorded and saved inside will materialize.

This was not the typical "meet the teacher" event, where I, as the educator, would stand and deliver my rules and routines for the year. Instead it was an opportunity to make connections as we began to know one another. Perhaps because we met outside the institutional space of the school and people were involved hands-on with making something, it felt more like a gathering of people than a teacher-directed information session.

Pages in a Family Album

I held as an important value that families would be a tangible presence in our classroom. In addition to framed photos, families were asked to create a few pages for our family book that described activities they enjoyed together, such as celebrations and rituals, favourite stories, and so forth. As each page was completed and arrived at school, we read together the stories, bios, and images that were included. Children eagerly asked each morning if we had any more pages to add to the family album. This was also a way of keeping families accountable to contribute. One album page was created by both parents and all four children in a family, including the baby who finger painted the background for the page of photos and text. This book quickly became a treasured favourite among children and adults alike. Hearing the stories helped me to learn more about the families in our classroom community and strengthened the bond between the children and their families. The stories also became a touch point for children who felt sad, distressed, or just missed their family members. In one situation, a girl from our class was away overseas for a number of weeks. A classmate found her page in the family album, removed it, and carried it clutched to his chest for days.

Another community-building effort involved asking families to tell the story of how their child received the gift of his or her name. These stories could be written, tape recorded, videotaped, or told in person. Every family participated, with the majority choosing to come into our classroom to tell their stories. I recorded these, along with a few photos, and sent them home via our class listserv (an electronic community conversation forum, subscribed to through e-mail). The members of our classroom community got to know each other just a little better as the stories were told and histories, family traditions, ethnicity, and sense of humour unfolded. These storytelling episodes certainly nudged folks out of their comfort zone initially, but they became significant in terms of helping people to connect with one another. Equally important, families began to see themselves as valuable contributors to our curriculum.

A Community of Learners

Following the success of the name story invitations, I encouraged families to accept an invitation to research and plan a science experiment to offer to the class. These experiments could be demonstrations or hands-on explorations. Aware that not every family member is able to leave their other responsibilities during school hours to come into the classroom, I offered to videotape the "scientists" at home or conduct the family's planned experiment myself. Having earlier taken the brave step to come into class to do some storytelling, families readily accepted this challenge to be "mad scientists." I was delighted when every last family made the effort both to plan an experiment and to come into class themselves to engage in this learning activity with the children. This spoke volumes to me about how seriously families were taking up the invitation to "cross the threshold" and be involved in the life of our curriculum and our classroom community. In fact, community was *becoming* the curriculum of the class.

Again I recorded these science explorations and shared the stories via e-mail. Many families commented on how significant this challenge to be a scientist was in promoting a sense of genuine contribution and partnership. Children began to speak of each other and their family members as all being scientists and teachers, a true community of learners.

A Circle of "We"

Throughout the year, we used the tea mugs the families had lovingly made for semi-regular tea parties. These parties were loosely organized and purposefully not connected to any particular holiday or event. They were casual affairs to which anyone could come as their schedules would permit, and they often included grandparents, nannies, and siblings. My intention again was to create occasions for gathering that had the sole purpose of building relationships.

Casual picnics in the park also became part of the culture of the classroom community. A few were planned around particular occasions, but as friendships developed, families began to initiate these events with some frequency. After-school gatherings at a nearby beach became a regular Friday happening, with different individuals participating as their schedules would allow. Siblings and extended family members were included and friendships deepened. I was advised by the school administrator not to take part in these "social events"—she was operating under the assumption that distance between parents and teachers should be maintained to foster the aura of professionalism described earlier. This belief system was common among educators in my school district, but it was clearly contrary to the values I espoused for building alliances with families, so I took part in the gatherings whenever I could.

Families developed a strong sense of connection with one another that went beyond the typical friendships that might form between classmates. Genuine caring developed among this little community of 20 families, and a deep sense of collective looking out for one another became a hallmark of the group. Family members began talking about our little group as "a circle of we." Relationships created a sense of community and shared responsibility for the children.

Family involvement is typically viewed as individualistic: it's about a parent's support of her own child at home or about the connection between one parent and his child's teacher. In the approach discussed here, family engagement becomes a shared responsibility. Individual actions still matter, of course, but they are set in a collective context. When families view themselves as a group, as a community bounded by similar interests and desires, a drive to act collectively for the benefit of all children can emerge. Families can enter schools not as isolated individuals standing alone on the school's turf, but as powerful actors who belong.

Connor's Name Story

Connor and his family (Nancy, David, and Aidan) came to tell us the story of Connor's name. Connor's whole name is Connor John Dae-Ryung Chapman. His mom and dad looked at a book that has 50,001 names in it. David would suggest a name and Nancy would say "no." David would suggest another name and Nancy would say "no." Then they found a name in the book, *Connor*, that they both said "yes" to. Then David and Nancy chose John for Connor's second name. John was David's best friend who was a police officer who passed away in a tragic accident shortly before Connor was born. The name Dae-Ryung is Korean, and means "Big Dragon." Connor was born in the year 2000, and according to the Chinese Zodiac calendar, this is the year of the dragon. Every sixty years, in the Chinese Zodiac calendar, the dragon is considered a golden dragon. Connor's grandfather is a member of a golden dragon club (all members are born in 1940), and Connor is now the newest and youngest member of that club! And the name Chapman is the family surname for all of Connor's family – David, Nancy, Connor, Aiden and their newest addition to the family, Finn, all have the same last name.

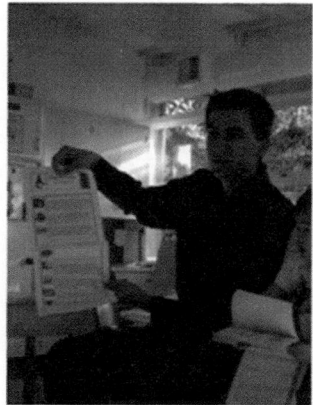

○ Sharing Ordinary Moments

One of the most effective practices that has evolved in my teaching practice is pedagogical narration.[2] Recognized as a hallmark of the Reggio Emilia educational project, where it was first refined, pedagogical narration gave me a way to share "ordinary moments"—vignettes from daily events or from ongoing, more elaborate project work—with the families of the children in my class. Ann Pelo (2006) describes her thinking about the practice of pedagogical narration:

As teachers—people committed to inquiry—we strive to pay attention to the *every-day, ordinary moments* of each day. These ordinary moments are the fabric of children's lives: they offer glimpses into children's hearts and minds. When we pay attention to ordinary moments, we begin to know the children deeply. (p. 180)

Sharing pedagogical narrations is a key piece of creating community. I encouraged families to read the narrations that were posted around our classroom and elsewhere in the school and that I also shared via our listserv. I believed that, over time, a series of these moments would paint a picture of life lived in community in our classroom. I asked families to respond to the stories, not only with me as the educator, but also with one another.

I have tended to focus a lot of my pedagogical narration on relationships and community, pointing out the ways in which children are making connections with each other. I make sure that I include things that involve families, whether it's a big gathering that we've had, or an interaction that a family member had when hanging out in our room, or a particular activity that they've been part of. The idea of "parents as protagonists" that the Reggio Emilia teachers speak of has made an impact on me: Families are not just involved or just participating—they are actively shaping the life of the classroom.

I let families know that there won't necessarily be something about their child in every day's documentation, but I also remind them that it's really useful for them to read the stories anyway because it gives them a flavour of our classroom culture that their child is spending his or her days in. This is an avenue for families to understand their child and their child's experience at school. It also gives them a connection with the other children and a sense of who they are, which builds community and a deeper investment in the program. Over time, parents shift from being interested only or primarily in their own child, to being concerned with other children and the whole group, to being interested in childhood in a broader sense. One of the family members described how pedagogical narration "brought me into my son's classroom, and also made me learn and care deeply about the other children, such that they became mine also." Another observed that "these small pieces were frequent, symbolic reminders of the collective connection: the connection to the children's learning, linked to the classroom, and the community around it—and back again."

In my own context, setting up an electronic listserv has been very valuable. All of the families had Internet access easily available to them, so this was an accessible and effective way to communicate. The listserv made it possible for me to post the stories and photos that I captured on a nearly daily basis. There are several advantages in this way of sharing pedagogical narration. Initially it was a convenient and quick way for me to share information, but it soon became a communication vehicle for everyone involved. Families could download and save stories, discuss them with their children, forward them to other family members, and generally become more aware of what was happening at school. Birthday invitations, birth announcements, and community events were the initial postings, but soon the listserv became a virtual meeting place where individuals would discuss life and school events, philosophy, and pedagogy—and, of course, the pedagogical narrations that were posted.

Achieving Equity through Dissensus

When families feel they are listened to, they can enter into a reciprocal relationship with educators. The listening becomes active, not passive, producing debate, exchange, and idea sharing. A heated debate occurred in our classroom community about how to handle an incident I had documented in which one child had said to another, in the midst of play, "I'm going to kill you." I was concerned about the incident on several levels: the comment affronted my pacifist tendencies; the child on the receiving end was visibly upset; and the child who had delivered the words—and who I chose not to identify in the narration—was from a Middle Eastern country, making me concerned about racial profiling given recent world events. Families had a variety of responses ranging from surprise and shock to amusement to concern. Some felt that it should be "nipped in the bud" immediately, that such language was simply not tolerable. Many were very concerned that the offensive comment might have come from their own child. Some had mixed feelings about how to handle violence with children, wanting to learn more about the effects of media and computer games on young children. A few took the incident lightly, saying "boys will be boys," and insisted, rather strongly, that it was hardly worth fussing over. Others expressed their sense of the importance to confront these difficult situations head on. Ultimately there was an acknowledgement of the range of opinions that were stirred up, which led to some negotiation of how to respectfully disagree with diverse perspectives. This is an example of the kind of philosophical conversations that arose and continued in the virtual meeting place of online conversation.

Most issues concerning young children and their educational programs will evoke a variety of responses from parents, many of them strongly held and expressed. Such diversity of opinion, Lyotard believed, creates change, emancipation, and, therefore, greater equity. Applying Lyotard's emphasis on dissensus, as opposed to consensus, to early childhood education, Lubeck (1998) writes:

> To speak of contradiction, ambiguity, and complexity, to call attention to other ways
> of seeing is not to unleash chaos but simply to name what happens as a matter of course

.... Modern ways of thinking orient us to value stability, certainty, and consensus, to write down guidelines and standards ... yet, arguably, we are most likely to grow in our practice when we are exposed to different interpretations and different ways of doing things. (p. 287)

Through this practice of sharing pedagogical narration, both digitally and in other formats, I believe that we as a community have generated the sense of safety, energy, and possibility that Isaacs (1999) deems necessary to create a "container"—the psychological space in which dialogue can take place. These conversations took us somewhere new in our collective understanding of issues as they relate directly to our everyday lives with children, parents, and one another. As Ann Pelo (Hilliard & Pelo, 2001) says, "it feels important to name the work we are doing as community building in a pretty revolutionary way. It's not just about providing a service of education or child care, but, in fact, it can be about becoming a community with each other" (p. 51).

Curriculum for Life

It was a very interesting day today...

Mackenzie B. received a very precious note in her lunch kit from her mom. The highlight of her day is to find a surprise note, lovingly prepared, and these notes are so special to her that she saves them in a special box at home. As she went to show her note to a classmate, some sort of altercation occurred, and the note was torn. This was devastating to Mackenzie, who was quite inconsolable for several minutes. The "offender" was quite taken aback. After several minutes, a plan was struck to repair the note with a glue and paper "bandage." This act of restitution seemed to calm Mackenzie somewhat.

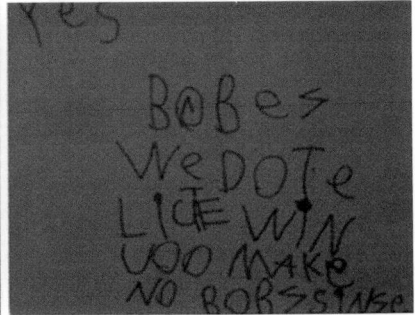

But there is so much power in written communication! Something in that event triggered a new writing episode, and suddenly a cluster of kids (of the male variety) began making notes to add to the "No Tigers Allowed" collection that read "No Barbies Allowed." With the newfound knowledge of being able to spell these words, several started making tickets, or messages, that were surreptitiously passed along to some of the girls, reading "No Barbies Allowed." This caused an uproar – and an upset girl tore up one of the notes. Now, the writer was the same who had torn Mackenzie's note earlier – but suddenly his note was destroyed, and tears were the result. A different experience with the shoe on the other foot. But the girls were quite angry at being told that no Barbies are allowed (although they are not part of our classroom environment), and with great animation stated that they did NOT agree with this new ruling. Another boy wrote several notes saying "you are wrong," and "incorrect." He was sticking by his no Barbie ruling. Quietly, thoughtfully, one of the girls penned a new message, which says "Yes Barbies. We don't like it when you make no Barbies signs."

So, we have an ongoing argument taking place in print. My challenge is to model that it's okay to have differing opinions, and to state your opinions – but to do so respectfully. And the kids have become very passionate about using the power of the pen to express themselves!

Such is the real curriculum of school, and of life!

When Did God Get Alive?

I can remember the moment so clearly when Ana approached me as I stood at the sink mixing up fresh paints. She had an important question burning on her heart. After she asked her question, I suggested we take it back to the other children and ask for their ideas. The transcript of that conversation follows:

- ◻ When did God get alive?
- ◻ I know when he got alive…in three days of being alive.
- ◻ God got alive when Santa got alive
- ◻ He did? Santa's not real!
- ◻ Yes, he's real. His magic gets him down the chimney!
- ◻ He's just a fairy tale.
- ◻ She's lying. Don't listen to her.
- ◻ Santa and Rapunzel and Magic – those are all not real.
- ◻ Then who brings the presents?
- ◻ Your mom and dad do. They trick you. And reindeer can NOT fly.
- ◻ Yes, reindeer can fly!

- And Santa didn't die on the cross.
- How did God get born? Is God and Jesus the same thing?
- Yeah. How did God get born?
- I wonder how God got born if he made Jesus get born? How can that be if both of them weren't born, who made all the people? Then they wouldn't have any moms or dads if they weren't born yet. There wouldn't be any people.
- Nobody would be in this world if God didn't get born.

Recently I read an article by Dr. Carlina Rinaldi, an educator from Reggio Emilia. Her words came to mind as I transcribed this conversation that tool place amongst a group of children today. They were invested in pursing the question that Ana had initially raised, and while each spoke passionately, they were able to listen to each other closely, while yet clinging to their own positions. Clearly, here the children are wrestling with issues of philosophy, theology, and magical thinking as they propose their theories…

How can we help children find the meaning of what they do, what they encounter, and what they experience? How can we do this for ourselves? These are questions about the search for meaning that influence the development of our identity. Why? How? What?

We don't have to teach children to ask "why?" because inside each human being is the need to understand the reasons, the meaning of the world around us and the meaning of our life. There is a mix of practical and philosophical concerns in their questioning attitude, in their effort to understand the meaning of things and the meaning of life.

But children not only ask "why?" They are also able to find the answers to their whys, to create their own theories. Observe and listen to children because when they ask "how?" or "why?" they are not simply asking for the answer from you. They are requesting the courage to find a collection of possible answers.

This attitude of the child means the child is a real researcher. As human beings, we are all researchers of the meaning of life. Yet it is possible to destroy this attitude of the child with our quick answers and our certainty. How can we support and sustain this attitude of children to construct explanations? If a child says, "It's raining because God is crying," we could easily destroy his theory by telling him it's because of the clouds.

How can we cultivate the child's intention to research? How can we cultivate the courage to make theories as explanations?

Elizabeth (a parent) contributes her thoughts:

There is so much going on in this document at so many different levels and layers it's hard to know where to begin. Points which touched me immediately (having 4 very little kids myself) were:

- ◻ Listening
- ◻ Finding meaning
- ◻ Building theories…finding a collection of possible answers
- ◻ Cultivating conversations, exploration through dialogue, co-construction of language which allows children to discuss an idea
- ◻ Education, truth – the whole notion of coming from within which relates to the next point…
- ◻ Symbolic life
- ◻ Intent – the process of getting to the big idea – which I guess loops us back to conversation, dialogue and listening. There's a great big circle being drawn here – there you go; circularity in form and function.

Lastly, what is the parent role in all of the above – how to participate (I want to be a part of this with my kids!), how to help facilitate and then watch them reach out, explore, dream and be excited and inspired about life.

○ Living in Authentic Relationships with Families

During the writing of this chapter, families expressed a desire for more informal encounters that take the child out of the equation and allow educators to be seen as everyday people. While "professional" and "approachable" might seem to be incompatible attributes, especially to families intimidated by the perceived authority of the school, our experience has shown that it is possible for families to see teachers as both. The opportunity to interact in less formal and less scripted situations is seen as an avenue to foster an appreciation for the professionalism of educators while also "humanizing" them, thus easing the power differential inherent in so-called professional–client relationships (Strike, 1993).

Complexity, understanding, and compassion can develop when teachers and parents engage in relationships rather than merely a string of episodic interactions. Mutually responsive relationships are likely to flourish if programs focus on the interconnectedness of families and educators through their mutual commitment to children and on exploring ways to enhance and celebrate this connectedness (Haseloff, 1990; Henry, 1996). This focus might involve providing opportunities for educators to participate in informal exchanges in which they are able to share stories of their experiences and explore concerns within a mutually supportive environment. Such exchanges can generate new possibilities about how current practices might be enriched (Blenkin & Kelly, 1997). Opportunities for families and educators to exchange experiences could be even more useful in promoting an understanding of different perspectives and fostering empathy.

As my thinking about building alliances with families has shifted, I've found myself wanting to be known in more personal ways. I ask: Are there things you want to know about me? I want to clarify that I don't expect to be only a recipient of their sharing, but to offer things about my life as well. It's powerful to hear family members ask me questions. My protective shield of "professionalism" is gone. I've started inviting families to do things with me, like going to cultural events in our community, sharing meals together, or participating in fundraising projects outside the boundaries of school. I think when you have those experiences together, experiences that build relationships and friendships, families are able to invest in what they want to see happening in the classroom. What I have been seeing is that the more I allow for opportunities to be together, whether it be to talk about the children's experiences in the program or just generally about our lives, the more they feel invested. Family members have commented that children, too, seem to benefit from seeing their parents/caregivers and teachers collaborating as partners who have personal connections with one another. The mutual commitment to children that I share with families seems to act as a conduit that inexorably connects us.

It is a challenge to risk sharing ownership of my work by opening myself up to family opinions and voice. Doing so involves becoming truly available for the concerns, joys, and questions of parents, and realizing that families and educators together are responsible for children's optimal growth. It involves making myself vulnerable. I find myself continually thinking, and thinking again, about what I choose to post publicly. Even if my voice does not appear in a particular transcript, for example, I am not invisible—I am present by virtue of what I choose to pay attention to, what I choose to highlight and make visible.

The practice of pedagogical narration alone does not ensure that curriculum is empowering for families. This practice must sit alongside efforts to build reciprocal relationships with families so that they feel they are able to participate safely (Gould & Pohio, 2006). It takes time, sensitivity, and an appreciation of families' diversity to create spaces where families reach a level of engagement that is comfortable for all. I must accept that not all families will engage with pedagogical narration with the same expectations, willingness, or understanding, and certainly I have experienced this. Some families feel as if it's too much information for them to receive on a regular basis, while others would prefer to receive stories about only their children. In addition, with each new school-year intake come new children, families, and staff, requiring us as educators to "build on the past and construct anew a culture of democratic engagement" (Fleet, Patterson, & Robertson, 2006, p. 356). And yet, I have profoundly experienced that the use of pedagogical narration can promote stronger relationships between educators and families. As Katz (1998) explains:

> Documentation makes it possible for parents to become acutely aware of their children's experience in the school. The enthusiasm of the children and the interest of the parents in children's work help strengthen the involvement of parents in the children's learning, provides a rich basis for parent-child discussion, and deepens parents' understanding of the nature of learning in the early years. (p. 39)

In partnership with the child and with each other, educators and families can co-construct knowledge. As such, they find new rhythms with which to be both teacher and learner, parent and learner. These partnerships, not easily achieved, have to be founded on trust and confidence (Hall, Oleson, & Gambetti, 2001). Through their collaboration and respective perspectives families and educators can more deeply understand the thinking child and the ways in which each child co-constructs knowledge.

Pedagogical narration is also about leaving traces, about giving visibility to actions. Families can see what their child is doing and what other children, learning in collaboration with their child, are doing as well. When the families become curious and interested, they become more skilful in posing questions, seeking answers, and offering answers themselves. Malaguzzi (1998) insists that "this steady flow of communication, largely through documentation, introduces to families a quality of knowing that *tangibly changes their expectations*. They take on a new and more inquisitive approach to the whole school experience, re-examining their assumptions" (pp. 69–70).

○ From Learning Community to Activist Community

Fidler (1995) defines a learning community as

> a group of colleagues who come together in a spirit of mutual respect, authenticity, learning, and shared responsibility to continually explore and articulate an expanding awareness and base of knowledge. The process of [a] learning community includes inquiring about each other's assumptions and biases, experimenting, risking and openly assessing the results. (p. 4)

When we share and compare our understandings of the world with someone else (a colleague or a parent), we implicitly hold our sense of ourselves up to scrutiny because each of us defines ourselves in terms of the way we understand the world and our place in it. If the other person understands the world differently from us, we lack the common ground from which to make sense of each other. In contrast, if the other person shares our views of the world, then they confirm our identity, we confirm theirs, and on the resulting common ground we can begin to build an interpretive community. Conversations that took place among the group of family members and educators described in this chapter indicate that people experienced just such an interpretive community.

A learning community in which democratic communication occurs can transform knowledge-power links between educators, families, and others. Should "meaningful, substantive discussion," as Lightfoot (1978, p. 27) puts it, take place, families and educators might find that they could support each other in ways that go beyond the everyday issues of the classroom. Mutual concerns about broader educational issues have galvanized families and educators to take action on matters they have a vested interest in. For example, when the administrative body announced a plan that would see our school reconfigured and no longer be able to accommodate all of the families who had been part of this particular learning community, the families mobilized. Although other very desirable educational settings were available in the surrounding neighbourhood, the families advocated fiercely to stay together as a community rather than be moved to different contexts. A letter-writing campaign was undertaken, along with repeated telephone calls to those who held decision-making power. A rather heated appearance by the families at an administrative meeting made the front page of the local newspaper, and the administrators agreed to reconsider the proposed changes. Ultimately the decision was rescinded, allowing this strong group of families to remain together. It is hard to imagine that families would have been able to act so quickly and with such confidence and organization if relationships had not been built and parents did not see schools as places to exercise their leadership.

When families view themselves as a community bounded by similar interests and desires, a foundation to act collectively and to become more powerful agents in the educational setting emerges. Relationships are at the core of bringing this power to families. But to gain the necessary power to become active participants, families must also develop their individual capacity to be leaders within this community. New relationships among families and newly developed leadership capacities have brought about changes in the collective sense of power and agency.

○ Relationships Take Time

The lack of time is a major obstacle to meaningful family–educator involvement. Without frequent, direct communication, the prospect for establishing communities in which both educator and family perspectives are valued and where honest, open discussion and healthy disagreement can occur is poor. Traditional forums, such as report card pickup days and open houses, are inadequate for building relationships.

This suggests that children's programs and their administrators need to consider opportunities for parents and educators alike to develop their capacity for interaction, or pleas for family involvement will ring hollow. Room is needed for families and educators to come together for extended periods of time to work on a project, to share information, to write a report, to somehow talk.

If program administrators were to see their mission as fostering community, if they recognized the importance of "restructuring schools and communities toward enriched educational and economic outcomes ... and inventing rich visions of educational democracies of difference" (Fine, 1993, p. 707), they would see things very differently indeed. Policies would begin to reflect a recognition that appropriate outcomes are not only about achievement test scores, but about the kinds of adults we want children to become in the kind of society in which we want them to live. It is time for researchers and scholars to take the lead in portraying families and educators as something other than "natural enemies" (Waller, 1932) whose relationships must be managed. It is important to demonstrate that community can exist and communication can flourish in early childhood spaces.

Throughout this chapter I, with my co-authors, have described our shifting understandings of family–educator relationships, acknowledging the disruption of traditional norms that our experience has engendered. This case has offered a distinct relational approach to parent engagement. This community-based approach highlights relationship building, develops the capacity of family members to be leaders, and works to close the gaps in culture and power between educators and families. These three functions are related. Strong relationships among families create mutual support and a sense of community out of which parents can develop as leaders; the assertion of their leadership can then produce change in power relationships and the culture of schooling.

This relational approach to power moves us away from a dichotomy in our current understanding of family engagement: that of participating either passively inside or combatively outside schools. This approach recognizes the reality of potential conflict between families, community leaders, and educators, but invites them into a collaborative process that fosters the power to create solutions together.

Increasing family power through collaboration requires authentic processes of relationship building and engagement with families and community leaders. Rather than approaching families with the agenda of teaching them how to be better parents or to simply support the school's agenda, the relational approach engages families around their own interests and values and respects their contributions. In this process, both educators and families can grow and change, and a new kind of relationship can emerge—one that centres on shared understandings of children's learning.

ENDNOTES

1   To avoid overlooking the many individuals other than parents who lovingly assume the task of rearing and caring for children, I use the terms *family* and *families* rather than parents throughout this chapter.

2   See Chapter 5 for the steps involved in the pedagogical narration process.

REFERENCES

Apple, M. W., & Beane, J. A. (Eds.). (1995). *Democratic schools*. Alexandria, VA: Association for Supervision and Curriculum Development.

Birrell, J. R., Young, J. R., Egan, M. W., Ostlund, M. R., Cook, P. F., Tibbitts, C. B., & DeWitt, P. F. (1998). Overcoming parental resistance to change in a professional development school. *Teaching and Teacher Education, 14*(3), 323–336.

Blase, J., & Anderson, G. (1995). *The micropolitics of educational leadership*. London: Cassell.

Blenkin, G. M., & Kelly, A. V. (1997). *Principles into practice in early childhood education*. London: Paul Chapman.

Bourdieu, P. (1977). Cultural reproduction and social reproduction: A model. In J. Karabel & A. H. Halsey (Eds.), *Power and ideology in education* (pp. 485–511). New York: University Press.

Bryk, A., & Schneider, B. (2002). *Trust in schools: A core resource for improvement*. New York: Russell Sage Foundation Press.

Cagliari, P. (2002). Lecture. International study tour. Reggio Emilia, Italy, February 14.

Cagliari, P., & Giudici, C. (2001). School as a place of group learning for parents. In C. Giudici, M. Krechevsky, & C. Rinaldi (Eds.), *Making learning visible: Children as individual and group learners* (pp. 136–141). Reggio Emilia, Italy: Project Zero and Reggio Children.

Coahran, M. M., Kay, P., Kay, J., & Fitzgerald, M. D. (1999). *From communication to conversation: A call for personal relations between parents and teachers*. Burlington, VT: University of Vermont.

Comer, J. P. (1996). *Rallying the whole village: The Comer process for reforming education*. New York: Teachers College Press.

Crozier, G. (1998). Parents and schools: Partnership or surveillance? *Education Policy, 13*(1), 125–136.

Dehli, K. (1995). What lies beyond Ontario's Bill 160? The politics and practice of education markets. *Our Schools/Our Selves, 9*(4), 31–42.

Delpit, L. (1995). *Other people's children: Cultural conflict in the classroom.* New York: New Press.

Epstein, J. L. (1995). School/family/community partnerships: Caring for the children we share. *Phi Delta Kappan, 76,* 701–712.

Epstein, J., Coates, L., Salinas, K., Saunders, M., & Simon, B. (1997). *School, family and community partnerships: Your handbook for action.* Thousand Oaks, CA: Corwin.

Fidler, M. (1995). Building a learning community. *Association Management, 47*(5), 40–47.

Fine, M. (1993). [Ap]parent involvement: Reflections on parents, power and urban public schools. *Teachers College Record, 94,* 682–710.

Fleet, A., Patterson, C., & Robertson, J. (2006). *Insights behind early childhood pedagogical documentation.* Castle Hill, Australia: Pademelon Press.

Gould, K., & Pohio, L. (2006). Stories from Aotearoa/New Zealand. In A. Fleet, C. Patterson, & J. Robertson (Eds.), *Insights behind early childhood documentation* (pp. 77–86). Castle Hill, Australia: Pademelon Press.

Grumet, M. (1988). *Bitter milk: Women and teaching.* Amherst, MA: University of Massachusetts Press.

Hall, E., Oleson, V., & Gambetti, A. (2001). Including parents in the process of documentation. *Child Care Information Exchange, 3*(1), 52–55.

Hargreaves, A. (1997). Rethinking education change: Going deeper and wider in the quest for success. In A. Hargreaves (Ed.), *Rethinking educational change with heart and mind. 1997 ASCD Yearbook* (pp. 1–26). Alexandria, VA: Association for Supervision and Curriculum Development.

Hargreaves, A., & Goodson, I. (1996). Teachers' professional lives: Aspirations and actualities. In I. Goodson & A. Hargreaves (Eds.), *Teachers' professional lives* (pp. 1–28). London: Falmer.

Hargreaves, A., Earl, L., & Ryan, J. (1996). *Schooling for change: Reinventing education for early adolescents.* New York: Falmer.

Haseloff, W. (1990). The efficacy of the parent-teacher partnerships of the 1990s. *Early Childhood Development and Care, 58,* 51–55.

Hemmings, A. (2000). High school democratic dialogues: Possibilities for praxis. *American Educational Research Journal, 37*(1), 67–91.

Henry, M. (1996). *Parent-school collaboration: Feminist organizational structures and school leadership.* Albany, NY: State University of New York Press.

Hilliard, D., & Pelo, A. (2001). Changing our attitudes and actions in working with families. *Child Care Information Exchange, 3*(1), 48–51.

Hughes, P., & MacNaughton, G. (2003). Preparing early childhood professionals to work with parents: The challenges of diversity and dissensus. *Australian Journal of Early Childhood, 18*(2), 14–20.

Isaacs, W. (1999). *Dialogue and the art of thinking together.* New York: Currency.

Kahne, J. (1996). *Reframing educational policy: Democracy, community, and the individual.* New York: Teachers College Press.

Katz, L. G. (1998) What can we learn from Reggio Emilia? In C. Edwards, L. Gandini, & G. Forman (Eds.), *The hundred languages of children: The Reggio Emilia approach—Advanced reflections* (pp. 27–45). Norwood, NJ: Ablex.

Lightfoot, S. L. (1978). *Worlds apart: Relationships between families and schools.* New York: Basic Books.

Lubeck, S. (1998). Is developmentally appropriate practice for everyone? *Childhood Education, 74*(5), 283–293.

MacNaughton, G., & Hughes, P. (2003). *Shaping early childhood: Learners, curriculum, and contexts.* Maidenland, UK: Open University Press.

Malaguzzi, L. (1998). History, ideas, and basic philosophy: An interview with Lella Gandini. In C. Edwards, L. Gandini, & G. Forman (Eds.), *The hundred languages of children: The Reggio Emilia approach to early childhood education—Advanced reflections* (pp. 49–97). Norwood, NJ: Ablex.

Miretzky, D. (2002). *Parent-teacher perspectives on parent-teacher relationships.* Unpublished doctoral dissertation, University of Illinois, Chicago.

Moore, M., & Klass, P. (1995) Understanding parents' expectations on hurrying: United States and England, *International Journal of Early Childhood, 27*(2), 30–36.

Nias, J. (1999). Teachers' moral purposes: Stress, vulnerability, and strength. In R. Vandenberghe & A. M. Huberman (Eds.), *Understanding and preventing teacher burnout: A sourcebook of international research and practice* (pp. 223–237). New York: Cambridge University Press.

Ogbu, J. (1993). Variability in minority school performance: A problem in search of an explanation. In E. Jacob & C. Jordan (Eds.), *Minority education: Anthropological perspectives* (pp. 83–111). New York: Ablex.

Payne, C. M., & Kaba, M. (2001, February). So much reform, so little change: Building-level obstacles to urban school reform. *Journal of Negro Education.* Retrieved December 17, 2009, from http://www.ccsso.org/content/PDFs/So_Much_Reform.pdf

Pelo, A. (2006). At the crossroads. In A. Fleet, C. Patterson, & J. Robertson (Eds.), *Insights behind early childhood pedagogical documentation* (pp. 173–190). Castle Hill, Australia: Pademelon Press.

Rinaldi, C. (1998). Projected curriculum and documentation. In C. Edwards, L. Gandini, & G. Forman (Eds.), *The hundred languages of children: The Reggio Emilia approach—Advanced reflections* (pp. 113–125). Norwood, NJ: Ablex.

Shpancer, N. (1998). Caregiver-parent relationships in daycare: A review and re-examination of the data and their implications. *Early Education and Development, 9*(3), 239–259.

Strike, K. A. (1993). Professionalism, democracy, and discursive communities: Normative reflections on restructuring. *American Educational Research Journal, 30,* 255–275.

Strozzi, P. (2001). Daily life at school: Seeing the extraordinary in the ordinary. In C. Giudici, M. Krechevsky, & C. Rinaldi (Eds.), *Making learning visible: Children as individual and group learners* (pp. 58–77). Reggio Emilia, Italy: Project Zero and Reggio Children.

Thorne, G. B. (1993). *Parent involvement in the schools: A new paradigm for preservice and inservice education of teachers and administrators.* Unpublished doctoral dissertation, University of Connecticut, Storrs, Connecticut.

Waller, W. (1932). *The sociology of teaching.* New York: Russell & Russell.

Whitty, G., Power, S., & Halpin, D. (1998). *Devolution and choice in education: The school, the state, the market.* Buckingham, UK: University Press.

○ Notes on the Contributors

Editor

VERONICA PACINI-KETCHABAW is Associate Professor and Coordinator of the Early Years Specialization in the School of Child and Youth Care at the University of Victoria, and the co-director of the Investigating Quality Project and the BC Early Learning Implementation Framework Project. She has worked professionally in the field of early childhood education for over 15 years and taught at different levels in a variety of educational settings in Argentina and Canada. She teaches and conducts research on issues related to poststructural, feminist, and postcolonial theory-practice in early childhood education.

Authors

IRIS BERGER has been involved in the field of early childhood education for the past 15 years, where she taught children between the ages of 2 and 5 years in a variety of settings. At present she is a lecturer and a coordinator with the Institute for Early Childhood Education & Research (IECER) at the University of British Columbia, Canada. Iris is a doctoral student with the Department of Educational Studies at UBC. Her main interests lie in working towards expanding the notions of childhood and early education by interrogating the underlying assumptions of current early childhood policies and practices.

KIRSTEN HO CHAN is the project coordinator at the Unit for Child Care Research and Professional Development in the University of Victoria's School of Child and Youth Care. Kirsten primarily works with the Investigating

Quality Project and the BC Early Learning Framework Implementation Project. She is also the executive director of a local nonprofit organization, Restorative Justice Oak Bay, which offers alternatives to the traditional justice system and gives youth a voice in dealing with crime and dispute resolution.

ENID ELLIOT has been an early childhood educator for many years. She has worked in Turkey, California, New York, and British Columbia in a variety of programs. She finds herself continually surprised, intrigued, and inspired by the children, families, and early childhood educators with whom she engages. Babies and toddlers are a particular source of joy and inspiration. Going back to do a doctorate helped develop different perspectives on that inspiration and her dissertation resulted in the book *We're Not Robots: Listening to the Voices of Daycare Providers*. Currently she is working/playing with a group of educators to naturalize outside playspaces.

SYLVIA KIND is an artist and educator. She is an instructor in the Department of Early Childhood Care and Education at Capilano University, where she teaches art, curriculum, and teacher inquiry classes. In 2006 she received a PhD in Art Education and Curriculum Studies from the University of British Columbia and was awarded the Gordon and Marion Smith Award for Excellence in Art Education. Her dissertation research explored Emmanuel Levinas' ethics of relationality and emphasized teaching and art practices as processes and instances of inquiry. Sylvia has published in numerous journals and contributed chapters to books. She is particularly interested in studio research, art as living inquiry, and the role of the *atelier* in early childhood. She is an exhibiting artist, working primarily in textile/fibre processes and photography, and she works closely with the Capilano University Children's Centre as an *atelierista*.

LAURIE KOCHER writes from the perspectives of a teacher of young children and a researcher who focuses on the practice of pedagogical documentation/narration. Both perspectives strongly inform her chapter. Laurie currently teaches in the faculty of Child, Family, and Community Studies at Douglas College near Vancouver, British Columbia. Her doctoral research focused on how and where hermeneutic phenomenology intersects with the practice of pedagogical documentation that emerges from the early childhood educational project of Reggio Emilia, Italy. She has been associated with the University of Victoria's Investigating Quality and Early Learning Framework projects. Paul Cabaj, David Chapman, Nancy Chapman, Carmen Ryujin, and

Elizabeth Wooding are all parents of children who were in Laurie Kocher's kindergarten class which was located in a public school in West Vancouver in 2007.

KATHLEEN KUMMEN is a lecturer in the Department of Early Childhood Education at Capilano University, North Vancouver, British Columbia, and a doctoral candidate at the School of Child and Youth Care, University of Victoria. Kathleen is part of Research in Early Childhood Care, Education and Health (REACH), a consortium of early childhood researchers at the University of Victoria. She has worked professionally in the field of early years for over 25 years and has held a variety of positions. Kathleen's research interests focus on exploring theory and practice in the preservice training and ongoing professional development of early childhood educators. In her dissertation research she hopes to focus on how to support preservice teachers in reflecting on their image of children and how that image connects to their understanding of theory and practice.

FIKILE NXUMALO is a caregiver practicing in family child care. Her main pedagogical interests are in practising for equity and social justice. From coursework taken through the University of Victoria's School of Child and Youth Care, she has been inspired by poststructural ideas as they relate to daily practice. As a participant in the *Investigating Quality* project, Fikile has become particularly interested in theories on the materiality/embodiment of race and how they could help to create an openness to multiple possibilities for ethical actions in encounters with difference.

MARY CAROLINE ROWAN is a Masters student at the University of Victoria and a recipient of a University of Victoria Graduate Fellowship as well as a Research in Early Childhood Care, Education, and Health scholarship. Carol has been involved in developing early childhood policy, planning programs, delivering training, researching, and creating curriculum materials related to early childhood education in Inuit communities for 22 years. Presently she is curious about the potential of narrative assessment as a connector in building relationships in the childcare centre/community and is excited about the possibilities in creating educator-made Indigenous language books for young children.

DEBORAH THOMPSON works as an early childhood educator in a multi-age childcare centre, a pilot project at UBC Child Care Services, in Vancouver, British Columbia. She is also a part-time instructor in the Early Childhood Care and Education program of Vancouver Community College. Since 1978, she has worked in the field of early childhood care and education as a caregiver, a college instructor, and a coordinator of programs. As a doctoral candidate in the School of Child and Youth Care, University of Victoria, Deborah will be leading an action research project examining multi-age grouping in the organization of child care services at UBC Child Care Services.

CRISTINA D. VINTIMILLA is a PhD candidate at the Centre for Cross-Faculty Inquiry in the Faculty of Education at the University of British Columbia. She is also an instructor in the Department of Early Childhood Care and Education at Capilano University. Her areas of interest are philosophy of education, teacher education, and curriculum. Her work engages with poststructuralist theories, particularly the work of Jacques Derrida. She is also very involved and committed to developing research projects in her home country of Ecuador.